Pulling the Temple Down

"We have pulled a temple down that has been built these three-quarters of a century."

Andrew P. Calhoun
Charleston, South Carolina
20 December 1860

Pulling the Temple Down

The Fire-Eaters and the Destruction of the Union

David S. Heidler

STACKPOLE
BOOKS

Published by
STACKPOLE BOOKS
5067 Ritter Road
Mechanicsburg, PA 17055

Printed in the United States of America

10 9 8 7 6 5 4 3 2 1

First Edition

For Jeanne

Library of Congress Cataloging-in-Publication Data

Heidler, David Stephen, 1955-
   Pulling the temple down : the fire-eaters and the destruction of the Union / David S. Heidler.—1st ed.
      p.   cm.
   Includes bibliographical references (p.) and index.
   ISBN 0-8117-0634-6
   1. Secession. 2. United States—Politics and government—Civil War, 1861–1865. 3. Confederate States of America—Politics and government.
   I. Title.
E459.H45 1994   94-18588
973.7'13—dc20   CIP

Contents

Preface		vii
Acknowledgments		ix
CHAPTER ONE	*"A Disposition to Dissolve the Union"*	1
CHAPTER TWO	*"Leadership of This Generation"*	21
CHAPTER THREE	*"A Partial Affair"*	39
CHAPTER FOUR	*"That We Were All Such Traitors!"*	57
CHAPTER FIVE	*"Ungrateful, Cowardly, Stupid State"*	79
CHAPTER SIX	*"The Sympathy of Angels"*	101
CHAPTER SEVEN	*"Glory Enough for One Day"*	121
CHAPTER EIGHT	*"One of the Most Aristocratic Cities of the Union"*	139
CHAPTER NINE	*"Instruments in the Hands of God"*	161
CHAPTER TEN	*"We Will Stand by You to the Death"*	183
Notes		189
Bibliography		233
Index		253

Preface

The radical secessionist occupies a unique place in antebellum American politics, and not because of the zeal with which he purveyed his doctrines. The fire-eater achieves uniqueness because he exuberantly advocated Southern state secession as a solution to problems that most Americans sought to resolve with compromise and accommodation.

The fire-eaters' persistently similar message provides us with an illusion of unity among them throughout the Southern states. That illusion creates the notion of a long-standing radical conspiracy to dissolve the United States. Actually, the fire-eater was ever the renegade, often compelled to his wild tactics by an inability to attract local state constituencies. In different Southern states different circumstances guided and goaded the activities of individual fire-eaters. Frequently, those activities were as starkly different as the personalities and temperaments of individual fire-eaters.

At the end of the 1850s, fire-eaters found themselves riding a massive secession movement the likes of which they had been trying unsuccessfully to create for over a decade. But even at the end, the movement arose out of fear and anger, a reaction to events that menaced traditional Southern institutions. When that happened, the fire-eater in his moment of seeming triumph lost his uniqueness. Only briefly did he enjoy power and influence amidst the storm of secession. Arrogant and uncompromising, his extremism was suited for turmoil, and so the disruption of the

Union found him in the role of the catalyst, the agent that sparks but does not enter into the reaction.

Anyone familiar with the antebellum period of American history knows its inherent confusions and complexities. Here is the story of a few of the men who helped make that so.

Acknowledgments

So many friends, colleagues, and critics (some of whom happen to be all three) have helped me that I could not begin to thank them properly. However, I must express special gratitude to a few people for their exceptional efforts.

Professor Thomas A. Belser, Jr., suggested the topic and suffered through the first clumsy drafts to help make it presentable for Professors Joseph H. Harrison, Jr., Robert R. Rea, and Allen Cronenberg. Every one of their suggestions marked an improvement, and for their equanimity and good cheer, I cannot find words adequate to express my indebtedness.

The people at the Southern Historical Collection at the University of North Carolina in Chapel Hill are as efficiently helpful as they are charming, and anyone fortunate enough to encounter the friendly staff of the South Carolina Historical Society in the Fireproof Building will know why Calhoun chose to spend the rest of forever in Charleston. Nelson Morgan at the University of Georgia Libraries promptly answers questions with detailed letters, and Elaine Owens at the Mississippi Archives phones and faxes with an alacrity I can only describe as saintly. Joanna Norman at the Florida State Archives made my search for photographs easier, and when bibliophile-without-peer David Coles found an unpublished photograph in a private collection, it was merely another sign of his abundant thoughtfulness that he remembered me and made sure I got a print. Mrs. Eleanor M. Richardson at the South Caroliniana Library spoke to me on the phone for a glorious ten minutes during which the delicate cadence of her voice made this Southern boy, so far from home, homesick. Chuck Auck provided the computer technology and Atlanta Braves fan Sam Caldwell the time to manipulate floppy disks and thus save me countless hours of work.

I must thank the kind people at Stackpole, specifically William C. Davis for his suggestions and encouragement and Sylvia Frank for her patience and help. I can hardly fathom the good fortune that placed me in such delightful company.

My mother and father imparted to me a deep love of history and have done much to guide me toward the path that I have taken. Their support has been unstinting and unconditional, and I know that merely saying thank you will never be enough precisely because they have never expected it to be said at all.

I have dedicated this modest offering to Jeanne. She knows why. Has it been only a few years that we have been married? Or days? I forget. She knows why.

CHAPTER ONE

"A Disposition to Dissolve the Union"

Breaking up the United States of America was no little task and was not taken lightly. A mainstream of sentiment and tradition bound the Union together throughout the antebellum period. So long attuned to what Abraham Lincoln called "mystic chords of memory," that sentiment and tradition had to receive multiple and resounding shocks before a substantial part of America would find the "chorus of Union" intolerably dissonant. Nobody could have thought in 1816 that forty-five years later an Illinois politician from the banks of the Sangamon River would have to remind Southerners, in an air of quiet desperation, that they were "not enemies, but friends."[1]

Yet that happened, and Americans have asked themselves why ever since. By 1865 President Lincoln decided what had caused the conflict. It was the slaves of the South "who constituted a peculiar and powerful interest." Further, he maintained that "all knew that this interest was somehow the cause of the war."[2] From the first bloodshed, opinion in the North was that somehow the slavocracy of the South had cajoled, panicked, goaded, and betrayed its calmer neighbors into the impetuous folly of secession. This view represented the main thrust of Civil War historiography during the nineteenth century. It has recently reappeared in the scholarship of neo-revisionism.[3]

Lincoln was a perceptive observer of American politics, but he was also a politician wrestling with dire concerns. We should take his view of the situation, as well as those of his contemporaries, with some degree of skepticism. That the belief in a Southern conspiracy should reappear in modern scholarship, however, is surprising. Even in the face of more sophisticated analyses, the notion of a Southern conspiracy perhaps persists because of the nature of the secession crises. As early as 1850, a group of radicals in the South was urging the doctrine of secession. Over a period of five months at the end of the 1850s, Americans met in conventions in virtually every Southern state with the express purpose of achieving the secessionists' goal. By this time, the small band of conspirators apparently had shaped a multitude.

The presence of that multitude has obscured many subtleties surrounding the causes for and the method of Southern secession. The advent of the Confederacy gives the impression that secession presaged nation making. It thus implies concerted effort, a widespread conspiracy working toward a common goal.

There was not, however, a conspiracy to dissolve the Union. There were instead some people who tried to compel individual states to secede from the Union. The South did not secede; particular states did. Those states later confederated not to make a new nation, but rather to construct a league whose primary purpose was to counter the anticipated coercion of the federal government.

Further confusion over the nature of secession results from the foremost common interest the seceded states had: the institution of slavery. By late 1860, enough Southerners believed that all alternatives for protecting slavery had been exhausted. But many Southern planters who had a cogently direct interest in the institution's safety were not persuaded and insisted that the crisis was the manufacture of scheming politicians scrambling for dominance in both the North and the South.[4]

The picture of the antebellum Southern fire-eater as a principled fanatic, wild-eyed and hoarse-voiced, whipped to his activities by the altruistic—yet immoral—imperative of protecting the ownership of slaves, ignores the truth that the fire-eater was a politician. He was not a prophet, except in the self-fulfilling sense. He was not an intellectual, for none of his group ever produced a significant innovation on the theories that purportedly guided his course.[5]

Perhaps the political motives of the fire-eater are often neglected because he was, with some notable exceptions, a dreadful politician. After all, for more than ten years he could not turn the explosive issue of the antebellum period to his advantage. The multitude he apparently shaped by 1860 resulted from provocative events surrounding slavery instead of fire-eater manipulation of Southern fears. In short, events finally made the radical secessionists' advice seem plausible.

The fire-eater never shaped events with his rhetoric, and he frequently found himself without a constituency. The conservative planter class of the South, for whom the fire-eater presumed to speak, rejected his radicalism. The Democratic party in the South disowned him because of the unpopularity of his exaggerated views both at home and in the North.

All that changed suddenly in 1860 because slavery had thoroughly disrupted sectional political accord for almost six years. The so-called "blundering generation" of traditional politicians—not the fire-eaters— caused that turbulence. The notion that the politicians of the 1850s were blundering, however, suggests that they were stupid, which they were not, rather than irresponsible, which they were. The use of the most dangerous issue of the age—and hence the most potent issue of the age— marked a high degree of complacency, opportunism, and irresponsibility among men who sincerely professed love for the Union. Each time they used slavery to secure support for or ensure antipathy against a piece of legislation, used it to make attractive or unacceptable this or that candidate for the highest to the lowest elective office, locally or nationally, they honed the issue to such sharpness that it became positively Damoclean. At that point the fire-eater emerged from the periphery of the political arena, not ranting or raving, but with calm determination, to grasp this weapon and cleave the Democratic party.

The failure of the American democratic system to deal effectively with the slavery problem was the result of traditional activity that used the problem for political advantage. Early on, slavery established itself as a potent political weapon, as the generation that had a living memory of the Constitutional Convention discovered. The flushed glow of nationalism at the end of the War of 1812 appeared so propitious that it earned the inaccurate label "Era of Good Feelings" for a period too brief to be an era and marked by alarming incidents of discord.

In 1820 Representative James Tallmadge of New York disrupted congressional discussion concerning Missouri statehood with a twenty-one word amendment to the Missouri Enabling Bill. Tallmadge wanted to restrict and gradually extirpate slavery in Missouri as a condition for her statehood. Whether or not New York Federalist Rufus King, whose bidding many assumed had prompted Tallmadge's initiative, sincerely believed slavery to be immoral was beside the point. Representative John Holmes of Massachusetts believed that the New Yorkers had raised the slavery question to divide Northern and Southern Democratic-Republicans. They could then proceed to create a sectional Northern party under established Federalist leadership.[6]

The speculation carried weight, considering the events of the previous twenty years. The election of Thomas Jefferson marked the beginning of Republican dominance that saw the harassment of Federalist judges, the potential shift of political power to the West with the Louisiana Purchase, and finally the War of 1812. And on the eve of the war's conclusion, New England Federalists met in an antiwar convention at Hartford, Connecticut, a convention that many elsewhere saw as possibly treasonous, certainly stupid.

Whatever motives caused them, the tone of the 1820 Missouri debates alarmed the politically sensitive. "It would seem," wrote Virginian James M. Garnett, "as if all the devils incarnate, both in the Eastern & Northern States, are in league against us."[7] Goaded by such concern, Southerners achieved a remarkable concert in an atmosphere of glaring acrimony. They found little comfort in the belief that their adversaries argued this issue for political advantage. Federalist opportunism took the form for Southerners of Northern perfidy. Charles Tait of Alabama declared that "hereafter the North can expect no act of liberality on this subject from the South. Touching on this matter the Sword has been drawn and the Scabbard thrown away."[8]

Talk of drawn swords might have been exactly the response for which the instigators of the Missouri crisis were hoping, but it simply would not do for the calmer congressmen with a national agenda. So a compromise was crafted with an astounding degree of difficulty since its principal author, Jesse B. Thomas, found himself having to answer a host of subsidiary complaints that had nothing to do with slavery directly, but had everything to do with Southerners' minority status because they owned slaves. The division of the Louisiana Purchase along the latitude of 36°30' created that line that Jefferson warned would be impossible to obliterate, but at least in the immediate sense it calmed the suspicions of Southern politicians worried over the sectional balance in the Senate.[9]

The Missouri Compromise also sought to retire the slavery issue from political discussion. It was divisive. It paralyzed political debate with towering difficulties and emotions that required generally unsatisfactory solutions. It was an inconvenience, and a dangerous one at that, for a political system whose Northern and Southern members wanted to deal with economic and social problems on a national level.

Some Southerners, however, were not prepared to deal with anything but the protection of their rights. The seriousness of proponents calmer than Charles Tait provided a foundation of theoretical protest for those of a later generation who would strive to draw the Southern sword. St. George Tucker, the distinguished Virginia jurist who married John Randolph's widowed mother, outlined his justification for secession in "View of the Laws as a Member of the Federal Union" in 1803.[10] Another Virginian, John Taylor of Caroline, began theorizing on the relationship between Americans and their government in 1814 with his *Inquiry into the Principles and Policy of the Government of the United States* to be followed by *Construction Construed and Constitutions Vindicated* (1820), *Tyranny Unmasked* (1822), and *New Views of the Constitution of the United States* (1823). These titles testify to Taylor's growing dissatisfaction with the nation's political direction. He came to view that direction as ominously inclined, under Republican auspices, toward the same overweening federal apparatus that Republicans had warned was the objective of the Federalist party.[11]

Taylor's dissent from the growing nationalism of the Republican party indicated substantial Southern discontent with the party of Jefferson and Madison. After the War of 1812, Taylor, Nathaniel Macon, and John Randolph loosely combined in a group frequently called the Tertium Quids because they stood apart from both moribund Federalists and National Republicans. In spite of stark differences in personality and temperament, this peculiar group's members shared the common bond of rejecting a shift in Republican ideology and practice. One had only to compare Madison and Jefferson as they were in 1798 with what they had become two decades later to see the point.

Randolph became the most prominent activist of the Quids because he was the most vehemently critical of postwar activity. His political career is mostly illustrative because he foreshadowed the kind of politicians who became known as fire-eaters.[12]

Randolph entered the House of Representatives in 1799 as a staunch and fiery Republican. During Jefferson's first term, Randolph demonstrated that he took too seriously the ideological imperatives of the so-called Republican Revolution of 1800 by leading the Jeffersonian assault on the Federalist judiciary. He prosecuted the impeachment trial in the Senate against Supreme Court Justice Samuel Chase, botched the job, and in the process suffered a humiliating dissection by the superior legal mind of Luther Martin. He also experienced the growing chilliness of party superiors.[13]

Soon enough he became an outsider, too uncompromising and therefore too dangerous to inspire a cohesive political following. With dramatic suddenness, he shifted his ire away from the Federalist party to his own Republican leadership. Ultimately, he regarded Republican policies as so unacceptable that he would say that Jefferson had never had a worthwhile opinion on anything except a new plow design.[14]

Randolph rapidly became an anachronism in an age that presaged the dramatic political realignments of Jacksonian Democracy. When Northern antagonists in the Missouri debates accused Southerners of aristocratic superciliousness, the charge could not have disturbed Randolph as much as the spirit that prompted it. From a Southern background tempered by his own disposition, he never altered his opinion about the ruling class's political rights and obligations. Randolph did not campaign; he stood for election. He cared nothing for political popularity and found contemptible those who catered to the desires of constituents or to the strictures of party policy.[15] As a particular kind of Southern Republican, Randolph abhorred the mass appeal of the French Revolution and admired the exclusive nature of British politics. As a perceptive observer without fear of electoral reprisal or party discipline, he rejected scornfully, while others accepted eagerly, the illusion that the Missouri Compromise had ended the disruptive slavery debate. In 1824 he insisted that "it is a thing which cannot be hid. You might as well try to hide a volcano in full eruption; it cannot be hid; it is a cancer in your face."[16]

Because Randolph was erratic in his personal and political life, he was never taken seriously for any length of time. By the 1820s, his strange appearance reinforced a reputation for eccentricity bordering on madness. Tall and too thin, a victim of sexual impotency and the correspondent afflictions that made him peach-faced and high-voiced, he appeared gradually to wizen and wrinkle rather than age. He drank too much and took narcotics to kill pain, the remedy racking his body as it glowed in his eyes. He ate too little anyway, but at times of high excitement, such as during the Missouri debates, he could take only crackers and gruel. He reserved his appetite for opponents whom he gobbled up in nasty courses served with cruel, if cool, sarcasm. Southerners liked Randolph best when he perceived his South threatened and went "for blood." He shouted at the North:

> We know what we are doing. We of the South are united from the Ohio to Florida, and we can always unite; but you of the North are beginning to divide and you will divide. We have conquered you once, and we can conquer you again. Ay, sir, we will drive you to the wall, and when we have you there once more we mean to keep you there, and will nail you down like base money.[17]

No fire-eater of the late 1850s could have engaged in more vehemence and inaccuracy, and his immoderation became a musical lyricism for a rising generation of reckless men. They also would assert that they knew what they were doing and would proceed upon the assumption that by their saying something, it instantly became so. The South was not united in the 1820s, in spite of Randolph's assurances, nor would it be united in the 1850s, in spite of the fire-eaters' insistence.

The importance of a belligerent Randolph and even the influence of the meditative Taylor should not be overestimated, for politics proceeded apace in the wield of more traditional men. In the South, John C. Calhoun already was achieving a heroic stature. His political power in South Carolina would become nearly absolute, and his political theory, often only vaguely understood, would shape in some degree the thinking of virtually every antebellum Southerner, even if some were unwilling to admit it.

One of the patriotic War Hawks of the 1812 Congress, Calhoun believed that the peace of 1815 was only a respite. The surge of nationalism following the war found him an eager participant. He supported the tariff, internal improvements, and other national measures calculated to draw the country together. Other Southerners came to feel their own interests had been neglected and thus abandoned their nationalism, but Calhoun clung to his position longer. Perhaps his persistent nationalism resulted from political necessity, because his presidential ambitions required a broader electorate than was available through exclusive Southern popularity. Yet the protective tariff continued to hurt Southern agricultural interests, especially in South Carolina, and Calhoun finally had to choose between his loyalty to home and his credibility in the North. His choice, a reluctant one, was compelled by the emergence of a serious crisis.

Because it served as the principal source of revenue for the federal government, most Americans viewed the tariff as a tolerable necessity. But mid-Atlantic state manufacturing interests had always desired a protective tariff to shield them from foreign competition. The Panic of 1819 and the ensuing depression provided protection advocates the basis for dominance in 1824. Gradually, Western farmers, New England merchants, and Southern planters complained that manufacturers enjoyed disproportionate considerations. Southerners felt the economic damage most acutely, so in 1827 South Carolinian Robert J. Turnbull wrote *The Crisis,* a series of pamphlets protesting a protariff convention in Harrisburg, Pennsylvania.[18]

At this point, political opportunism again played mischief maker. Jackson partisans planned to alienate congressional politicians from their protectionist constituents by proposing such a high protective tariff that it would be impossible to accept. Nevertheless, the tariff bill passed. A palpably worried Calhoun took Turnbull's arguments, whose theory of state interposition had impressed him, to fashion *The South Carolina Exposition and Protest* of 1828, a justification for a state's ability to nullify federal law.[19]

Neither Turnbull nor Calhoun put forward an innovation. Since the Constitutional Convention the fear of tyranny by a numerical majority had activated protests from the South, most notably Jefferson's and Madison's Kentucky and Virginia Resolutions that protested the Alien and Sedition Acts in 1798. These resolutions served as the philosophical ancestors of Calhoun's theory of Nullification. When Northern population growth, especially in protectionist strongholds, resulted in irresistible legislative majorities, would not participation in national councils become pointless? Calhoun proposed Nullification as an alternative. A state, perceiving itself harmed by a national statute, could interpose its authority between the federal government and local citizens to nullify federal law.[20]

Northerners challenged this theory almost immediately. At the end of January 1830, Senator Robert Y. Hayne of South Carolina attempted to wed Western discontent over public land policy to Southern protests against protectionism by extolling Nullification as a remedy for both.[21]

Daniel Webster argued against this reasoning and initiated the Webster-Hayne debate, mostly remembered for the New Englander's stirring peroration on the sanctity of the Union.[22] Yet, the debate served as only the dramatic precursor to the apogee of the turmoil, for two years later Hayne, then governor of South Carolina, presided over a state whose legislature, captured in the 1832 elections by Nullifiers, called a convention that challenged federal authority to collect tariff duties in South Carolina ports.

Ostensibly, economic protests fueled the entire issue, but a larger impetus loomed behind it. Southerners feared that unchecked national authority would eventually affect the fortunes of slavery. A siege mentality that characterized the activities of the South in later years was conspicuous in the South Carolina Low Country during the 1820s and early 1830s. Simply put, wherever there was a large body of slaves, there were Nullifiers.[23] James Hamilton, Jr., who presided over the Nullification Convention in 1832, described the tariff fight as "a battle at the outposts, by which, if we succeeded in repulsing the enemy, *the citadel* [of slavery] *would be safe.*"[24] Likewise, John C. Calhoun considered "the Tariff, but as the occasion, rather than the real cause of the present unhappy state of things." Instead, the fear that an unrestricted national government could tamper with "the peculiar domestick [*sic*] institutions" of the South made South Carolina, in Calhoun's view, move toward radical solutions.[25]

Confronted by an intensely angry Andrew Jackson, who threatened invasion if national authority were thwarted, the Nullifiers realized that Western concern over public land policy had not translated itself into a coincidental affinity with South Carolina radicalism, nor had Southern distress over the tariff generated support for the Palmetto State in neighboring legislatures. Alone and threatened, ultimately outmaneuvered by the Compromise Tariff legislatively engineered by Henry Clay and cautiously endorsed by Calhoun, and facing a voluble and increasingly belligerent element of pro-Union sentiment within their borders, the Nullifiers quickly reassessed their situation.

In convention in March 1833, South Carolina backed away from its stand on Nullification. Robert Barnwell Rhett exhibited a marked unhappiness over how the crisis had concluded and would not make excuses, as others were, for the abandonment of Nullification. Instead, he jumped angrily into the fray with a violent speech on the merits of disunion. "Sir, if a confederacy of the Southern States could now be obtained, should we not deem it a happy termination?" Rhett asked. He proclaimed that "South Carolina must be an armed camp. She has no rights under this government, but what she is prepared to assert in the tented field."[26]

This sort of talk shocked the convention and brought on attacks even from leading Nullifiers. The timidity of his colleagues disgusted Rhett, especially since those who now disowned him had applauded his ringing voice only months before. Rhett was not now nor would he ever be reconciled to the abandonment of a position because it was unpopular, unfeasible, or dangerous. Ignited by the Nullification movement and encouraged by the grateful approval of its leadership, he raged on, mindless even of the damage he did mostly to himself. Rhett, like Randolph at the end of his career, quickly became an outsider precisely because he could not be controlled and because he exhibited a political immaturity that inclined him toward impetuosity rather than calculation, toward dogmatism rather than persuasiveness. Already in 1833 he was prepared to pull from beneath a shroud of euphemisms what he was sure was the central fear of virtually every Southerner, that "every stride of this government over your rights, brings it nearer to your peculiar policy. . . ."[27] The staunch Unionist Benjamin F. Perry watched Rhett's fiery attempt to revive a crisis that had already passed and looked beyond the political miscalculation to a dark portent. "There is a disposition to dissolve the Union and form a Southern Confederacy," he recorded in his journal. "It will show itself more plainly in the course of a few years."[28]

True enough, some men believed that if federal domination could not be resisted by innovative political techniques within the Union, the injured state would have to seek its fortunes without it. As early as 1827 South Carolinian Thomas Cooper suggested that "the question, however, is fast approaching to the alternative, of submission or separation."[29] A year later, James Hamilton echoed the sentiment in Walterboro, South Carolina. The rejection of Nullification in favor of disunion by men like William Drayton and the respected Langdon Cheves represented the views of many who thought that South Carolina had to guard her constitutional liberties, even if by leaving the Union.[30]

Many antebellum Americans regarded the theory of secession valid, but they considered the act of secession an unacceptable remedy for even substantial injury. On the other hand, there was much confusion—not only among theoretical secessionists, but among Unionists as well—as to just what the Union meant and what it was supposed to do. For instance, Webster, John Quincy Adams, and Andrew Jackson all perceived the Union differently. Webster saw it as tied to tradition to bring about order. Adams maintained that it was a positive force that could improve life. However, Jackson conceived of the Union as national sovereignty, equipped with a constitutionally restrained method of expressing its will and the means to frustrate attempts at thwarting that will. Adams's view was prophetic, but given the nature of his active presidency, Jackson's concept of Union prevailed for the time being, though not without immediate dispute, one example being the pamphlets written by Littleton W. Tazewell, governor of Virginia.[31]

Tazewell, boyhood friend of John Randolph, produced a series of thirteen articles between December 1832 and February 1833 in which he traced a constitutional basis for the Union to counter Jackson's definition of a sovereign people with one describing the nation as a compact of states. In affirming the right of secession, Tazewell condemned coercive threats designed to stifle withdrawal. "The security of the Union," he insisted, "is to be found in the common affections and common interests of the States, not in the bayonets of its soldiery."[32] This idea that the Union would be held together in high crisis by local fear of the national military proved an ugly legacy of the Nullification crisis. It eventually became a potent weapon for radicals who could charge that Southern Unionists acted not from principle but from cowardice. Robert J. Turnbull had already instructed South Carolinians that "there is not an atom of disgrace in being vanquished, but there is meanness in submission."[33] Turnbull died in 1833, but Barnwell Rhett was left to carry on.

The disposition to dissolve the Union did not show itself as quickly as Benjamin F. Perry thought that it would, but the provocations to do so appeared almost immediately. In January 1831 abolitionist William Lloyd Garrison first published the virulent *Liberator,* evoking an immediate and angry Southern response. After all, Southerners recalled that Denmark Vesey's Charleston conspirators had been well versed in Rufus King's antislavery sermons delivered during the Missouri debates; and now there were rumors, fed by coincidence, that Nat Turner's murderous spree in Southampton County, Virginia, had ended when the perpetrator was apprehended while clutching a copy of Garrison's publication.[34]

In 1835 the Georgia legislature passed resolutions declaring that Congress should not allow the post office to circulate abolitionist literature, and that the federal government had no right to interfere with slavery in the District of Columbia or the territories.[35] And when the Texas Revolution succeeded in establishing the Lone Star Republic, the annexation of Texas began to occupy the South's attention as a means of preserving the sectional balance in the Senate to offset the population advantage of the North in the House. Such a necessity became more apparent when Northern antislavery petitions began peppering the national legislature. Southern-sponsored "gag rules" called for immediate tabling of such petitions, much to the annoyance of constitutional purists.[36]

If Andrew Jackson "wanted the government to leave the people alone," it was also true that he "provided no way to make the people leave the government alone."[37] The annexation of Texas provided both the circumstances and the motive by which David Wilmot refused to leave the government alone. Upon the annexation of Texas, the United States quickly embroiled itself in a messy border dispute with Mexico. Because of James K. Polk's territorial ambitions, the controversy soon mounted to a major crisis. When Polk sent General Zachary Taylor's command to the Rio Grande, the *Charleston Mercury* mused that "this certainly looks like an invasion, but it will pass quietly."[38] Local Mexicans, however, could not refrain from attacking Taylor, giving Polk a reason other than his own impatience to send a war message to Congress.

By making war on Mexico, Polk marched into politically dangerous domestic territory. The Texas problem had created factions in the Democratic party. Polk's inclination for annexation had secured him the nomination in 1844, and although Van Buren's supporters had stayed in the party, they were not happy. As the possible acquisition of Texas crowded the final days of John Tyler's administration, Polk wavered, finally feigning indifference about whether Tyler should act or wait. Upon Secretary of State John C. Calhoun's recommendation, Tyler acted. Polk then announced for immediate annexation, and the Van Buren wing had its first evidence of Polk's bad faith. Those perceptions were reinforced, for upon Polk's inauguration, Van Burenites chafed under slights concerning cabinet appointments; there then followed the passage of a reduced tariff (the Walker Tariff), the veto of the Rivers and Harbors Bill, and the settlement of the Oregon question.[39]

Oregon provided a nettlesome prelude to the troubles that enveloped Polk's administration in the Mexican War. In Oregon as in Mexico, the central issue was the situation of the boundary. Where would American territory end and British West Canada begin? Prominent abolitionists, such as Joshua Giddings, wanted to secure all of Oregon to balance the entry of Texas, and Southerners feared that Northern extremists would promote war with Britain to that end. Charges of warmongering were hurled at those who cried, "Fifty-four Forty or Fight!"[40]

This sectional aspect of the controversy, seen as in the South's worst interests, prompted William Lowndes Yancey of Alabama to speak against impetuosity. It was an uncharacteristic display of moderation for Yancey, but he could not resist explaining to Westerners that the Northeast could not be relied upon in a war with Great Britain. The Northeast only wanted eastern Canada, he said, not the protection of Oregon's rights.[41] He joined Rhett to warn Congress about the horrors and the expense of such an enterprise. Apparently Calhoun orchestrated these Southern performances because Yancey's counsel of patience and his advice that an American population surge would resolve the matter imitated exactly Calhoun's suggestions for the Oregon Territory.[42] Antislavery men in the North felt cheated when Polk resolved the dispute by reducing the American claim to the 49th parallel. They caviled when the administration that had so assiduously avoided war over Oregon openly courted it with the Mexicans.

David Wilmot was probably as angry with the Polk administration's pro-Southern bias as anyone in the North. Upset over the administration's distribution of patronage, the Pennsylvania Democrat habitually sided with Van Burenites led by New York's Preston King.[43] When the administration put a bill before the House requesting money to persuade Mexico to make peace and cede her northern provinces, Wilmot reopened the slavery issue.

In an amendment to the appropriation bill, the Pennsylvanian stipulated that Congress would supply the money only if slavery were forever prohibited in any territory acquired from Mexico.[44] Because many considered the Wilmot Proviso as nothing more than a political ploy, it did not cause an immediate uproar. Yet when the administration's attempt to squelch the amendment only quashed the appropriation bill, Southerners realized that the Proviso was not merely a stratagem of disaffected Northern Democrats; it was becoming a celebrated cause among their most feared enemies in the North.

In the second session of the Twenty-ninth Congress, John C. Calhoun attempted to remove slavery from discussion. He directed Armistead Burt to argue in the House a constitutional position that Congress had no authority over chattel slavery in the territories. Van Burenites vigorously opposed this effort to calm national debate. John Petit of Indiana dismissed appeals to the Constitution and glared at Southern threats (so far inferred) of disunion. Northerners rejected Burt's proposal.[45]

When the appropriation bill came before the Senate on 1 March 1847, Northern Whigs renewed demands for the Proviso amendment. Lewis Cass, searching for a way to make political capital out of the controversy, admonished his colleagues to stop their agitation for the good of the country and, although Cass did not mention it, for the good of the Democratic party. The Michigan senator had good reason to worry about party harmony. Looking toward the 1848 Democratic Convention, he knew that a nomination from a party broken by discord over slavery would be worthless. Some Northern Democrats followed Cass, abandoning their principled reservations to nurture amity and defeat the Proviso. Northern Democrats in the House also followed the pattern there by either changing their votes or abstaining through nonattendance.[46]

The appropriation passed without the Proviso, but at a high cost to Democratic unity, in spite of Cass's efforts. Yancey became convinced that both the North and the West were faithless. He resigned his seat in the House in August 1846, remarking that the South should ignore national conventions. He wanted nothing more to do with party operatives; rather, he preferred men whose views were sectionally correct.[47] Here again Yancey sounded the Calhoun line. The old South Carolinian had kept South Carolina away from national party conventions since their appearance two decades before. Now he talked about a united South to counter Northern political aggression. In only a few months, Yancey was guiding an Alabama nominating convention to precisely that object.[48]

Of prime importance to Yancey was the Democracy's stand in the presidential contest of 1848. Whigs, gleefully contemplating yet another chance to gain the White House amid Democratic discord, had already inclined themselves toward the hero of Buena Vista, the redoubtable old Indian fighter Zachary Taylor. So Yancey's course in the coming year would be a weaving one, dictated by necessity and political reality. He toyed with the idea of bipartisan support for Taylor, following Calhoun's lead to abet a man with no demonstrable political ideas and hence who would be perceived by many Southerners as perfectly malleable on the territorial issue.[49] But Yancey did not trust the Whigs, so he backed away from the tentative alliance and sought to mend Democratic fences along acceptable boundaries. An Alabama meeting for harmony on 3 January agreed that the state's interests would have to be protected at the national convention. Yancey aimed to make certain that those Northern men friendly to the South would be seated in Baltimore.[50]

The Alabama State Convention, scheduled to meet on 14 February, itself posed a problem for Yancey because many present perceived him as an unreliable chameleon. However, other voices helped him. John A. Campbell and Percy Walker, L. P. Walker's younger brother, believed— or said they did—that all Northern Democrats wanted to bar slavery from the territories. Yancey also questioned the fealty of Northern Democrats. He could not abide Lewis Cass, the Michigan senator who in fact received the nomination, so he planned to bind Alabama delegates to support a "dark horse," Levi Woodbury of New Hampshire. Although most delegates exhibited little enthusiasm for Woodbury, the state platform, written by Yancey and Campbell, pledged support for him. Attacking the territorial issue with proslavery arguments, the so-called Alabama Platform, turned congressional nonintervention in the territories on its head. The platform demanded that Congress protect slavery in the territories even from local interference. Delegates were to reject any candidate who did not agree, thus rebuffing not only the Wilmot Proviso, but also the "squatter sovereignty" trumpeted by the Cass forces. Woodbury was agreeable to the plan, judging from a private letter to Alabama Senator Dixon Hall Lewis. So Yancey deftly wove a persuasive speech that convinced weary delegates to endorse a platform that simply made no sense from a traditional Southern position. Congress would protect slavery in territories where Southerners had stoutly insisted Congress had no authority.[51]

If Yancey and Campbell designed the Alabama Platform to secure Southern rights in the Western territories and to elevate Levi Woodbury to the presidency, they were laughably naíve. The platform could not have had any purpose other than the destruction of the National Democracy. If the national convention embraced the platform, Northern Democrats would have to disown it; if it were rejected, Yancey had at least his state's delegation under instructions to withdraw. Either occurrence proposed a broken convention and a disrupted party.

The scheme did appear feasible considering the Democratic divisions. On the eve of its gathering in Baltimore, Florida Senator David L. Yulee thought it would not be surprising "if the convention exploded."[52]

Baltimore itself was primed for such an event. A plan to publish a Southern newspaper, the *Western Continent,* was hailed as necessary because "the Southern people are no longer safe in trusting to the Northern press" because "the influence of such papers is pernicious, and for our best interests we ought to use effectual means to *check it.*"[53]

The appearance of two rival New York delegations also did not bode well for amity. From Utica an antislavery, or Barnburner delegation, adherents of the Van Buren wing, competed with the Syracuse delegation—proslavery, or Hunker—for the right to participate in the convention. Yancey's involvement in the Hunker-Barnburner dispute brought the convention to the brink of chaos, for much to the chagrin of nationally minded Democrats, slavery became the nucleus of disputes over the Western territories. Preston King of New York assured the convention that his state would not desert the Democracy's candidate over the slavery issue, but Yancey would not be mollified. He shouted that "if New York does not choose to go with us, we will go without her."[54]

If Yancey believed that his plans were the plans of the South, he was badly mistaken. His disruptive scheme suffered a major setback when a compromise cobbled together members from both delegations to represent New York. The solution did not please anyone very much, but at least it steered the convention away from internecine debate. A reiteration of the platform resolutions of 1840 and 1844 ignored the Wilmot Proviso problem, so Yancey in committee tried to insinuate the Alabama Platform. Louisianan John Slidell, alarmed by the prospect of a broken convention, quashed this mischief, so Yancey brought his platform to the floor in a minority report. Only Florida and Virginia supported him, and the cautious convention rejected his report in a 216 to 36 vote.[55]

Yancey should have sat quietly, abided the sense of the convention, and begun repairing the self-inflicted damage. But having committed the politically deadly sin of futile troublemaking, Yancey compounded it with the even deadlier sin of obstinacy. He quixotically walked out of the convention accompanied by only one other delegate. Even the Alabama delegation ignored him and disregarded its instructions.

Yancey angrily raced south, first stopping at Charleston to protest the convention's actions to a grumbling crowd, then proceeding to Alabama to persuade the state to repudiate the Democracy's nominee. In Montgomery on 19 June, he extolled his platform to a Democratic meeting and lamented its violation. Yet, Alabama would not desert the Democracy, despite Yancey's persistence for an independent nomination.[56] "In Alabama the best kind of feeling prevails," Stephen A. Douglas wrote to Cass after travelling through the state. In noting the rejection of Yancey's ideas, Douglas glowed that even Montgomery was assured for Cass; as for the rest of the Alabama, "even the Whigs concide [*sic*] the state to you . . . as against Taylor even."[57] All Yancey was gaining with his renegade campaign was popularity with the Whigs.[58]

"I did not think your speech at Charleston a judicious one," Dixon Hall Lewis chided Yancey.[59] Lewis himself knew the potential perils awaiting those who deserted the party in an election year, especially this election year. His allegiance to Calhoun's no-party support of Taylor had angered Alabama party members, some of whom suggested that William R. King take the nomination for Lewis's Senate seat. In spite of a 428-pound bulk that required two railroad tickets and a special chair in Congress, Lewis had moved easily into a prominent position in Alabama politics. He had helped frame the Walker Tariff and had led the Polk administration's attempts to stop the Wilmot Proviso in the Senate. His weight did embarrass him, especially at campaign time when he had to be lifted onto speaker's platforms, fanned, and, on one occasion, doused with a bucket of water against the Alabama heat. Yet it had not deprived him of a good marriage, and his sister-in-law was Governor Benjamin Fitzpatrick's wife.[60] However, none of this—neither family connections nor previous services—mattered in light of his support for Taylor, so he quickly rejected Calhoun's initiative, declared for party, and assured his reelection.[61]

Lewis then advised Yancey to stop his efforts for an independent nomination, for no other influential Democrat would follow. Jefferson Davis was "quietly beginning . . . to acquiesce in the *necessity* of supporting Cass," as were Littleton Tazewell and James A. Seddon in Virginia, David L. Yulee in Florida, and even Barnwell Rhett in South Carolina, all out of the need for defeating the candidate who, unlike Cass, had refused to commit himself on a veto of the Wilmot Proviso.[62] In short, all of the influence in the world amounted to nothing when one was cut off from the Democratic party, a fact of political life to which Yancey resigned himself in 1848, but not, as it happened, forever.

The Free Soil candidacy of Martin Van Buren helped augment Democratic disunity and lose the election to Taylor in November, but Southern dissatisfaction with Cass indicated another dangerous diver-

gence of Northern and Southern opinion. The fate of the Western territories catalyzed disagreement now not only on the theoretical constitutional level but on the level of functional national party policy as well. In
Virginia, Edmund Ruffin, Jr., had planned to vote Democratic but
scratched out Cass's name and substituted Calhoun's as a personal statement while remaining in the Democratic fold. As the forces arrayed
against the South's institutions grew stronger and more aggressive, the
political process had presented for many only unpleasant choices. The
younger Ruffin told his father, "Southerners ought to pause."[63]

Everyone should have paused. The election of 1848 offered dark por-
tents. The emotional impact of slavery issues befuddled the political
system and made it dangerously vulnerable to disruption. Yancey went to
Baltimore to cause trouble, and the convention should have dismissed
him as a hapless malcontent. Instead, he threatened and alarmed the
National Democracy with less than 15 percent of the delegates sympa-
thetic to his position. He had made it heatedly debate an issue it wished
to ignore.

Yancey's tactics imperiled not just the Democratic party but the South
as well. If he really wished to defend Southern rights within the Union,
his performance was most dubious. John Calhoun had seen the dangers in
Northern attitudes as early as 1828, and the outcome of the Nullification
crisis had only enlarged his apprehensions. In the face of growing abolitionism, he became a staunch defender of slavery, bringing to the Southern argument a logical precision rendered in his characteristically calm,
expository style, always seeking to instruct rather than persuade.[64] Yet the
injection of slavery into national discussion consistently alarmed him, for
he sensed that within the climate generated and dominated by Northern
agitation, any notice taken of Southern slavery presaged only another
assault. He initially opposed the Mexican War for fear that territorial
acquisitions would lead inevitably to just such a controversy as that
caused by the Wilmot Proviso.[65]

Calhoun recognized that the slavery issue isolated the South as a peculiar sectional minority. It was not really the Wilmot Proviso that was
dangerous. Rather, it was the temper of opinion in the North that railed
against Southern property rights and created the spirit of assault upon
Southern political rights. To defeat Wilmot and leave the other "unre-
sisted and in full operation" would be worse than outright failure. There
could be no compromise because compromise meant little beyond spu-

riously reassuring the South "without removing, or even diverting, the danger."[66] He labored strenuously in his last years to persuade Northeastern conservatives that Southern concerns were not exclusively sectional, but rather were founded upon a larger issue than that of Negro slavery. He wanted to show that a coalition of minority interests could protect any of its members' political rights. An exiguous community would otherwise find itself beleaguered by its own diminished influence in an increasingly hostile national environment.[67]

The supreme tragedy that attached itself to the old South Carolinian was that he deeply believed that the destruction of slavery, whether immediately through its outright abolition or inevitably through its restriction, meant the strangulation of the South. Only through a united South, forgetful of its "wretched party strife," could the North be made to listen out of a fear of retaliation. There lay the safety of the Union.[68]

After 1848 events began to move so quickly that Calhoun saw an immediate need to buy his section some time, even if purchased with threats dire enough to frighten Northern opponents into offering concessions. Convinced then that the only way to preserve the Union was by menacing it, he sought to unite the South in an implacable front sensitive to violations of its proper constitutional rights.[69]

He was confident that if the movement succeeded, the Union and his South would both survive. Some who fervently enlisted in his cause already had different ideas.

CHAPTER TWO

"Leadership of This Generation"

Antebellum Washington was, according to one observer, "in all social and industrial aspects a Southern town."[1] While the Southern character of the city did not please all Southerners—J. H. Hammond always preferred the cleaner and more elegant Philadelphia[2]—one particular characteristic, the unhappy presence of the slave market, seemed to Northerners a shameful exhibition of hypocrisy in the capital of a nation that embraced the philosophy of human liberty. By 1848 many Northern reformers considered that the time was right to strike legislatively at this condition. When New York Whig Daniel Gott brought a resolution condemning the slave trade before the House of Representatives, Southern members had heard enough. They anxiously sought some form of protection against what they saw as a near miss (the Gott resolution was tabled) bound eventually to find its mark. So in December 1848 the representatives and senators of the slaveholding states caucused, Whigs and Democrats alike, and the first serious move toward Southern unity began.

Although there were others involved in this move, John C. Calhoun assumed a special prominence. Calhoun was much older than when, as an ambitious politician, he had drafted the *South Carolina Exposition and Protest* in 1828 and had reluctantly joined South Carolina's ill-fated confrontation with Andrew Jackson; correspondingly, he was also wiser, for he realized that South Carolina alone did not possess the kind of influence necessary to stand against a powerful federal apparatus. No state alone had that much power. It was better to act in concert, drawing upon the collective strength imparted to a whole section's action. In the 1848 meeting of Southerners from the national legislature, Calhoun was pleased to see a widespread indignation taking hold. Here in this meeting he tried to impress his colleagues with the seriousness of their circumstance. Always an imposing orator, Calhoun stood a full six feet and could wither an opponent by scowling his dark, gray eyes. His manner in the Senate was unerringly deliberate, a fixture of intellectual meditation, as calm as the morning clothes he habitually wore to legislative sessions. However, now voicing the grievances he felt the South subjected to, he shouted, gestured broadly, stamped his foot. The effect, though surely arresting, was not altogether successful.[3]

Although a Committee of Fifteen, with Calhoun appointed its chairman, drafted what was eventually known as the Southern Address, some Southerners refused to sign such a sectional document. Whigs, not wishing to foul the lines of Zachary Taylor's incoming Whig administration, backed away from the Address. And many Democrats, under instructions from President James K. Polk to avoid a sectional statement that was sure to divide the party, also abandoned the cause. In any event, there was a rival address in circulation from a committee of which Senator John M. Berrien of Georgia was chairman. The latter appealed to the nation, rather than exclusively to the South, to arrest the anti-Southern agitations of the North. The distinction was not so subtle as it might appear, the latter address being more moderate—or, as the Calhoun people said, more timid.[4]

The factiousness of this early attempt at Southern political unity affirmed the existence of a strong sense of Jacksonian nationalism among substantial numbers in the South. Unfortunately, the sectional strife that characterized the slow division between the North and the South had been subjected to too many irritants for certain men in both sections to remain calm. They became determined to dwell on differences rather than common interests. Perhaps this was unavoidable, because the fundamental difference between the two regions was a testament to an age caught in all respects between the old and the new. Hence, paradoxes abounded as the natural manifestations of change. Southerners who resisted change and Northerners who impatiently pressed for it encouraged difference and division. Provocation and response began to spread from the politicians' forums to the population in glaring, dangerously perceptible ways. Earlier, state legislatures and conventions had mounted protests. Now groups of ordinary citizens gathered to declare that they would not tolerate the antislavery movement and that slavery was a positive good.[5]

Northern universities and colleges, such as Princeton where the faculty consisted of Northern Whigs almost exclusively, opposed Southern interests and had no compunction about letting Southern students know the error of their ways.[6] Likewise, Southern universities instilled in students the idea that the Union was not as valuable as the sovereignty of the state.[7] Where before there had been mutual, even if grudging, respect for Northern adversaries, there now was contempt arising from imputations of hypocrisy. David Yulee, once staying in the same hotel as the Stephen Douglases, noted that Douglas had two servants and mused that "these Northern men like the luxury of slaves, when they can get them."[8] It mattered little that Yulee later saw one of the "slaves" and discovered that she was a white servant.[9] Too often the mistakes went uncorrected and the judgments unamended. Inevitably the community of America became alien for many ordinary Southerners. Even the glorious Fourth of July lost its national significance for those who could not abide a society that countenanced—and seemed gradually to encourage—abolitionism. A new generation emerged and came to prominence, finding adamancy easier than amiability, combat more desirable than compromise.[10]

One such member of the new generation was Robert Barnwell Rhett of South Carolina. Discouraged by the failure of the Southern caucus to achieve unity, Rhett nonetheless supported Calhoun's efforts and lobbied against the Whigs as they began to drift away from the movement. Yet the poor performance of the Southern Address, which gained only 48 of 121 possible signatures, reaffirmed Rhett's belief that separate state action was the best way to secure Southern rights.[11]

Rhett had been among the few—perhaps he was the only man—who lately had crossed Calhoun in South Carolina and politically lived to tell about it. Tall with blue-gray eyes, Rhett liked to smile and laugh, but many found him imperious, aloof, and affected. In 1837 he had changed his name from Smith to Rhett, following the lead of his brothers who wanted to preserve the name of a distinguished ancestor, Colonel William Rhett. The gesture struck some as ostentatious.

Although he had a quick, nervous temper, he was a self-controlled man with extraordinary abilities, not the least of which was the capability of speaking at considerable length without spending his voice. Thin, yet erect, and with good shoulders and narrow hips, he made a striking figure, his soft, white hands appearing curiously bleached relative to a rather florid complexion. This was so noticeable that Rhett would explain that the ruddiness was not due to drink, but instead that "the Englishman is not out of me yet."[12]

Rhett had always done in politics fairly much as he pleased, and—apparently living a charmed life—he had usually escaped any consequences. Thoroughly schooled in radicalism, he had joined protests over the tariff in 1827 and had been a Nullifier in 1832. In the early 1840s, he led the abortive "Bluffton Movement" in South Carolina, an unsuccessful attempt to break with Calhoun and force separate state action on the tariff question. But Rhett's most overt challenge to Calhoun's authority in South Carolina occurred in the 1848 presidential campaign. Calhoun's no-party support of Taylor kept South Carolina from the Baltimore Convention, but ultimately Taylor's Whig candidacy proved unthinkable to Democratic loyalists. By September 1848 Rhett was covering all his political bases. He officially deserted Calhoun by bemoaning the alienation of Southern Democrats into the Whig Party. The call for party loyalty earned the Colleton firebrand a new popularity even in conservative, Calhounite Charleston. Citizens crowded into Hibernian Hall to hear Rhett stump for Cass even as he still insisted that the South must look to its own protection.[13]

Rhett was now forty-nine years old and probably at the height of his powers.[14] Yet he was gloomy as he watched the attempts for a unified Southern movement with a certain amount of detached sorrow. In the summer of 1848 he wrote to Calhoun, who evidently could never stay angry with Rhett for long, that neither the Wilmot Proviso nor the abolition of slavery in the District of Columbia would issue from the Thirty-first Congress scheduled to convene in December. He had hoped that Southerners, irreconcilably provoked, would be willing to face "the contest, and end it once and forever." But this was too much to ask for. Northerners, Rhett believed, would commit "no such blunder."[15]

This was loose, harsh talk, very impolitic, and it must have chagrined the old senator to hear Rhett in such a condition. The red-faced South Carolinian was accustomed to framing this kind of independent fantasy, but Calhoun, for all his particular failings, was a practical man. Rhett had his fellows of like mind with wild hopes for a quick showdown with the

North—indeed, the spring and summer of 1850 would bring them blossoming like so many wildflowers in an untended meadow—but Calhoun and many others sincerely worried that at last the North would inflict its will on the South, even if that meant the dissolution of the Union. Georgia, Alabama, and Mississippi all exhibited sizeable evidence of discontent, and even the border states of Missouri and Kentucky had joined Virginia in vocally protesting the controversies left by the inactivity of the Thirtieth Congress. As Northern state legislatures, one after another, passed resolutions demanding the prohibition of slavery in the Western territories and the abolition of the slave trade in the District of Columbia, anger, growing more intense, swept through the South. Kentucky's October 1848 Constitutional Convention provided a forum for those who wanted to use the occasion for constitutional emancipation. The issue was fought out county by county, and the result was an adamantly proslavery convention.[16]

Rhett's immoderate mood concerned Calhoun because of South Carolina's precarious position in any Southern movement. Although unity of discontent existed in the South, it was fragile and undefined. A strong thread of Unionism veined states like Alabama and Georgia, not to mention North Carolina, Virginia, Florida, Louisiana, and the Border States. Healthy Whig partisanship in these states could easily reassert itself with a veto of the Southern movement as it had the Southern Address.

The National Whig party was a peculiarity. It owed its creation to a dislike of Andrew Jackson and the political trends he represented. But the hold exerted by the party over the wealthy planter class in the South became more paradoxical each year as it became apparent that National Whig policy often ran counter to Southern interests. Irritated by the onset of abolitionism, the party began to divide along sectional lines. Soon distinctive labels like "Cotton" and "Conscience" Whig delineated people who belonged to the same party more out of habit than political affinity. Yet the habit was strong. In the old Southwest, Louisiana had possessed a competitive Whig organization as early as 1837. After 1840, however, Whigs represented only a minority in Arkansas, Alabama, and Mississippi, and even in Louisiana after 1842 the Whigs never elected another governor. Still, wealthy and influential Southern Whigs constituted a powerful minority that could keep pace with the Southern Democracy in all but two states.[17]

The Whigs would have been stronger in South Carolina and Virginia if not for the remarkable hold over state politics exerted by Democratic cliques. Virginia gave Democratic presidential candidates her votes from 1828 through 1856, and South Carolina would have had an equally unblemished record except for Calhoun's defection in 1832. Indeed, in South Carolina John Calhoun ruled the roost of a Democratic party that only seldom resisted his will.[18] As efficient as this might have seemed, it was also dangerous, not because of Calhoun, but rather in spite of him. The absence of national political parties left South Carolina virtually bereft of internal opposition. Its behavior thus inclined toward compulsive truculence at the slightest provocation.[19]

The majority of South Carolina's leaders recognized that their overt role in a Southern movement could taint it, scornful memories of the Nullification debacle still fresh in nearly everybody's mind.[20] So South Carolina intended, at Calhoun's urging, to disguise a nearly unanimous desire for secession. Rhett, from a different kind of Carolina tradition, voiced the minority sentiment: South Carolina should bravely forge ahead and be done with it, ignoring the activity (or inactivity) of other Southern states. Charleston, reflecting the attitude of men like Robert W. Barnwell and Andrew Pickens Butler, desired secession, but only if it did not risk commercial and political isolation.[21] Calhoun was altogether different. The old man loved the Union only a little less than he did the South, and he wished, if possible, to see both flourish. In the long term, the only way for that to occur was through the formation of a national political coalition. But first an immediate threat had to be dealt with, and Calhoun sought to do so by forming a Southern league within the United States.[22]

The fate of the Western territories caused this imperative urgency. Two years after the introduction of the Wilmot Proviso, the organization of the Oregon Territory demonstrated that the Proviso, while officially failed, was still potent in principle. Hence, when the discovery of gold in California triggered a tide of emigration and a self-generated convention framed an antislavery constitution, Southerners simply exploded. Amazed and appalled to discover that a place existed where "mere labor" could earn three dollars per day, James H. Hammond believed that stable government could not survive in California's hyperactive economy. In fact, not "for a century—perhaps centuries to come, unless the mines give out" would it be possible to place responsible government there.[23] One had to ask why such an attempt was being made now, and the answer, most regrettably, seemed provided by coincidental crises that took on the appearance of concerted Northern political aggression: the question of the slave trade in the District of Columbia; the boundary dispute between Texas and the New Mexico Territory; and the issue of whether or not the New Mexico and Utah Territories, like California, would wish and be allowed to become bastions of Free Soil. Under the weight of these combined controversies, the national government stumbled with inactivity through the latter part of 1849 while some Southerners salved apprehensions with elaborate plans for a Southern movement.[24]

Only one other state felt as strongly as South Carolina did about Northern attitudes on slavery. In Mississippi discontent had come very close to obliterating the lines separating Whigs and Democrats, and the slavery issue had become paramount in the state's elections. Albert Gallatin Brown's campaign in 1849 against his Whig opponent the Reverend Dr. William Winans for a seat in the United States House orbited such concerns. Brown was not an easy adversary, and his record attested to electoral invincibility. He had held elective office without a single defeat since 1832 (a successful run he would continue until 1865). Unlike his fellow Mississippian, Senator Jefferson Davis, Brown was not an aristocrat, and his constituents were a conglomeration of poor whites, small slaveholders, and nonslaveholders from the piney woods section of the state. His face resembled Davis's, and though it lacked the chiseled prominence of high cheekbones, it was a good face with clear eyes, a clean-shaven jaw, and a chin partially obscured by a thick rectangular beard jutting over his necktie. Notwithstanding that he was a marvelous political fighter in a state remarkable for its rough-and-tumble politics, his devastating trouncing of Winans in the November election undoubtedly was due not so much to his attractiveness but rather to Winans's having made antislavery remarks in a speech several years earlier.[25] The electorate in Brown's district had a long memory for such transgressions, and even as the *Mississippi Free Trader,* also in Brown's district, curiously proclaimed the evil of slavery, Brown argued for the institution's positive good and declared the efficacy of state sovereignty.[26] He reflected his constituents' views and held sentiments that conformed with those of his Mississippi colleagues in the national House and Senate. These Mississippians did not always match the fervor of South Carolina's politicians, but the potential was there.

Because of this potential that boded so well for bipartisan support, Mississippi became the likeliest candidate to lead a concerted Southern protest. At Calhoun's veiled instigation, a group of discontented Whigs and Democrats met in May 1849 with the distinguished William Sharkey presiding. Calhoun described Sharkey as a "very able man" who was, best of all, a Whig.[27] This meeting advocated a bipartisan state convention to meet in October. Calhoun's suggestions for Mississippi remained confidential, lest knowledge of South Carolina's influence spoil the plan. "I dropped a note to General [Henry S.] Foote stating that it had occurred *in Mississippi* that a Southern convention was the most important action required," a friend reassured Calhoun. "You will understand this."[28]

At the same time, Calhoun did advise Mississippi to address its call "to all those who are desirous to save the Union and our institutions, and who, in the alternative (should it be forced upon us) of submission or dissolution would prefer the latter."[29] The October state convention took the advice, even if some grumbled about the provenance. Sharkey, presiding in October as he had in May, summed up discontent by asking, "Shall we submit to farther degradation, or shall we seek redress? If the latter, how is it to be obtained?"[30] The convention answered with ten resolutions, the seventh calling for a Southern convention in Nashville on the first Monday of the following June. The convention also approved "The Address to the Southern States" that proclaimed not only the right of secession, but the possibility of its occurrence.[31]

So by the fall of 1849, Calhoun was exulting, and this mainly because the Mississippi call for a Southern convention had crossed party lines, Whigs and Democrats participating. Here, at last, the prospect of a Southern party acting as a bloc against Northern political aggression seemed realized. A convention two states removed (and, as far as most people knew, thoroughly removed) from South Carolina's influence had taken the first step, signalling the chance for the South to act. The clamor of the times suggested that all the slave states might grab the opportunity.[32]

Yet it was not to prove that easy. The idea of the Nashville Convention reached its greatest appeal long before the June meeting date. Such a circumstance resulted, in part, from compromise efforts in Washington during the first half of 1850. Otherwise, internal conditions caused people to lose interest in the convention. Southerners held some of these in common, while some were unique to particular states.

Texas, for instance, was unique. That this vast land had been a sovereign republic between its independence from Mexico and its annexation by the United States made Texans especially egocentric. This habit of sovereignty was hard enough to break in relations with the United States government, let alone a mere section of the United States. Texas Senators Sam Houston and Thomas J. Rusk refused to sign the Southern Address in 1848, and Houston, that giant of a Texan who was as large as the state, was adamant about the matter. "I am the big dog of the barnyard. I am the big dog of Texas," Houston once allegedly crowed, prompting enemies to refer to him as "his dogship."[33] In any event, threats of disunion had ceased to scare his dogship—or so he said. And as for sectional interests, he proclaimed himself a nationalist, argued for bills accordingly (with at least the tacit approval of most Texans), notably squaring against Calhoun on the Oregon territorial bill in 1848.[34] He habitually argued for the rights of Texas, never for slavery, and just as he had voted against the extension of 36°30' in 1849, he was willing to vote for a free California in 1850. Furthermore, the idea of the Nashville Convention alternately bemused and disgusted him. Rusk, on the other hand, usually voted with Southerners, despite his refusal to sign the Southern Address.[35]

But Houston was not Texas. A strong pro-Southern group lived in the state. In January 1848 in preparation for the state convention that would send delegates to the Democratic National Convention in Baltimore, a county meeting in Galveston issued a set of angry resolutions protesting federal interference in the territories and proclaiming the right to settle them with "property" (meaning slaves). The resolutions recommended that should the Democratic nominee in Baltimore reject these notions, Texas should reject him. The committee that drafted these resolutions was not really very representative of Texas, but it did contain at least one individual destined for prominence in the Southern rights movement—Louis T. Wigfall.[36]

Of more profound influence in 1850 was the rather sizeable group of pro-Southern advocates in Marshall, one of Texas's larger towns, situated in Harrison County, the largest county in the state. Here Robert W. Loughery's *Texas Republican* churned out pro-Southern agitation that embraced Calhoun's ideas while encouraging young radicals like Wigfall. The paper applauded Marshall's citizens for denouncing Houston's and Rusk's refusal to sign the Southern Address, and it now urged Texan attendance at Nashville.[37]

Newly elected Governor Peter H. Bell also wanted the state represented at Nashville. A feisty Democrat who had defeated Houston man

George T. Wood in November, Bell won by promising a galled electorate that he would take an aggressive stand on the New Mexico boundary problem, a promise that would almost cause a civil war. Bell told the legislature in December 1849 that Congress had no right to tamper with the spread of slavery into the territories. The Virginia Resolutions,[38] passed in March 1847, appealed to him as a model for Texas to emulate, but he did not specifically include in his program Texas participation at Nashville.[39]

So the legislature dithered on the Nashville matter, studying and reporting and wrangling on how and by whom delegates should be chosen. Finally legislators scheduled an election (to coincide with legislative nomination) for the first Monday in March, the same day Texans would choose the permanent site for their capital. The hasty announcement combined with the capital site question made for slim returns on the Nashville Convention.[40] And, of course, many Texans simply wanted to stay out of Nashville for other reasons. As one correspondent wrote Governor Bell, "Texas having so recently come into the Union, should not be foremost to dissolve it, but I trust she will not waver, when the crisis shall come."[41]

Such wavering sentiment also frustrated those trying to build a successful Southern movement in other states. Louisiana did not look promising even though the state's retiring governor, Isaac Johnson, felt "a proud assurance" that the state would support "any measure the Convention might adopt."[42] Conservative and affluent, Louisiana contained a ruling elite as anxious to leave undisturbed a prosperous trans-Atlantic trade as it was suspicious of South Carolina radicalism.[43] Not until late February did the state Senate pass "slavery resolutions" advising each parish to send a representative to Nashville and protesting congressional interference with slavery in the territories. The Louisiana House, more attuned to the state's cautious mood, did not even vote on the resolutions, opposition and promotion crossing Whig and Democratic lines.[44] To the north, Arkansas was much the same way. New and raw and needing the federal government more than the South, Arkansas stayed clear of the sectional movement, despite the powerful pro-Southern voice of Congressman Robert W. Johnson.[45]

Offering some surprise early in 1850, the Whig *Wilmington* (North Carolina) *Commercial* warned that "unless there is reform, and that speedily, there will be found an immense majority in all the southern states, who will very readily entertain a proposition for disunion."[46] Such pro-Southern press sentiments in North Carolina, however, ran counter to the people's conservatism. North Carolinians were staunch in their love of the Union and would not be willing to see it dissolved. To be sure, Southern rights meetings took place throughout the state during the congressional controversies of 1850, but these meetings did not represent most North Carolinians. When the crusty old states righter Abraham W. Venable carried his district against the attacks of Whigs and Union Democrats in 1849, he had felt sufficiently proud of the achievement to write to Calhoun about it.[47] Venable and Thomas L. Clingman in the House spoke passionately against the proposed compromise measures in January and February, but they did so with little support from their constituents.[48]

For a while, though, old North State Whigs and Democrats supported the Nashville Convention—Democrats because they were angered over the slavery issue and Whigs because they either agreed or could see a tide of resentment sweeping the state. Conservatives manned both parties, however, and they meant to use the convention at Nashville as a symbol of resistance, never as a prologue to secession.[49] As the compromise began its torturous journey through Congress, even the inclination for resistance evaporated, and opinion grew hostile toward the Southern movement. The disunionists, wrote one observer in North Carolina, "have tried to break up the Union & the only reason they did not succeed is that the People are not willing."[50]

Likewise the people of Kentucky, though sentimentally inclined toward the South, steadfastly opposed disunion "as a remedy for any evil."[51] This was no surprise coming from the state of Henry Clay, just as it was expected (or should have been) that the people of Missouri, home of the towering old Unionist and Jacksonian Thomas Hart Benton, would have no desire to participate at Nashville.[52]

Signs that at least Missouri and Kentucky would not join the sectional movement must have relieved the nervous editor of the *Boston Daily Advertiser* who, late in February, was remarking that "everything is to depend . . . on the course of Kentucky, Tennessee, and Missouri."[53]

For its part, Tennessee presented a peculiar set of contradictions. The state's summer elections of 1849 had delivered a Democratic House and a Whig Senate, and the Senate accordingly stifled all resolutions to centralize the choice of delegates to the June convention. So local meetings had to carry out selections. Overall, Tennessee Whigs opposed the Southern movement and necessarily the proposed convention. For instance, there was the "calm and cautious" John Bell in the Senate.[54] Bell, a good Whig who was also a good nationalist, opposed anything hinting at disunion—and the convention, according to Whigs, sponsored more and more solely by Democrats, seemed disunionist. Bell repudiated the convention and supported the compromise measures before Congress. Meanwhile, Hopkins L. Turney, Tennessee's Democratic senator, quarrelled with any kind of compromise. In the state itself, the Democrats were, after a fashion, for the convention because the memory of Andrew Jackson's nationalism was still a strong bulwark of the Tennessee party. Hence, the lines were drawn in Tennessee, and no radical voice of sufficient influence could erase them. Whigs packed the local meeting held in Nashville's Davidson County. Although Andrew Jackson Donelson, nephew by marriage of Old Hickory himself, presided, the Whig majority boisterously rejected the whole idea of the convention. Donelson and company tried again, this time without the unruly Whigs, and managed to elect twenty-nine delegates for the county. Most of the enthusiasm was out of it, however.[55]

If Tennessee was bereft of radical voices, young Florida, the southernmost state, had Senator David L. Yulee. He was from a heavily Democratic area outside of St. Augustine, was almost forty years old, and was of Portuguese and Jewish antecedents.[56] He had become a Calhoun follower around 1845 and since then had grown so angry with what he regarded as Northern treachery that by 1850 he inflexibly opposed any kind of compromise. The North had violated the trust of the Missouri Compromise, he maintained, and if the North would not now agree to a constitutional amendment protecting slavery, he saw secession as the only answer.[57] He insisted on the preservation of an equal balance between slave and free states.[58] As for the Nashville Convention, Yulee joined with Whig Representatives Edward C. Cabell and Jackson Morton, the latter a somewhat befuddled man who frequently followed Yulee's lead, in writing a persuasive pro-Southern letter to Governor Thomas Brown.[59] Brown, a Unionist Whig, wanted to protect Florida's position more than the South's rights, and he refused to promote the convention, denying that he had any right to appoint delegates to it.[60] As in Tennessee, the matter was left to local meetings.[61]

With so many states deemed depressingly lukewarm (if not slightly chilly) toward the Southern movement, radical and moderate states righters alike surveyed Georgia and Alabama with warm optimism. These were the keystone states between hot Mississippi and red-hot South Carolina, and what they would do in relation to Nashville and the impending compromise in Washington would be of extreme importance.

In Georgia, circumstances looked, up to a point, especially promising. Even Whig Representative Robert Toombs, disgusted with events in the House of Representatives, finally cried out that "the *Union* is the masked battery from behind which the Constitution and the rights of the South are to be assailed."[62] Toombs's anger proved exaggerated and temporary, but the actions of the Georgia legislature, nearly evenly divided between Whigs and Democrats with the latter in a slight majority, encouraged those who favored Southern rights. Although conservatives dominated the Democratic party in Georgia, news of California's constitutional prohibitions on slavery had acted as a balm on Whig and Democratic differences. Radical fervor gripped both houses of the legislature, and taking their cue from newly elected Governor George W. Towns, they smelted resolutions stamped with earmarks of possible secession. Whigs and Democrats alike found common ground, and if they were occasionally discordant over whether to call a state convention or how to choose delegates to Nashville or if they should list California's admission among their grievances, these were mere matters of method to a common end.[63]

Alabama appeared a likely prospect for extreme radicalism because of the activities of William Lowndes Yancey.[64] Yancey had controlled the actions of the three conventions in Alabama—two official and one informal—that had met between May 1847 and February 1848 to draft and verify the Alabama Platform. The platform was popular in several Southern states. The Georgia legislature had endorsed it as had Democratic party conventions in Florida and Virginia in 1848.[65] Despite his rambunctious activity in the 1848 campaign, Yancey still wielded considerable influence because of his ability to make speeches that simplified complicated matters even as the "tamer natures" of his audience were "transported."[66] A uniquely passionate orator in an age when passionate oratory was the standard, Yancey had a vocal range that could preserve a staid conversational cadence and then leap into high tones of fervid declamation. He moved nervously but never stalked about the platform.

His straightforward, rather long sentences were remarkable for a virtual absence of adjectives, and though he seldom wrote out his speeches, he meticulously prepared anecdotes. Yancey was deadly with his voice, and it was injudicious to cross him on the speaker's rostrum.[67]

Alabama had gravitated toward Yancey's ideas after Taylor's victory. The state legislature protested Northern agitation on slavery, and Senator Benjamin Fitzpatrick signed Calhoun's Southern Address.[68] Yet Governor Henry W. Collier's suggestion of an ultimatum to convince the North that the state meant business was defeated by a timid legislature that refused even to provide for participation at Nashville. An informal (meaning extralegal) meeting of the legislature later selected delegates, but the state opposed disunion. Secessionists became more vehement in the face of resistance, and large, angry meetings calling for Southern rights tried very hard to act like a majority. The act was good enough to alarm Alabama Whigs. They began asking the embarrassing question of why Nashville delegates had not been selected by a popular referendum. Henry W. Hilliard, that cultured and intelligent Alabama Whig, expressed the widespread feeling in the state when he wrote that "no convention ought to be held in *advance* of some act of aggression on the part of the government."[69]

Affairs in Congress most dramatically impeded the Southern march to Nashville. Early in the year, the mood of Southerners in Congress mirrored the anger of their section. At the start of the session, the House spent day after exhausting day in a pitched battle over the speakership, and in February a Southern filibuster blocked all discussion on California.[70]

Finally, Henry Clay put his compromise measures before the Senate. The old Kentuckian formally broke with the Taylor administration to seek an amicable settlement of the California issue, the Texas and New Mexico boundary dispute, and the slave trade irritant in the District of Columbia, while presenting to the South a new, tougher fugitive slave law—all of these in one package. The plan had many weak spots (and indeed would fail as a package), but the earliest obstacles to its success were Zachary Taylor's intransigence and the Southern Democrats' machinations. The Whigs in Congress were a different matter, and those Southern Whigs, whose participation in the fall of 1849 had so pleased Calhoun, suddenly backed away from the Southern movement and the Nashville Convention. Everyone should work for a compromise solution, so why have this convention? Especially *this* convention that now appeared, in light of the happy flush of compromise, superfluous at best and tainted at worst.[71] As events progressed, Whigs accused Southern Democrats of outrageous sectionalism, and those Southern Democrats, politically cornered, had to defend themselves against the charge of supporting disunion—a charge that many of them half-suspected was true.[72]

It was no secret that John C. Calhoun was not a well man in 1850. He had collapsed the previous year, crumpling to the floor of the Senate chamber, a casualty of the taxing advocacy for his Southern Address. Doctors had diagnosed the trouble as a bad stomach, but nobody was deceived—his lungs were bad, his heart weak, he was an old man. The "stomach" trouble kept him out of the Senate off and on, and now a bout with pneumonia forced his absence after the first two weeks of the current session. "We are glad to learn," wrote the *Charleston Mercury,* "that Mr. Calhoun . . . is recovering his health."[73] But only those clinging to illusions could have believed that he was. He coughed and spat frequently, and although traces of pneumonia still veined his lungs, he could not resist the chance to have at this great controversy in one last speech. He would argue the cause for his Southern homeland, true, but also for the Union.

When he limped into the Senate on the arm of James Hamilton shortly after noon on 4 March, a countenance more skull than face revealed that he was dreadfully ill. Yet the gray eyes still snapped fire, and in a surprisingly firm voice he delivered a brief preamble to a quietened, solemn audience that saw before them now a dead man, but for the dying. That preamble was an apology for having to call upon James M. Mason of Virginia to read the speech, a strong speech that eschewed the idea of any compromise—the South had none to give—and demanded, for the sake of the Union, concessions that would forever still the slavery question.[74]

Three days later Daniel Webster carried out the design of pacification that had been his settled plan for nearly a month: to break with the Taylor administration, throw his influence to Clay and the Compromise, and chide the radicals of both camps, North and South, for agitations that could only work to sunder the Union.[75] Yet Calhoun was not satisfied even so. There was no issue of compromise here, he insisted, and there was the dispute at its base, as ever, on the indissolubility of the Union. The South Carolinian dragged himself to the Senate chamber again, almost for the last time, to contest Webster's words, to argue the right of secession; and, after a brief exchange with Webster, still contesting, he left, to die twenty-four days later.[76] In the minds of some—those who were with Calhoun—nothing was settled. While in the minds of many, everything had been given a great opportunity, perhaps conclusively, to settle right. The latter sentiment was due to Webster's amazing and, for him, politically damaging performance on 7 March. The former sentiment was that of the Southern Democrats who, at the end of March, lost the leader of their cause.

Even though activities in the Southern states had occupied the fretful attention of many during the early months of 1850, all of the frenetic activity was not so much a prologue to the attempted realization of a Southern movement as it was the crescendo leading up to the speech of Webster and the end of Calhoun. "Webster's speech," remarked Robert Winthrop, "has knocked the Nashville Convention into a cocked hat."[77] The observation, as the mood of the Southern Whigs shifted toward the Compromise, turned out to be mostly true. The notion of a united Southern bloc ignorant of Whig and Democratic party lines evaporated as quickly in the spring of 1850 as it had suddenly appeared in the fall of 1849. This was the immediate impact of Webster's effort, the effect of which was measurable and obvious. Calhoun's death, on the other hand, remained shrouded in dark ambiguities about what it meant for radicals and moderates alike.

He was the first of the great triumvirate—Clay and Webster were the other two—to pass from the scene, and in that, his passing marked the beginning of the end of a legislative era. Concerning the South, his death definitely marked the end of something else. Calhoun had been the driving force for all widespread Southern initiatives up until now. He had formed ideas of sovereignty that had drawn intellectual force from the Jeffersonian doctrines enunciated in the Virginia and Kentucky Resolutions of 1798 and had used those ideas to formulate Nullification two decades before 1850. It had been Calhoun's doctrines that had so unwittingly, yet so pervasively, schooled South Carolina politicians in the habits of radicalism. The logical maturation of state interposition, upon the theory's rejection, was secession as an alternative way to resist Northern domination. Yet Calhoun meant for it to be the very last resort. "We ought rather than to yield an inch," he wrote in February 1849, "take any alternative, even if it should be disunion, and I trust that such will be the determination of the South."[78]

He never thought that it would come to that, or at least he hoped that it would not. He planned merely to create a Southern sectional unanimity that would be impossible for the North to ignore or challenge in the same way that Andrew Jackson had challenged South Carolina in 1832. Secession, as the ultimate weapon, was the saber to be rattled, but Calhoun was sure that a love for the Union exemplified by Northern statesmen of his day would never force the sword to be drawn. Although he had put on a foot-stamping, shouting performance before the Southern caucus in 1848, this was the angry Southerner getting the best of the Southern statesman. "He did not create but only formulated and expressed the attitude of the planter class to which he belonged," wrote Calhoun biographer Charles Wiltse, "seeking always to direct Southern discontent into nonviolent channels."[79] Indeed, his last speech in the Senate in March 1850, probably the best statement of the Southern position from anybody up to that time, was remarkable for its calmness. James H. Hammond, the South Carolina secessionist who was, moreover, a practical politician, admitted that the speech contained ideas that were "the only safe and sound ones."[80] Yet for all its calmness, it contained that warning shot across the bow of the advancing North.

Calhoun's death left the South with a legacy it only dimly understood; for in this void, it was the radicals, the fire-eaters, who remained to draw aim with secession, not as a warning, but as an end. The North likewise was not without rash men who would impatiently await the voids they sought to fill in their own section. Webster, whose exit was not far away, included with Southern radicals the "Northern abolitionists & free soilers" as the most "reckless men" he had ever met in public life.[81] North Carolinian Bedford Brown was convinced that the strength of the abolitionists derived from the intemperance of the fire-eaters who were only using the Wilmot Proviso as a pretext. He blamed the radicals' attitude for driving off friends in the North, especially the Northern Democrats. Brown was especially incensed by Calhoun's activities that left Southern Democrats with few friends. "This can mean nothing but *Disunion!*" he cried. "*Disunion! Slave question or no Slave question!*"[82]

Brown was only partly right, because while men like Webster and Calhoun and Clay disagreed, they generally understood each other. The radicals of both sides, as the giants passed away, would make no such effort, because what they wanted to accomplish required that they make no such effort.

"Events may now be controlled," wrote Calhoun at the end of 1849, "but it will be difficult, if not impossible to control their course hereafter."[83] The old man was not, in this case, apprehensive about the behavior of the fire-eaters, but he might as well have been. The fire-eaters viewed Calhoun's influence as a harmful restraint upon their ultimate goal of secession. "I am no Calhoun man," Henry L. Benning, one of Georgia's most passionate secessionists, had declared in the summer of 1849. "He is in fact off the stage; the coming battle is for other leadership than his, a leadership of this generation, not of the past."[84]

The effort to throw off any impediments to disrupting the Union would indeed put events largely out control for much of 1850. Whether or not Calhoun, in the face of this radical discontent with his leadership, could have effectively regulated the forces of Southern nationalism is conjectural, but also it is mostly immaterial. Edmund Ruffin's son lamented that "the South has lost in him its ablest Champion. How great the loss is, time only can reveal."[85]

The loss soon proved very great indeed because Calhoun's death unleashed radical zeal. Even if its uncontrollable nature meant that it would remain largely undefined, it still ran unchecked, threatening to crash the political system. "The man I most dread is Calhoun," wrote Beverley Tucker in Virginia.[86] Tucker was generally far ahead of his fellow radicals on every subject, so far ahead that he often appeared not in his right mind. Yet his dread of Calhoun was not so much directed toward the Carolinian as it was against moderation in any degree or form. In that crystalline world of men possessed with an undeviating vision, it now seemed as though a grand opportunity to cleave the Union was at hand. A few looked toward Nashville.

CHAPTER THREE

"A Partial Affair"

After Daniel Webster's speech, the South watched suspiciously, some of its citizens anxious for thorough abatement, others seeking to maintain the excitement. The skin of conciliation only thinly shielded even Congress. Sixty or seventy members of the House of Representatives reportedly went to their desks armed.[1]

In mid-April Senator Henry S. Foote of Mississippi leapt up in Congress and denounced Senator Thomas Hart Benton for calling into question the patriotism of the dead Calhoun. This was a scene of high irony because Foote had endorsed the plan for a Southern convention only to break with Calhoun and side with the compromisers in March. Perhaps Foote's fervent dislike for fellow Mississippi Senator Jefferson Davis, a Calhoun man, prompted his action as much as anything else.[2] As Foote sang the praises of John C. Calhoun and vented indignant admonitions toward Benton, the formidable Missourian stalked across the Senate floor to confront his accuser. Foote, a small man with a large, bald head within which fulminated a violent temper, happened to be carrying a pistol in his pocket, for he had acquired early in life the habit of shooting at people he did not like.[3]

A deafening clamor erupted as Foote, pistol or no, ran away from Benton, not by scampering across the chamber, but by backing down the aisle toward the president's platform, all the while continuing his verbal assault. Amidst the uproar, Millard Fillmore bellowed for order, and finally someone grasped the pistol away from Foote.[4] Everyone calmed down, more or less. In the short span of three and a half months, the men of the Thirty-first Congress had witnessed an exhausting floor fight over the speakership of the House, James Mason delivering Calhoun's swan song, Daniel Webster arguing tacitly for the slaveholding South, and Henry Foote threatening to shoot Thomas Hart Benton. Now, presumably they thought they had seen everything—everything except, of course, disunion. But then, the night was young.

In the South, the mood passed from ugly in late fall of 1849 to determined in the first quarter of 1850. Yet there were promising signs of moderation. "Is this the way to unite the South?" the *Columbus* (Georgia) *Enquirer* complained when arrogance became a Democratic habit in the Georgia legislature.[5] And when five hundred citizens crowded into Concert Hall in Columbus on 18 April, the four-hour meeting accomplished nothing except to show that fire-eater manipulation—managed by Henry Benning and Walter Colquitt—could not produce a majority to say that the South should convene before some "hostile act" from the North.[6] By the end of April the *Mobile* (Alabama) *Advertiser,* the *Richmond Whig,* and the *Hillsboro* (North Carolina) *Recorder* had come out against the convention as unrepresentative of the South.[7]

Southern rights advocates were in a high dudgeon over the clear signs that the movement was faltering before it was getting started. The Georgia elections in April were a paramount disappointment. In the first place, almost nobody voted; only 2,500 out of an electorate of some 95,000 cast ballots. District nominating meetings had been bad enough, but the elections were comical in that some counties did not even conduct polls, while others tallied a distressing number of votes for "no convention" or, even worse, "no disunion." Then, some of the delegates who had received the smattering of votes ultimately refused to go. Some districts, particularly in southern Georgia, were to have no representatives.[8] The convention "will be a partial affair, and without any results," the *Concordia* (Louisiana) *Intelligencer* noted. "The really intelligent masses . . . will not be slow to discover when their rights are really invaded."[9]

In 1850 Virginia had fire-eaters who, in at least one instance, rivalled even the radicals of South Carolina. Virginia too felt the galled outrage when Northerners attacked slavery. Divisions within the state, however, promised little success for a Southern movement. These divisions were not so much along party lines—as was the case in other Southern states where Whigs backed away from the essentially Democratic movement—

but rather reflected the sectional squabble that pitted western against eastern counties. Those western counties in 1832 had turned thumbs down on Nullification, and now they rejected any move toward disunion, which is what they saw as Nashville's purpose. Democrats and Whigs alike condemned the Southern movement. "Beyond the mountains both parties have one voice," said the *Richmond Whig.*[10] And that voice did much to moderate passions in the East.

But to what extent could those eastern passions be moderated? Thomas Ritchie, conservative Democrat and editor of the influential *Richmond Enquirer,* favored the meeting in Nashville, but that was all he and his followers had in common with fellow, more radical Democrats. M. R. H. Garnett, Nathaniel Beverley Tucker, and Governor John B. Floyd went far beyond the wishes of the moderates, Tucker especially wanting the convention less for conciliation of Southern interests than for disunion. Tucker was even advising William Gilmore Simms and James H. Hammond in South Carolina to urge South Carolina's secession. Virginia, he dreamily maintained, would follow.[11]

As hopeful as old Calhoun himself (who had predicted that Virginia would support Nashville), John Herbert Claiborne had brought resolutions before the Virginia House of Delegates on 2 January for the appointment and popular election of delegates to the convention. Governor Floyd proclaimed to the legislature that "the time had already passed for the discussion of the question between us. . . ."[12] But the Whigs, along with Virginians from the western counties, frowned, shook their heads, and muttered, "This is disunion."

The seeds of western discontent—that vague feeling, bolstered by statistics not unlike those Hinton Helper would later use, that slavery in the east economically harmed the west—bore fruit in the election of delegates. Edmund Ruffin, the radical Democrat who was beginning to turn his slate-gray eyes away from agricultural innovation to political agitation, was so angered by the stand of the western counties that he argued against participation in Nashville. Even a sham of unity was impossible when "the recommendation of the legislature has not been responded to by a single county west of the Blue Ridge except for Jefferson."[13]

Of more profound impact across the whole state were the two occurrences in Washington of Henry Clay proposing the compromise measures and Daniel Webster delivering his 7 March speech. "I think Webster deserves a great deal of credit for taking the position he has on the slavery question," Julian Ruffin wrote to his father.[14] But Julian's older brother, Edmund, saw nothing creditable in a performance that made "the people [of the South] seem drugged . . . and seem to think that all is satisfactorily arranged." As he watched Southern anger ebb, Edmund feared "that the South will be gulled and glad of the chance to be gulled."[15] Similarly, Beverley Tucker complained that "our politicians have gone over to the compromisers."[16]

And so they had. Most irksome was that moderate Virginians wanted to participate in Nashville to check radicals from the lower South. Even this mood was dispirited. Only seven out of fifteen conferences chose to send delegates, and of the fourteen men selected by sparsely attended meetings, only six planned to travel to Tennessee. Henry Wise rejected his nomination and, apparently unaware of the urgent need for representatives of the Old Dominion's moderation, chose Beverley Tucker as an alternate.[17]

Nathaniel Beverley Tucker was not troubled that he would attend Nashville only because Wise did not want to. At last he would participate in something he regarded as profoundly worthwhile. Possibly the most rabid fire-eater in the South in 1850, Tucker surely ranked among those who first proclaimed the joys of disunion. In fact, he maintained that he had hated the Union since the Missouri debates in 1820. Tucker lived in Missouri at the time of the acrimonious exchanges over the territory's fate, residing in the Flourisant Valley where he had cut and roofed a hollow sycamore tree for a law office. From this makeshift post he proclaimed his already full-blown antipathy for the North. Using his position as territorial judge for the Northern Circuit, he tried to influence opinion in Missouri, seen apprehensively by him as wavering between the Tallmadge restriction and proslavery. He made certain that grand juries got a good dose of sectional animosity along with his general instructions. Tucker told Missourians to keep Yankees out of the territory at all costs, a task easily enough accomplished, he mused, by requiring travelers on the Illinois side of the Missouri ferry to say the word "cow." A Yankee would reveal himself with his nasal passages.[18] "I vowed then," he would write in February 1851, "and I repeated the vow, *de diem in diem,* that I will never give rest to my eyes nor slumber to my eyelids until [the Union] is shattered into fragments."[19]

Of course, very few Virginians seriously considered seceding so Beverley Tucker could, after thirty years, finally get a good night's sleep.

Tucker was anything but popular in the soberer councils of Virginia politics. While it bothered him to have so little influence, he was probably accustomed to it. His father, the venerable St. George Tucker, had never managed to consider his son as anything beyond adequate. This was a sharp judgment for young Beverley, who lived in the shadow of his older, more facile brother, Henry, not to mention his brilliant half brother, John Randolph of Roanoke. Tucker never managed facility in any endeavor, and he never achieved brilliance. John Randolph had dissipated into an alcoholic curmudgeon, while Beverley, growing old, did not even distinguish himself in degeneration. To many he was just what Henry S. Foote thought him to be: a "newspaper scribbler" and a "sort of political harlequin."[20]

By 1850 Tucker had spent years teaching constitutional law at the College of William and Mary in Williamsburg. He openly confessed that he tried to instill disunion in his students, and if he had been unsuccessful in all other undertakings, he was resoundingly effective in this one. A small core of states rights extremists, containing a surprising number of Tucker's former students, prodded the Virginia legislature in February 1847 to pass proslavery resolutions to protest the Wilmot Proviso. These former students were not frequently a moving force in Virginia politics, but their day would come.[21]

Regardless of his influence over his students, Tucker was a lonely man who ardently wished for an important role in the sectional struggle. He wrote letters to whoever would have them, Tucker finding it easier to agitate through the mails than from the stump. Twenty-five years earlier, several abscessed teeth languished in his lower jaw until they deformed it and reduced him to communicating with chalk and slate. After several weeks, when he again could speak, the skewered line of his face was matched by an impediment that would slur his words for the rest of his life. Except for classroom lectures, Tucker rarely spoke in public.[22]

Yet his letters reached everywhere. He only required that his correspondents answer and that they fundamentally agree with him. He limited himself to people like Thomas R. Dew, Edmund Ruffin, Duff Green, William Harper, James Hammond, and William Gilmore Simms.[23] These last two men, both South Carolinians, inspired in Tucker more trust and confidence than anyone else. Simms especially enjoyed frank exchanges with the old Virginian, encouraging him even while sympathizing with the pessimistic diatribes that issued from Williamsburg with the regularity of a soured clock chime. Lately the letters always dwelled on the North's villainous attempts to interfere with the South's right to own slaves and populate, with those slaves, the Western lands.

Simms and Tucker were alike in some respects. Both were novelists and evidently compulsive letter writers. Simms wrote quickly, if carelessly, a habit that made him punctual with his mail even if it did make his fiction occasionally silly. He rarely took time to revise anything he did, but rather flitted from one project to another, whether a novel or his editing chores for the *Southern Quarterly Review*. He regularly carried his tall, straight body to his writing table where he would write another letter full of concern to Williamsburg.[24]

Both men had their streaks of eccentricity. Simms's favorite daydream was to imagine himself in a boat drifting out to sea away from land but not toward any destination. It was a strange vision for a novelist who, by necessity, must accustom his mind to beginnings and endings. It was an even more peculiar vision for a man who could not swim.[25]

It is too kind a judgment to label Beverley Tucker as only an eccentric. Something had happened to Tucker by 1850, as though an inexpendable cog in his mind had suddenly snapped, causing it to tilt and whir into irrationality. Perhaps this had been in 1848, the year that his older brother Henry died. For whatever reason, events in the sectional struggle overwhelmed Tucker's perceptions of reality. He began to entertain daydreams far more bizarre than that of endlessly drifting around in the ocean, more bizarre because Tucker imagined himself destined to assume great responsibility in resolving the sectional conflict. He went to Washington in March 1849 on Zachary Taylor's inauguration day to meet the new president and advise him of the proper course to take with the South. After intermediaries delivered Tucker to an evening reception at the White House, he was bitterly disappointed when Taylor virtually ignored him. Tucker blamed chattering guests for distracting the president, not that he and Taylor had never met prior to that brief introduction beside a punch bowl.[26]

Anger nearly consumed Tucker in the first months of 1850. He called Henry Clay a "charlatan" and a "humbug" for, in his view, trying to perpetrate a series of compromises that provided all real advantage to the North.[27] Tucker placed his largest hopes in the Nashville Convention, refusing to believe what was obvious to anyone with political acumen: that Webster's 7 March speech had indeed "knocked the Nashville Con-

vention into a cocked hat."[28] Instead, Tucker formulated complex stratagems for the convention to promulgate. For instance, the convention
could recommend constitutional amendments that would be unacceptable to the North. Southerners could keep the issue alive until the presidential election of 1852. Then a bloc vote for a Southern candidate could
throw the election into the House of Representatives. Southern congressional delegations would withdraw, leaving the Union with neither an
executive nor a legislature—in short, without a government. The consequent centrifugal disorder would sling away states like gobs of clay from
a runaway potter's wheel.[29]

The plan was exceedingly unrealistic because it assumed too much
support for an irresponsible course obviously designed to destroy the
United States. The hesitancy of many Southerners about Nashville belied
any enthusiasm for disunion, and the anger that swept across the South in
the fall of 1849 had already dissipated. Tucker plotted the maintenance of
a studied assault on the national government that would require the undi-
vided allegiance of Southerners for at least two years. If he had dismissed
the naiveté of trying to talk sense into a stranger on the day of his inauguration, he only embraced a larger, more unreasonable naiveté.

Yet no child ever awaited Christmas with higher expectations than
did Beverley Tucker await his departure for Nashville. In late May, he
excitedly left Williamsburg to travel overland to Wheeling. From there a
steamboat took him to Cincinnati. The journey itself was quite a treat
for Tucker: he had not been out of Virginia in years. He observed everything carefully to record his journey in letters to his wife Lucy. Those
letters were a sadness because in them Tucker, without the slightest trace
of unction, described events to make himself appear important to Lucy.
He promised her that except for his arguing down a New Yorker who
had scoffed at the idea of the coming convention, he was preserving
"great reserve and mildness," which was not quite true. Cincinnati, cold
and ugly and unimpressive to him, prompted harsh remarks. He described
Ohio as "a foul cess-pool" where a free Negro was hated until prospering,
at which time a white man would give his daughter in marriage to him
"and she too will thankfully take him to her obscene and lustful bosom."[30]

Tucker arrived in Nashville on 2 June and immediately found James
H. Hammond, with whom he stayed the night. Hammond discovered
that Tucker was a lively companion during that first night, when they
talked into the wee hours, but the South Carolinian must have noticed that

Tucker's mind was not altogether sound. Hammond later introduced him to the South Carolina delegation. Tucker boasted to Lucy that he was "much looked to" and "as much depends on me here as on any other man."[31]

James Henry Hammond's attendance at Nashville marked his first participation in public affairs in five years. A young lawyer who hated the law, Hammond married in 1831 Catherine Fitzsimmons, a plain seventeen-year-old whose lack of pulchritude was made tolerable to James by a substantial dowry consisting of Silver Bluff, a 7,500-acre plantation complete with slaves and implements.[32] Hammond proved an innovative and tireless planter, and Silver Bluff prospered. Meanwhile, his interest in politics, first evident by support for Nullification, placed him in the House of Representatives in 1834 for one term, abruptly terminated when an ulcerous stomach compelled his resignation. In 1840 he unsuccessfully campaigned for governor of South Carolina and then captured the office in 1842.[33]

During his term as governor, Hammond's indiscretions generated a family scandal that forced his retirement from public life. Catherine's older sister, Ann, had married the politically powerful Wade Hampton II. Ann's death left several children dependent upon their Aunt Catherine for motherly attention, but Uncle James's primary concern fell upon four comely nieces, ages thirteen to seventeen, whose visits to Columbia were marred over a two-year period by Hammond's seductive caresses and wandering hands. These episodes approached but never reached intercourse.[34]

Perhaps because Uncle James finally went too far, the oldest girl told Aunt Catherine of these escapades, and lurid details filtered back to the Hampton family. The girls' brothers threatened Hammond with physical violence if he ever again showed himself in Columbia.[35]

Hammond left the governor's office with knowledge of the incidents still confined to the family. He explained his desertion of a promising political career to the curious by claiming that he did not want to hold office ". . . nor do I aim at popularity or desire it." He asked, "Haven't I served my time and earned my retirement?"[36]

What Hammond wanted was immaterial. The elder Hampton, perhaps not fully aware of the details, threatened ugly publicity unless Hammond withdrew from consideration for the South Carolina Senate seat in 1844.[37]

Hammond barely endured his retirement and variously railed against Hampton, South Carolina, and what he called the hypocritical standards of virtue, while remaining careful to continue his show of indifference toward political affairs. "I have no interest—no room for politics," he claimed early in 1850.[38] When he was elected to attend Nashville as a member of the South Carolina delegation, he explained that the secession issue was all that interested him about public affairs.[39]

He worried about the Virginia legislature's instructions that her delegates assure the security of the Union. That sounded preemptive and counter to what he wanted to happen at Nashville.[40] A "Union of the South" should be uppermost so that "almost everything should be sacrificed to it."[41] The possibility of South Carolina's acting alone worried him, and the success of the Compromisers' efforts in arousing Virginian moderation disappointed him to the point of cynicism. "An immense deal of gas will be let off, I suppose," he observed to Edmund Ruffin about the convention even as he urged the Virginian that he "must not give up the fight."[42]

Delegates had been arriving for about a week in Nashville when Tucker first sought out Hammond. Set among rolling hills and flanked on the east by the Cumberland River, it was one of the loveliest towns in the South in 1850. Overlooking roofs mingled with trees and terraces, higher even than the church steeples, was the deceased Polk's mansion, the columns only recently draped with black crepe. Below the hills, in the town itself, fast carriages bustled around the new capitol, years into its construction, and yet only a third completed. Fashionably exquisite examples of taste abounded, from the furnishings in splendid homes to the jewelry on exceptionally pretty girls.[43] Two years before, gaunt poles had stretched to Louisville and beyond to the coast linking Nashville to the comprehensible lightening of telegraph keys. The town, like the rest of its part of America, had begun shucking its frontier heritage in fits and starts so that it stood with one foot planted in a wilder past while the other advanced toward the amenities of city life. The University of Nashville planned a medical school while across town the section known as "The Jungle" clung stubbornly to the customs of earthier living. There, on the riverfront, everything from prostitution to confidence games mixed blithely with copious drafts of hard liquor to make for considerable caterwauling, stabbing, shooting, and sensuality.[44]

Yet Nashville confined the amusements of "The Jungle" to its area.

Assorted livestock meandered through the nice parts of town, but not to detract from the beauty of lush gardens meticulously maintained by the Horticultural Society, or a park, dappled by broken sunlight, where cool twilights brought sweethearts to stroll and spark.[45]

Nashville entertained the convention with mixed emotions. The Whigs, a majority in Davidson County, had made known their disfavor by attempting to vote down representation to the event, and the town reflected this sentiment with a chilly reception.[46] If the political complexion of the convention displeased a strongly Unionist citizenry, however, the fierce social hilarity mutual to any convention and its hosts gradually diminished the town's pique. There was plenty of theatrical entertainment for the delegates who could be amused by Swiss bell ringers or "a Mrs. Fogg [who], on account of the thinness of her audience, postponed to a more favorable evening her 'Ballad Entertainment.'"[47]

Mrs. Fogg had stiff competition from parties and socials held in the delegates' honor. As one observer put it, "At first the citizens of Nashville were opposed to [the convention], but day-by-day, as its sessions advanced, it grew into favor. The galleries . . . thundered applause, and the ladies smiled approbation."[48] One wonders how much the socializing, rather than the politics, had to do with this approbation. The ladies, in any event, had reason to be happy. When parliamentary exercises grew wearisome, delegates found flirtations with the pretty girls who filled the galleries an exhilarating relief. Parlor socials reinforced this activity, and with good effect, since it was perhaps the most constructive activity of the whole nine days the convention met.[49]

By the time the convention assembled, events had made it less a national danger and more a political pitfall. It had become a harmful embarrassment, and its chief victim was the Democratic party. Even while the delegates arrived at Nashville, meetings all over Tennessee advocated the acceptance of the compromise before Congress. One such gathering occurred in Nashville only two days before the Southern Convention's opening session.

Moderate supporters of the convention tried to explain that loving the Union had nothing to do with supporting a compromise that outrageously infringed on Southern rights. Southerners should support the convention "not to dissolve, but to save the Union."[50] Most delegates ignored the political disfavor, but they could not have been unaware of the change of mood, all across the South, away from their purpose.[51]

Except for South Carolina, every state at Nashville had trouble gathering delegates. South Carolina alone could afford to be particular in choosing some delegates. For instance, the Committee of Electoral Delegates in Hamburg's congressional district sent a list of questions to likely candidates to make sure no mistakes were made. The list included: a) Would the person accept an appointment to the convention? b) Would he make an issue with the North if the Wilmot Proviso passed or California were admitted as a free state? and c) If not, then "be so good as to say how far you [are] prepared to go on this issue."[52]

Elsewhere the hope that delegations would cross Whig and Democratic lines had withered.[53] Virginia's six delegates, besides Tucker and the less ardent states righter William F. Gordon, were all Unionist and pro-Compromise.[54] Texas had only one delegate in the wake of the conspicuous absence of enthusiasm for the convention. Forty-two-year-old James P. Henderson, the first governor of Texas, had made fiery speeches with Texas radical Louis T. Wigfall, but he was at Nashville with less than a thundering mandate. He did have a few more than the 140 votes Sam Houston derisively estimated as poor Henderson's constituency.[55]

Alabama's delegation of twenty-one (out of an appointed thirty-six) held only seven Whigs. William Lowndes Yancey and other fire-eaters refused to participate because of the delegation's instructions to arrest any extremism.[56] John A. Campbell, who would write most of the resolutions adopted by the convention, was at heart a moderate who argued for Southern rights but who disliked slavery and would later emancipate his slaves. He advocated the formation of a Southern party undiluted by the interests of Northern Democrats. But George Goldwaithe, originally from Massachusetts, was prepared to consider secession as an alternative in 1850, while Leroy Pope Walker, a strong states rights advocate along with John A. Winston, would experience a growing radicalism in the coming years. Jefferson Buford, an erratic activist, was also in the delegation, but his notoriety was waiting a few years away and farther west in the vast unorganized part of the Louisiana Purchase that would become Kansas. Florida's four delegates (out of the scheduled six) were all conservative.[57]

Tennessee's delegation of 101, nearly all of whom were Democrats, was the largest and the most conservative. It was committed to checking radical tendencies. Major William H. Polk, brother of the dead former president, was a member of the delegation. He spoke early in the convention, pronouncing with his deep voice distinguishable syllables for effect and enunciating his vowels with a crispness that nodded his head forward. And Gideon Pillow, out of his place of retirement south of Nashville where he lived elegantly, was there viewing the assemblage with his "happy eyes," strangely, considering the troublesome histories that seemed to attach themselves to him with a tenacious resolve.[58]

Mississippi's delegation faced an embarrassing problem. After all, it represented the state that had issued the call the previous October for the convention. All eleven delegates were strong states righters, but none was adamantly for secession. Indeed, Judge William Sharkey, the old Whig who would preside over the convention, had adopted a moderate stand. He had written to Senator Foote that should the Compromise pass in Congress, the people of Mississippi would acquiesce.[59] Hence, the delegation, if it chose a radical course, would be at odds with sentiments back home. In Washington, Foote had taken heed of the majority mood in his state, and had completed his shift of allegiance to the Compromise by April, agreeing to the "prompt consideration" of the admission of California.[60] This action significantly helped to turn away Mississippi from a secessionist tide, while it also effectively split away radicals who would have otherwise participated in the convention. John J. Pettus, who had been elected to attend, believed that any move toward a compromise was a sign of weakness, and he refused to go to Nashville as a way of protesting the moderation of the proceedings.[61]

While Mississippi and Alabama stood for moderation, the delegations from Georgia and South Carolina were the most extreme. The thirteen delegates from Georgia (numbering only five of those originally chosen) were as unrepresentative of the state as they were radical. Henry L. Benning was a blatant secessionist, as was Charles James McDonald. Walter T. Colquitt briefly admitted that disunion might bring on a civil war, but he also publicly doubted it.[62]

The South Carolina delegation was the most talented and thereby the most impressive at the convention. The seventeen delegates included venerable Langdon Cheves, now seventy-four, distinguished by a notable public career that included membership in the 1812 Congress and the presidency of the Second Bank of the United States. While Cheves had rejected Nullification in 1832, he had come to embrace secession by 1850 almost as avidly as he had embraced alcohol.[63] Robert Barnwell Rhett was also a member of the delegation, and even fellow South Carolinians thought him dangerous. Rhett advocated separate state action for South Carolina, urging its secession regardless of the mood in other Southern states. This was something no other South Carolina delegate could endorse, the embarrassing lesson of 1832 serving as a constant, grim reminder that separate state action meant dread isolation. So the appointed delegates at large had not included Rhett. He was there at the behest of loyal constituents in St. John's Colleton.[64]

The South Carolinians realized their precarious position in the Southern movement. They did not wish to taint any proceeding by evoking memories of an impetuous past, and so they were mostly in agreement to assume an inconspicuous role at Nashville. Hammond, his face as pale as "alabaster," was calm and conservative; Rhett was as uncharacteristically soothing as he was characteristically courteous; Robert W. Barnwell and Cheves said little if anything, and all were careful to present a patriotic manner that was, above all, calm.[65] In the best tradition of the Old South, they were thoroughly ingratiating guests at Nashville. The mayor of Charleston, who was not even a delegate, impressed the ladies with his good looks and delighted the whole town when, after visiting nearby Mammoth Cave, he described it as a "Niagara in repose."[66] And the delegation itself would win praise at the end of the session for thoughtfully presenting to the McKendree Church a "superb carpet to compensate for the wear of that which covered the floor during the session."[67]

It was only in the McKendree Church that the convention could find a large enough meeting place and still accommodate galleries. In front of Sharkey's chair, in the two front pews, sat the groups from Mississippi and South Carolina; left of Carolina sat Florida and behind was Alabama; Virginia was to the right of Mississippi, Georgia behind. Tennessee's huge number sat in a side pew to the left of the pulpit, in front of which, on a carpeted platform, were "a dozen little green tables . . . for editors and reporters." Sharkey, looking like Andrew Jackson, sat center.[68]

Thus it was on 3 June, a Monday, when the convention opened and proceeded to consume the next two days with the appointment of a resolution committee and the settling of voting procedures. Then on the third day resolutions came pouring in from, variously, John Campbell of Alabama and John McCrea of Mississippi. A strong set of resolutions full of radical fervor from Henry L. Benning added to the woes of the resolutions committee. Yet for all the diversity of the different sets of resolutions, they had in common the recommendation of extending the Missouri Compromise line of 36°30' to the Pacific.[69]

The extension of the Missouri Compromise line was in 1850 favored by Southern moderates and fire-eaters alike, and for different reasons. One moderate reasoned that extending 36°30' would felicitously change California's boundary, which he regarded in "its present delineation . . . a hideous deformity." [70] However, less frivolous thought prompted support among most moderates. They believed that a reapplication of the Missouri Compromise was the safest way to abate sectional fury; it had worked in 1820, and many believed that it could work again. An earnest desire for Congress to settle the Western question on this basis before the convention met in Nashville stemmed from the hope that the North would settle for 36°30'.[71] Such a hope, however, was misguided, and the radicals knew this. Some Southern fire-eaters had come full circle on the matter; for while they had pressed for just such an extension in 1847, they had abandoned their advocacy in 1848—as had most Southern Democrats—during the presidential campaign of Lewis Cass. In 1850 the extension reappeared on the radical agenda. "We are somewhat at a loss to know," remarked the *Charleston Mercury,* "why Southern men labor so hard to fashion all sorts of propositions of pacification."[72] But astute observers were well aware that the extension of 36°30' was unacceptable to both the North and Northern congressmen. James Buchanan had written to Jefferson Davis in March that "the truth is the South have [*sic*] got themselves into a condition on this questions [*sic*] from which it appears to me now they cannot extricate themselves."[73] In other words, once having jettisoned the extension of the Missouri Compromise line, the South could not reclaim it. The fire-eaters knew this and, though their tactics were not usually subtle, they adopted 36°30' as a demand for settlement, knowing that it was a demand that the North would reject.[74]

Resolutions and declarations continued to bombard the convention through Friday. Beverley Tucker, presumably tireless, introduced two long sets of resolutions independent of his delegation. The convention heard resolutions on everything from congressional jurisdiction and the inferiority of the Negro to the Texas boundary problem. By Saturday, the most notable characteristic of the proceedings was the squabble that had broken out among the Alabama delegates. Reuben L. Chapman wanted to adopt the thirteen resolutions approved by the committee, but others protested and managed to table the matter until Monday. Also tabled was consideration of the Address that would issue from the convention.[75]

The Address, directed to all slaveholding states except Delaware, became a major point of contention at the gathering because its author was the dangerous fire-eater Robert Barnwell Rhett. Rhett, following the South Carolina strategy, had participated only guardedly in the details of organizing the convention and had, with his state's delegation, demurred from discussion. He had grasped the opportunity to prepare the Address for the convention, however, seeking to use it as a lecture to the South. He accused the North of sixteen years of aggression, citing instances of congressional petitions designed, as he saw it, to overthrow slavery. Through all this, Rhett declared, the South had been patient, but now that exclusion of the South from the Western territories surely had as its ultimate purpose the abolition of slavery, the South could no longer abide its treatment. He then attacked Clay's compromise point by point. California's admission would upset the balance in the Senate and unwittingly enact the Wilmot Proviso. A ruling favorable to the New Mexico Territory on the Texas boundary would provide that territory with enough land for two additional and potentially free states. He saw the prophecy of abolition in proposals to end the slave trade in the District of Columbia, and he denounced the proposed Fugitive Slave Law as a fugitive victory, in itself treading down the rights of states through provisions for trial in federal courts. Finally, as a solution to the present predicament, Rhett slyly recommended the extension of the Missouri Compromise line.[76]

There was considerable opposition to the Address in this form. Even some within the South Carolina delegation were ambivalent. Hammond had written earlier that he was "decidedly opposed to any address either indignant or remonstrant, or conciliating to the North, and nothing need be said to the South after the Southern Address."[77] All that Hammond thought necessary for the convention to do was to draw up a brief preamble to a recommendation for a general congress of the South. The time for words was past, he believed, and action—concerted action—was now necessary. As it happened, his attitude on this issue had more to do with rivalry with Rhett than it did with ideological differences between himself and the fiery delegate from St. John's Colleton parish. John C. Calhoun was dead, and Hammond knew the void would have to be filled.

On the next Monday, the thirteen resolutions glided to unanimous passage. They were the gist of Southern discontent, citing the limitations of congressional authority in the territories and recommending the extension of the Missouri Compromise line. While the remaining business concerned fifteen additional resolutions as well as the troublesome Address, it was in the discussion over the Address that the convention finally abandoned its sedate demeanor.[78]

The unfortunate Gideon Pillow spoke first, expressing a wish to dilute the harshness of the Address with amendments. Then Thomas Judge advocated a change for the passages referring to the compromise before Congress. And finally when John McCrea, that "bright speaker" who was a friend—but no follower in this instance—of the radical Albert Gallatin Brown, brought forth more amendments designed to tone down the Address, the radicals had heard enough.[79] Walter Colquitt answered.

Here Colquitt was the fire-eater! The idea of any kind of compromise as well as the thought of muting the clarion of the Address enraged him, and he commenced a dramatic demonstration that stunned the convention. He charged the length and width of the center aisle, whirled and tore, stalked and stomped, lowered his voice to spitting whispers and exploded it like an angry trumpet that shook the audience at the McKendree Church again and again. "Wild, fierce, terrible, dreadful, *mad,*" remembered one observer, while admitting, "yet most wonderful to listen to."[80]

Then Beverley Tucker gained the floor, and like his behavior in the previous months, his actions for the next hour were clothed in the dim gauze of unreality. He had refused to believe that the convention was no longer important or that its course was inexorably fixed upon moderation. He had carefully cataloged the few times he had spoken on brief matters so that he could lay his contributions before Lucy in those letters for her approbation. One of those times had been his pathetic assurance to the convention that should it reassemble in November in Marietta, Georgia, he would go there—indeed he would go anywhere.[81] Moreover, he had fretted about doing well, better than his thick-voiced best, in a great speech he planned to make to the assemblage. Now he sensed the opportunity for this speech, but the opportunity was an illusion. Either because of Colquitt's fierce oratory or because the delegates were weary and wished to go home, the Address was safe on its way to passage, and it was with a mixture of surprise and chagrin that on the verge of adjournment, the convention realized that the old Virginian intended to make a sizeable statement. Pathos unwittingly fed on itself for Tucker at Nashville, because what he had envisioned as his (and the South's) finest hour was to be only an embarrassing afterthought to a meaningless event.

He gave the effort his all, and though he was worried enough over his poor enunciation to apologize, he launched into a discourse concerning what had been his dream for years. He painted a glorious portrait of a Southern Confederacy and prophesied a lovelier domino theory of secession than anyone like Rhett could have imagined in his wildest dreams. Although citing an anti-Southern conspiracy in Congress, Tucker declared that cotton was too valuable for the North to lose with a war. The formation of a Southern Confederacy would occur in peace because of Northern discretion. Tucker grew so excited that he forged leaden fantasies and made them soar like eagles. Illinois, Ohio, and Indiana would wish to join the South; he saw Pennsylvania coming into the Confederation, and then Cuba and Santo Domingo. Jamaica would join as well, he shouted, adding that England would not object. He shocked the pretty women in the galleries by maintaining that the binding together of these diverse entities would be as joyous as "a union like that of the sexes."[82]

Though he could have continued for hours more, after an hour his voice, unaccustomed to the strain, began to fail him. He concluded, and the convention summarily adjourned. Hammond came across the floor to congratulate the old man, though he privately thought that Tucker's voice had been poor and the speech worse. Tucker, unaware that he had made something of a fool of himself, was pleased with his performance.[83]

On the whole, the entire convention was pleased with its performance, although it had made little more than a fraction of a ripple in the events it had started out so brazenly to influence. The days in Nashville had accomplished, in one sense, nothing more than to produce a handful of resolutions formed by a group of men who, despite their professions of moderation, carried no resolute mandate from the states they claimed to represent. At the outset of the convention, Cave Johnson, the old Jacksonian Democrat who had been Polk's postmaster general, had visited for two days in order to determine the tenor of the Tennessee delegation and discern from this "what's best to be done" about the potentially dangerous proceedings. He prefaced his observations to his close friend

James Buchanan by remarking that he had "seen the elephant."[84] Johnson was being overly dramatic. The Nashville Convention, so feared as the juggernaut of Southern anger, had been rendered by events little more than a mouse.

In the immediate sense the convention had hurt the cause of the fire-eaters, for Rhett's Address attracted widespread attention. While Southern radicals thought it an excellent statement, conservatives saw it as a positively homicidal device that could, if taken too seriously, kill the Democratic party in the South.[85] The projection was prescient, if over-stated. Radical activity in the ensuing months would hurt Southern Democrats at the polls. But of more lasting impact was the ongoing distrust between radicals and conservatives in the South that would last for the remainder of the decade, preventing the possibility of a thoroughly united South.[86]

As the delegates trundled out of Nashville, there was little unanimity anywhere in the nation. The highly touted compromise was mired in Congress consequent to Zachary Taylor's refusal to endorse any part of it except the section, so hated by the South, that admitted a free California. Out in Texas, the border dispute with the New Mexico Territory was almost to the boiling point, and even though some of the South had met in convention, nothing seemed changed, nothing seemed accomplished.

Yet the fire-eaters who left Nashville, nestled among those hills along the Cumberland, were more than they had been before. They had met, had made acquaintance, had become friends of purpose. The thorny prize of a separate South hovered before these superpatriots who truly believed that with enough diligence they could win those too timid to take the necessary steps toward salvation. They were only beginning to warm to their work.

CHAPTER FOUR

"That We Were All Such Traitors!"

After the Nashville Convention the fire-eaters quickly moved to counter moderates. First, they severed connections with them. Then oblivious to the torpor of the people, men like Rhett and Yancey snarled their calls for disunion. Quitman in Mississippi, Henderson in Texas, and McDonald and Colquitt in Georgia, more discreet only in degree, urged action by Southern Rights Associations, such organizations springing up all over the South consequent to the agitations of this loud minority.[1]

The radicals' behavior alienated much of their potential support. On 21 June at Hibernian Hall in Charleston, Rhett declared that "to maintain the Union, is to acquiesce in the destruction of the Constitution; and to maintain the Constitution we must dissolve the Union." To rebut anticipated charges of treason, Rhett emphatically stated, "I have been born of Traitors, but thank God, they have been Traitors in the great cause of liberty, fighting against tyranny and oppression."[2] The response from the North was bitter, and Henry Clay, laboring in Congress to accomplish a compromise, angrily declared to applauding galleries that if Rhett meant what he said, he *was* a traitor.

A fluttering banner at a dinner in Rhett's honor in St. Helena Parish might proclaim, "Oh that we were all such traitors," but not everyone in the South agreed.[3] "Has such a man no respect for the intelligence and patriotism of the people?" marvelled the *Columbus* (Georgia) *Enquirer* about another Rhett speech. Phrases like "prepare for war and bloodshed . . . dissolve the Union . . . terminate the political connection . . . become at once a more military people" distressed enough Georgians to cause Howell Cobb to predict, according to some, that Georgia was sure to be Unionist if only to contradict the fiery South Carolinian.[4]

Rhett's crowing rhetoric battered even the precarious unanimity achieved in Nashville, especially when it should have been carefully preserved. He gloated that Tennessee's delegation obviously favored the Compromise at the outset of the convention. When Aaron V. Brown, himself a member of the delegation, observed in a toast at a dinner given by Gideon Pillow that "in five days the Tennessee delegation were [*sic*] brought into line" to support instead extending 36°30' and the pugnacious Address, Rhett claimed a victory. Brown lamely explained that he had been referring only to the seating arrangements at General Pillow's dinner.[5]

Alabama threatened to elude the fire-eaters' grasp as well. "The Mountain democracy," John A. Campbell noted in late 1847, "command the state and our politicians defer to their [*sic*] wishes."[6] Over two years later the situation had not changed. County leaders were not with the "talent," the Calhoun wing of the party, because almost as much as in Tennessee, Alabama Democrats were still in the thrall of Andrew Jackson.

In Montgomery, a little over a month after the Nashville Convention's adjournment, a meeting of citizens gathered from both town and country to hear George Goldwaithe explain the convention's work. A law partner with his brother-in-law John A. Campbell, Goldwaithe was respected in Montgomery, where three decades of residence had established him as a calm, capable member of the community. Expelled from West Point thirty years earlier because of a hazing incident, Goldwaithe had at the time dreamed romantic dreams of joining the Greek revolutionary movement against the Ottoman Turks, but had chosen to immigrate to Alabama instead. Now politicians, planters, and merchants gathered in the hot Montgomery courthouse perhaps to foment a revolution of their own.

Amity prescribed parity for the meeting's presiding officers—John A. Elmore for the Democrats and Thomas Williams, Jr., for the Whigs. Goldwaithe began calmly, explaining the cause for and the goals of the Nashville Convention. As he progressed, his delivery became more excited. Although he owned plantations in Texas and Mississippi, the transplanted Massachusetts native felt no particular sympathy for slavery and was not afraid of professing loyalty to the Union. Perhaps the residual excitement of Nashville now mingled with the charged atmosphere of the courthouse, or Goldwaithe wanted to prove that moderate conservatism was not timidity. He blurted out, "If the assertion of just rights brings disunion, let it come!"[7]

Yancey eventually spoke to the meeting, but only after waiting for a request to do so, remaining in his chair longer for the effect it would produce. He habitually began such addresses calmly and pleasantly, progressing gradually into a more violent argument that also, according to his admirers, grew more intellectually forceful. The effect on his audience was electric, for a Yancey speech, when all went correctly, could be magical. Even when things went wrong, Yancey was formidable, someone once remarking that "no one could have defended a bad cause better than . . . Yancey."[8]

On this occasion he battled overwhelming Unionist sentiment that served as the main bond of Southern unity. The proposed compromise before Congress sufficiently satisfied moderates to gain their conditional acceptance. Yancey scoffed at unity bought with submission. And while he was careful not to judge anyone's reasons for seeking agreement through compromise, he maintained that this was no time for party claims that sought advantage. Yancey's suggestion for separate state action, which the majority stiffly opposed, brought forth the most vehement response.

Yancey managed to have his own resolutions combined with the minority report of the meeting. Disappointed by efforts to elevate Nashville's "soft" resolutions over Rhett's Address, he objected to suggestions for nonintercourse, increasingly the focus of moderate protest. Also he argued that to delineate circumstances that would justify the governor's calling a secession convention only deceived the people into believing that *now* was not the time for action. Yancey stoutly declared that soon enough Texas would require help in resisting federal demands on her territory.[9]

If anything gave hope to radicals in the summer of 1850 it was the highly combustible dispute in Texas. It "will probably furnish a more conspicuous and fruitful issue than any other cause of quarrel," chortled William Gilmore Simms in July.[10] Indeed that issue of the Texas–New Mexico boundary had been brewing ever since the accession of Zachary Taylor, whose handling of the matter did little to calm tempers.[11] A disputed area in northwest Texas, consisting of El Paso, Worth, Presidio, and Santa Fe Counties, was at the center of the controversy. The normal revulsion over losing territory joined with the sectional controversy to heighten stubborn passions. The usually calm Unionist Whig from Georgia, Alexander H. Stephens, informed the *National Intelligencer* on 3 July 1850:

> You may consider the "gallant State of Texas" too weak for a contest with the army of the United States. But you should recollect that the cause of Texas, in such a conflict, will be the cause of the entire South. And whether you consider Santa Fe in danger or not, you may yet live to see that fifteen states of this Union, with seven millions of people, "who, knowing their rights, dare maintain them," cannot be easily conquered![12]

Governor Peter H. Bell, for his part, consistently took an aggressive stand regarding New Mexico. A Virginian by birth, Bell had participated in the 1836 Texas Revolution, developing a martial bearing to match his imposing physical presence. He presumably felt a special need to protect the interests of the western part of the state since voters there had been largely responsible for his victory in the governor's race of 1849. In February, he tried to preempt any dispute by dispatching a special commission to place the area under Texan authority. In April the commission had met stiff resistance in Santa Fe from Brevet Colonel John Monroe's military government and had to break off its mission. When Monroe then called for a New Mexican constitutional convention, presumably with Taylor's blessing, Bell was set on fire. Although the Texas legislature previously would not provide him with the military authority to cope with the problem, by June there was sufficient anger to justify a special session, scheduled for August. Radicals all over the South saw the potential for their moment.[13]

"The first hostile gun that is fired in this contest disolves [*sic*] the Union," declared William P. Duvall. "Every Southern state will stand by Texas." Duvall was spoiling for a fight and urged that "Virginia will have to lead the Southern confederacy. She has arms for herself and two [other] Southern states, and if the Union is broken, we will save the North all further trouble with California and New Mexico, for we will take them to our exclusive use."[14]

President Taylor remained intractable about Clay's Compromise, refusing to endorse anything other than California's admission under the terms of her constitutional convention. He had determined to adopt a harsh stand against Texas for its agitations respecting the border, threatening in the process to spark a conflict that many saw as dangerously prefacing a full-scale civil war. Then, during the first week and a half of July, fate intervened to remove him as a major obstacle to the settlement of the Texas controversy as well as the other crises. Taylor always had suffered from a fragile stomach, and when a blistering Fourth of July celebration compelled him to an icy refreshment of milk and cherries, his system rebelled. Within three days he was dangerously ill, and during the next three days he was vomiting up even the ice he crunched in attempts to quench an unrelenting thirst. Crippling cramps came and went with copious doses of calomel and quinine until on Tuesday, 9 July, he was dead.[15] Millard Fillmore, having no objections to the Compromise, now was president of the United States.

Fillmore's ascension meant that the Compromise had a better chance, but it did not mean that Governor Bell was more easily going to bully the federal government. Fillmore, through his new secretary of state, Daniel Webster, pressed Bell while helping to devise a way out of the problem. Fillmore's frank endorsement of the Compromise encouraged the work in Congress to proceed with greater vigor. Strong Union support in North Carolina, Tennessee, and Virginia also gave impetus to Compromisers' efforts.[16] Henry Clay spoke tirelessly throughout July for a package, the Omnibus Bill, that would have resolved all the sectional crises in one legislative stroke; but the Omnibus Bill, eliciting more varied opposition in its sum than its parts ever could, failed on 31 July by a dramatic majority. As opponents of the package exulted in both the North and the South, Compromisers entered August determined to rescue its separate parts.

Clay, however, was exhausted by the heat and the argument. When he retreated to Newport, Rhode Island, for recuperation, Stephen A. Douglas had his first opportunity to show frankly remarkable talents for legislative manipulation on a large scale. Despite bitter debate, on 9 August a boundary settlement that gave New Mexico the land and Texas ten million dollars passed the Senate, its proponents hoping that the gesture would calm the impending meeting of the Texas legislature.[17]

Nothing calmed down. In Texas, town meetings adopted increasingly belligerent resolutions, and the special session of the legislature reflected secessionist sentiment all over the state. On 25 August a joint committee passed a resolution stating "that Texas will maintain the integrity of her territory at all hazards and to the last extremity."[18] Thomas J. Rusk in Washington heard of the precarious situation, of Bell's determination to "not Sell a Bit of Land as large as a handkerchief for a Million of Dollars" and that among many in the state "a Dissolution of the Union is evidently wished for." County and community meetings continued to pass resolutions supporting Bell. Similar meetings occurred in Alabama, South Carolina, and Mississippi.[19]

Regarding the Compromise solution for Texas and New Mexico "as no worse than Mr. Fillmore's bayonets, because it is no better than a bribe," John A. Quitman was prepared to lead Mississippi's militia into Texas.[20] Only a short time before, Quitman, dressed in a uniform from the Mexican campaigns, had ridden his white horse while white-robed girls tossed flowers before him, so that he could be properly installed as governor. A man of abiding loyalties and deep tradition, Quitman each July 13 gave Harry, his "faithful body servant and slave," a five-dollar gold piece for having brought him chicken broth during the fight on the Tacubaya Causeway at Mexico City. Now Quitman offered Bell five thousand men in arms if Texas needed them to challenge the United States Army. "I am always ready to strike in her defense," he proclaimed, although he knew that the Mississippi legislature would have some say in the matter.[21]

Fillmore acted quickly to quell the growing belligerence by threatening to call out the militia, the army, and the navy to protect the nation's interests. Although he only sent reinforcements to Santa Fe, this was apparently enough. Either concerned about the consequences of rash action or swayed by the ten million dollars slated for the pathetically bare Texas treasury, Bell vetoed the legislature's military bill, apologetically giving technical reasons for doing so. The legislature adjourned on 6 September after taking no other definite action. Much of the state, primed for some action, was disappointed.[22]

Fillmore tried anxiously to buy some time, because Douglas' maneuvers in the Senate were achieving wonders. In rapid succession after the passage of the Texas–New Mexico Bill, there followed a bill for the admission of California, a bill for the organization of New Mexico, and finally, on 14 August, the Fugitive Slave Bill. Extremists from both sections made the accomplishment an ordeal, Southern senators especially protesting all along the way. On 2 August a caucus read an agreement signed by Hopkins L. Turney (Tennessee), Andrew P. Butler (South Carolina), David Yulee and Jackson Morton (Florida), David Rice Atchison (Missouri), Pierre Soulé (Louisiana), Jeremiah Clemens (Alabama), and Jefferson Davis (Mississippi). These men proposed blocking the admission of California unless the prospective state accepted 36°30' as its southern boundary. Fortunately for the Compromise forces, Southern unity proved as elusive in this instance as it had for all of 1850. When Soulé moved to resist the admission of California by all parliamentary means, Barnwell, Butler, Mason, Atchison, and R. M. T. Hunter broke ranks to cast nay votes, snarling the motion in a tie. In this way the fight against California's admission as a free state was lost. Southern Whig defections in the House provided enough votes to overcome the strange coalition of Southern and Northern extremists who had joined against the Compromise. Albert Gallatin Brown and the South Carolina delegation found themselves on common ground with men like William Seward, Joshua Giddings, and Preston King in attempting to block conciliation and hope for the best—or, as the moderates saw it, the worst. But the irresistible momentum of Unionism generated in the Senate rolled over the House as well, breezing the Compromise through the lower chamber in September to the noisy celebrations of approval in both the North and the South.[23]

Although some Northerners grumbled about the terms given to the South, particularly the Fugitive Slave Act, most felt that they had gained the best of the bargain.[24] So did the fire-eaters. In the midst of their neighbors' exultation, these radicals still agitated for active resistance.

Governor Whitemarsh B. Seabrook of South Carolina wanted a call for a Southern congress that would execute separation from the North the same as the Continental Congress had in the American Revolution. Seabrook had to contend with his state's noisy fire-eaters, Rhett, for one, demanding separate state action if no alternative presented itself. Such activity alarmed more sagacious South Carolinians, who worried that these indiscreet counselors were ruining the chance for Southern unity. James Hammond complained, "Such men spoil all movements."[25]

Seabrook definitely did not want South Carolina to act alone. The call for a Southern congress would have to come from Georgia or Mississippi. Robert Barnwell agreed that it would be "inexpedient for South Carolina to move alone in this matter."[26] Seabrook searched rather frantically for a likely provenance for secession sentiment.

"May I ask," he wrote Quitman in Mississippi, "whether Mississippi is prepared to assemble her legislature." Quitman expressed confidence that not only would Mississippi gather her legislature, but a secession convention would follow. Seabrook openly sighed with relief. "Your letter," he said, ". . . from its tone, has given me the assurance that Mississippi will be the banner state in the noble contest."[27]

Seabrook had misread the tone. Suddenly Quitman wanted South Carolina to lead the way. "The secession of a Southern state," he encouraged, "would startle the whole South and force other states to meet the issue plainly."[28] Seabrook could not have been so sure. He asked Georgia Governor George W. Towns how his state would receive such a move. Towns replied that he was doubtful that Georgia would agree to rash action. He counseled Seabrook to cool Carolina ardor lest Georgia be irrevocably lost to the cause of Southern rights. Anxious not to quash secession sentiment in Georgia, Alabama, and Mississippi, Seabrook resisted pressure to call the South Carolina legislature into special session. Although in October he prepared a proclamation doing so, he wisely submitted it to Towns, who presumably vetoed the idea since the proclamation never appeared.[29]

Quitman deserted his previous optimism because forces in Mississippi were clearly gathering for the kind of struggle that moderate Democrats had feared all along. While Seabrook tried to enlist the state's support, Quitman had indeed called for the special session of the legislature to meet on 18 November. In his proclamation he scrawled out complaints against the Compromise: Congress had denied the South equal protection in the territories acquired from Mexico, had appropriated public money to dismember territory from Texas and give it to a potentially free state while holding the sword to Texas to coerce its agreement to the bargain, and had abolished the slave trade in the District of Columbia. Furthermore, he was certain that Northern aggressions against Southern institutions would now continue. Despite urgings to "let Georgia and Mississippi take the lead and secede" and assurances that "gradually other states will join you," Quitman watched Compromiser celebrations in places like Natchez with growing alarm and disgust. "They shout hosannahs to cover their shame," he reassured himself while vowing that he would "not be the instrument of surrendering our birthright of liberty and equality."[30]

Mississippi Representative Albert Gallatin Brown became a secessionist after the Nashville Convention and addressed the special session of the Mississippi legislature accordingly, attacking the Compromise. Yet both Brown and the moderate Jefferson Davis avoided advocating separate state action or even petulant disunion, Davis especially maintaining that resistance should offer more than the stark alternatives of Union and disunion. The goal should be protecting the Union of 1787. Brown echoed the sentiment, reminiscent of Calhoun, simultaneously advising the South on how to restore equality with the North. Repeal the Compromise, he instructed, or the South, in concert, should sever all political ties with the North. A few weeks later, Brown, reiterating the theme, argued even more vehemently for Southern nationalism, out of the Union if necessary.[31]

Meanwhile, Henry S. Foote busily aroused and capitalized upon Mississippi's Unionist and pro-Compromise inclination. He took up Beverley Tucker's Nashville speech like a bludgeon to pound radical sentiment as treasonous. While the legislature met in special session, Foote's Unionist Convention gathered in Jackson City Hall to approve Foote's position on California, denounce disunion, and, for good measure, condemn Governor Quitman. The convention then formed the Mississippi Union Party.[32]

The legislature, taking up the challenge, proved full of Quitman's supporters by passing on 30 November the call for a convention "to consider the state of our Federal relations and the remedies to be applied." Election of delegates was set for the first Monday, September 1851, and the convention was to meet on the second Monday of the following November.

It was not quite what Quitman wanted, having become convinced by late September that nothing less than secession would do, but given the circumstance it was the best he could hope for. The legislature, taking no chances, voted down a popular referendum on the convention or on the Compromise. Quitman thus consoled himself by anticipating the simultaneous occurrence of the Georgia Convention and the meetings of the Alabama and South Carolina legislatures. He hoped to see communication established between these groups.[33]

Although Yancey's efforts in Alabama had accomplished nothing, he was undeterred. Macon County girls at a barbecue near Town Creek baked a cake adorned with a little flag proclaiming, "Secession! If this be treason, make the most of it." Crowds trundled down dusty roads in the mid-August heat to Montgomery to greet with "hearty and enthusiastic applause" Yancey's repeated objections to the Compromise, but all of the effort was futile. Upon the passage of the Compromise in September, Yancey recommenced his attack, succinctly stating, "I am for action . . . not talking." He then advised citizens to form Southern Rights Associations that he described, despite their penchant for much talk, as the "most efficient means of action." Anger did sweep over some radical enclaves in Alabama, giving Yancey some cause for hope. J. J. Seibels' father wrote from Columbia, South Carolina, that Georgians should tar and feather Toombs and Stephens for their affirmative votes on the Compromise, while the younger Seibels' *Montgomery Advertiser* supported Yancey's Southern Rights groups. In late October, businessmen, planters, and lawyers led by the "Eufaula Regency" met in that small southeast Alabama town to draw up a petition to Governor Henry Collier requesting that he call a special session of the legislature.[34] Collier, like Seabrook in South Carolina, managed to read the mood of the state and postponed any action until the Nashville Convention reassembled.

On 7 September, the passage of the California and Utah bills completed the despair of many radicals. The *Southern Press* in Washington, however, recalled the upcoming second session of the Nashville Convention, scheduled for 11 November; the paper took heart and again dared to think that this meeting might bring the answer, though this was clearly a minority opinion. Actually the success of the Compromise had so deflated the radical menace that many moderates who in June had chaperoned fire-eaters now saw no point in attending. Even some radicals stayed away. William Gilmore Simms counseled James H. Hammond that nothing would be accomplished there.[35]

"Bad would be our condition, if the Convention should fail for want of backing," John C. Calhoun had written a year before about the first gathering at Nashville; now his words seemed portentous concerning the second. The weather was colder in Nashville, and so was the hospitality, a more somber mood perhaps resulting from a midsummer cholera epidemic that had almost paralyzed the town. Entertainments had shut down, and citizens had resorted to medieval plague rituals such as burning tar and firing cannon. No parties or gaiety would greet delegates who made the difficult journey to Nashville. "The road to Nashville is not continuous," a South Carolinian later lamented. From Chattanooga a steamer ferried passengers to where the Nashville Road crossed the Tennessee River, and from there a railway stretched to the Cumberland.[36]

On Monday, 11 November, the convention met a block away from the McKendree Church at the Christian Church where its members took stock of their number and complexion. The ninety-five delegates were far more radical than those of the previous session. South Carolina had the largest delegation with sixteen, although Hammond had taken Simms's advice and stayed home. Mississippi's all-new delegation of eight appeared under the cloud of questionable credentials. Georgia's eleven-man delegation contained seven new members of whom one, James N. Bethune, had formed with Walter Colquitt the "Coffin Regiment," so named because its members vowed to march to the Missouri Compromise line determined to fight to the death, their own coffins conveniently strapped to their backs. Alabama returned only two original delegates among its present five. George W. Williams, a new delegate, was the probate judge of Henry County, had served thirteen terms in the state legislature, and was an outright secessionist. Florida's four delegates, of whom three were new, included John C. McGehee, a native of South Carolina transplanted to Florida's Madison County, a stronghold of Southern rights, where McGehee must have felt at home since Madison was virtually a little South Carolina. McGehee was not as radical as many, being rather a cooperative secessionist. Arkansas and North Carolina, as in the first session, sent no one, and Virginia sent only William F. Gordon, who had not ventured far from his plantation in Albermarle County since 1837 but presumably enjoyed a brief period of renewed public activity at the end of his life.

The number of the Tennesseeans had diminished, down from a hundred and one to fourteen, three of whom were new. But while the number was reduced, the delegation's moderation was not. Radical resolutions raised Tennessee objections, especially from A. O. P. Nicholson, Aaron V. Brown, and Gideon Pillow. The tone of the meeting, however, turned bitterly angry, despite the objections of the few moderates.[37]

Langdon Cheves, ignoring the ukase of the previous session against South Carolinian conspicuousness, let himself go on Thursday, offering a single resolution that proclaimed secession by Southern states in concert as "the only remedy for the aggravated wrongs."[38] In a three-hour speech that the *Charleston Mercury* hailed as the "final appeal to our love of country," Cheves begged for the formation of an independent Southern confederacy and mocked the Union, snarling that, as for Northerners, "there is no doubt that they have abolished the Constitution. The carcass may remain, but the spirit has left. . . . It stinks in our nostrils."[39]

The failure of Tennessee's moderate resolutions reflected the absence of the first session's conservative elements. The radically dominated Committee on Resolutions quashed Tennessee's recommendations so the session never heard them despite Brown's and Nicholson's attempts to bring them to the floor.[40] Eventually resolutions, primarily from Mississippi's delegation, followed a preamble supplied by the Alabamians. They affirmed the right of secession, denounced the Compromise, and recommended a Southern congress. Nicholson and Brown persisted in their objections by declining, in a symbolic move, to address the convention; but A. J. Donelson protested with an address. Although the session's presiding officer, Georgian Charles James McDonald, quickly called Donelson to order, the Tennessean was able briefly to criticize the convention to scattered applause from the gallery. The *Charleston Mercury*'s correspondent complained that "the galleries were full of [Yankee abolitionists]" and hoped that "the next Convention held in the South . . . will be where there are neither DONELSONS nor Abolitionists to disturb thier [*sic*] meeting."[41]

The convention hastily adjourned after McDonald had successfully reined in Donelson. The stated reason for the rapid closing of business was the impending arrival of a funeral party in the Christian Church, but this was a transparent excuse for the open manhandling and silencing of any opposition to radical objectives. In any event, some might have mused that a funeral of sorts had already been in progress.[42]

That the passage of the Compromise Bills in Congress did not abate the sectional fever was due, in large part, to a widespread belief in the South, even among Unionists, in the theoretical right of secession. In North Carolina, for example, Union Democrats, though eschewing its application, endorsed it as a principle.[43] William Rutherford, Jr., a Georgia Unionist, found himself in the same company as Governor Henry Collier in Alabama in endorsing the right of secession.[44] The *Natchez Free Trader* proclaimed that "we shall term the two parties SECESSIONISTS and SUBMISSIONISTS, for we believe that these are the only issues before the country."[45] In some places in Alabama there was the outspoken belief that the "compromise measures will warrant the secession of any slaveholding state from the Union." With the repetition of such rhetoric, gradually secession became more noticeable as a Southern Democratic doctrine.[46]

While secession remained a theory, radicals could expect its acceptance, but any move toward application caused wavering and resistance, much to the distress of the fire-eaters. In Virginia, the Whigs and "Democratic submissionists" were prepared to support the Compromise and oppose those who were not, noted Edmund Ruffin, Jr., "unless the repeal or equivalent alteration of the fugitive slave law opens their eyes."[47] Although Southern Rights Associations were organized to pursue policies of nonintercourse with the North, the sectional question had been overshadowed during the summer by the "struggle between the East & West for power" in the election of delegates to the Virginia Constitutional Convention. The state, meanwhile, had resolutely stood aloof from Deep South overtures, and the Compromise soothed all but the radicals. Edmund Ruffin, as angry as the South Carolinians, found Rhett's attitudes more agreeable than those of his fellow Virginians.[48]

As one radical Virginian had discovered, however, South Carolina was not peopled entirely with Barnwell Rhetts. Beverley Tucker spent most of July as James Hammond's guest at Silver Bluff, playing billiards and working on his Nashville speech. The visit was not altogether pleasant for Tucker, for although Hammond was fond of his friend and thus could overlook his lapses of rationality, apparently the neighbors only found him odd. William Gilmore Simms, whom Tucker ardently wished to see, was down with diarrhea (or so he said) during all of Tucker's stay and was unable to show him around Charleston.[49] Even Hammond could not ignore the speech defect that made Tucker a painful spectacle on the stump.

At the Fourth of July celebration at Barnwell, Hammond spoke for an hour from a stand set up under a shady grove, but Tucker excused himself from addressing the crowd because of weariness. When the time for toasts arrived, however, Tucker took his turn, standing to call out: "ZACHARY TAYLOR: A Southern President who has used the military power of the United States to sequester the whole of California, and the whole of New Mexico for the North." Many listeners did not know Tucker well and must have been mystified by the strange tribute delivered in South Carolina to the most unpopular president there since Andrew Jackson. But Tucker continued with a scriptural quotation he had used in his speech at Nashville: "What part have we in David! Neither have we any inheritance in the son of Jesse. To your tents, Oh Israel! Now look to thine own house, David!" To cover a performance that bordered very close on incoherence, Hammond quickly volunteered, "The Union of the South for the sake of the South."[50]

"When you were in Barnwell," soothed Simms after Tucker was safely back in Virginia, "you were in one of our most sterile precincts, morally and physically." Whether or not this calmed Tucker's worries over the impression he had created in South Carolina, he was soon obsessed by other apprehensions, such as imagining that the government was intercepting his letters.[51]

There was some Unionist sentiment in South Carolina. "It will not do," said Unionist Benjamin F. Perry, "to break up a government every time it goes wrong."[52] His voice, although a strong one, was lost in a fevered atmosphere that prompted men to ask not whether the state should secede, but when. The October election yielded a legislature filled with secessionists, although a division did exist between those advocating separate state action and those desiring cooperation with other Southern states. The former group, led by Rhett, was in the majority but was not sufficiently strong to muster the necessary two thirds to call a state convention.

A protracted series of negotiations and debates marked the growing fire-eater excitement at almost realizing their objective. Everything seemed to go their way. On 27 November four companies of artillery from Florida landed at Fort Moultrie and Castle Pinckney, causing a stir in Charleston that was transmitted to Columbia. As speculation about the soldiers' destination included that of Texas, a rumor surfaced that Seabrook had asked Washington why troops were being concentrated in Charleston Harbor and had been told by Millard Fillmore that it was none of the governor's business. "We are not so excitable here," yawned the *Mercury,* "and Mr. Fillmore might send the whole of his disposable forces without raising much anxiety."[53] But this belied an excitement that gained the separatists enthusiastic supporters. Was this not the overt act that moderates always cited as the prerequisite for action? "Wait with patience," counseled James Hamilton in a perceptive letter that explained why no other state would join South Carolina in secession. South Carolina apparently had lost all patience and was dreadfully close to taking herself out of the Union.[54]

Part of the cause for the South Carolina legislature's heated session was the evidence that the anticipated Georgia Convention would not deliver an ordinance of secession. After the Nashville Convention, the radicals had launched a campaign in Georgia in early June. First the fire-eater press editorialized against the Compromise and for the extension of the Missouri Compromise line. Southern Rights meetings heard speakers like McDonald and Colquitt delivering angry orations, but the subsequent attempt to form associations inspired little enthusiasm. The problem was transparent to the perceptive observer. Most agitation was the work of South Carolina transplants who had migrated to Savannah and the counties along the Savannah River. Unionists countered the propaganda of the "Old Nullifiers of '32" with meetings of their own designed, as they put it, to show the real sentiment of the state.[55]

During the summer Rhett and Yancey attempted to raise the cause's popularity in Georgia. A Southern Rights meeting filled Macon to over-flowing on 22 August with as many as twenty-five sharing a hotel room. The Macon and Western Railroad halved its round-trip fare and ran extra trains. Rhett and Colquitt appeared the day before the meeting but did not speak, preferring to save their thunder for the main event, which got underway at ten the next morning at the warehouse of Field and Adams. "The ladies" enjoyed reserved seating. Bands played and the aroma of barbecue wafted amidst the crowd that heard Yancey as well as Rhett speak, the first time the latter had addressed a popular assembly outside of South Carolina.[56] Sixteen windy resolutions, reported by the committee headed by Charles James McDonald, covered everything from approving of Nashville and recommending the call for a Georgia Convention to welcoming Alabama's representatives and soliciting subscriptions for the *Southern Press*. The ladies appreciatively waved their pocket handkerchiefs, the resolutions were passed unanimously, and everyone trailed off to eat the barbecue before returning for more speeches.[57]

The resolutions did not alarm as much as Rhett's call for disunion did. "It is melancholy to think that any portion of any party in Georgia could be so demented," muttered the *Southern Banner* in Athens.[58]

The plan put forward at the meeting called for the secession of Georgia, temporarily of course, to be followed by South Carolina. Rhett later explained the idea in more elaborate terms at Walterboro, South Carolina: Georgia would secede first, then South Carolina, then Alabama and Mississippi. Within eighteen months the rest of the South would join the seceders. Out west, New Mexico, Utah, and California would also secede because they would want access to the Atlantic, free trade, and slave labor for their mines. Rhett saw Mexico as a vast real-estate reserve awaiting Southern expansion.[59]

The Georgians who cheered this fantasy were a small minority. In fact, while the radical press inflated the attendance at the Macon meeting to as many as 10,000, most likely only about 1,500 attended, occasioning even the fire-eaters to explain that the intensity of mid-August heat had kept many away.[60] Described by moderates as a "stupendous failure," the meeting did alarm a large section of the Georgia Democracy, prompting Union Democrats to form coalitions with Whigs, particularly in the southern part of the state.[61] Hammond's fears seemed realized in that Rhett's decisive extremism was too elephantine.

But was it Rhett's extremism or Rhett's native state that caused Georgia to resist disunion? Georgia–South Carolina enmity had existed since colonial times and lately had been irritated by trade rivalry.[62] Now radical secession emanating from South Carolina added to this resentment. "It is not true," protested the *Charleston Mercury,* somewhat defensively, "that there is contempt and hatred between the people of the two States."[63] But there were complaints in Georgia that "the revolutionary spirit . . . of the people of a neighboring state has gradually insinuated itself into our midst, like the serpent into the garden of paradise."[64]

Aside from this reaction against South Carolina, no one could be sure how Georgia felt about the Compromise until November. Howell Cobb was told in July, "The people will be with you in supporting the Compromise." The Democratic radical press was "no more the voice of the people than the delegates to the Nashville Convention were their representatives."[65] However, after the passage of the Compromise, another correspondent, who had been "mixen [*sic*] amongst the people," was not so sure. The mountains in the northeast were Unionist, but the Democrats were "Ultras" and angry at Cobb, wanting to replace him. "This is rather provoken [*sic*]," it was observed, "but I think we will be able to stand up to them and in the mean time advance the true interests of our country."[66] Radicals countered that "the Georgia papers have a better tone, and our friends claim to be strong."[67]

Claims of strength, however, rested on a relatively narrow foundation of potential secessionists: Democrats enthralled by their radical leaders, members of the urban lower middle class who owned perhaps one or two slaves, professionals in cities who wished to appear prescient or desired prominence in a new movement, and illiterate poor whites populating the Pine Barrens. Such types composed the most malleable groups. Yet fear over starting a civil war (although "Ultras" scoffed at such notions) and, probably more importantly, the prosperity brought by cotton that was selling at thirteen cents a pound undermined radical initiatives not only in Georgia but all across the South. Georgians were apprehensive about the shape a Southern confederation would take—would it be more consolidated or looser than the Union? While Henry L. Benning thought "that the only safety of the South from abolition . . . is to be found in an *early* dissolution of the Union," secession in itself would not be sufficient; a Southern confederacy would only result in yet another sectional division within the South itself. Benning wanted a consolidated republic that would "put slavery *under the control of those most interested* in it."[68]

Such a prospect did not attract conservatives. Most Georgians, like most Southerners, wanted to resist moderately the "aggression" of the North, primarily through such methods as nonintercourse.[69]

"You see that her [Georgia's] Whig politicians are already playing the skunk," complained William Gilmore Simms as the campaign for the Union gathered momentum, causing Georgia radicals to back away from their extreme position.[70] By November disunion was rarely mentioned as a means of resisting the Compromise. Some went to the fight for nonintercourse, others to the proposal for another convention (like Nashville), but the majority decided to abide the Compromise. The political reality that all Georgia secessionists, with two exceptions, were out of office in 1850 dictated the decision. One of the exceptions, however, was Governor George Washington Towns.[71]

There was little that Towns could do by himself, even if he had wanted to. Already having warned Seabrook away from separate state action, Towns preferred a cooperative effort throughout the South. "My own opinion," he later explained, "was that the Union and the rights of the South could be preserved only by Union among ourselves and to this end were my efforts directed."[72] The legislature in February had empowered him to call a convention if Congress tampered with slavery, but the mood of the state had changed by fall. When Towns received the official copy of the California Act on 23 September and did call the convention, Unionists began pondering the wisdom of the move. But radicals throughout the Gulf States hailed the move as exactly what they had been waiting for. Georgia, they gleefully predicted, would lead the separation. Northern Whigs were manifestly unconcerned, but Democratic papers there openly worried.[73]

They did not have to worry. The election returns were counted on 26 November, showing a devastating Union victory of more than two to one. Less than one half of the Democrats had voted for Southern rights, even after the strenuous attempts to divorce the statement of such rights from secession. Moderates were sure that they had "got these ultras at last."[74]

The convention that gathered in Milledgeville on 10 December 1850 was composed of talented men, educated and propertied, many of whom were slaveholders. They were also, reflecting the election returns, over-whelmingly Unionist. On 11 December a pro-Union set of resolutions was read and referred to committee. The radicals were not to be ignored, though, for R. W. McCune protested the design to bury all radical resolutions in committee. He perceived "a disposition in the majority not to harmonize" but rather "to drive off members who are called 'fire-eaters.'"[75]

McCune and the few other fire-eaters present encountered the vener-able Thomas Spalding presiding over the convention. Spalding, the last surviving signer of the Georgia Constitution, was so much a Unionist that he proclaimed at the outset of the convention his preference to see not only himself but his family dead rather than participate in anything inclined toward disunion. He called McCune out of order, and after some haggling, the convention proceeded, bypassing the extremists.

Despite such debate, the Georgia Convention adopted a preamble and three resolutions with amazing rapidity on 13 December. The following day, after long and impractical delays caused by the fire-eaters, the fourth and fifth resolutions also passed with large majorities. Credit for these resolutions is usually given to C. J. Jenkins, chairman of the Committee of Thirty-three, but Alexander Stephens later claimed that he had writ-ten them. The resolutions were similar to those unsuccessfully proposed by the Tennessee delegation at the second session of the Nashville

Convention and those of an October rump meeting of Unionists who voiced Unionist dissatisfaction with the Compromise. The so-called Chatham Platform, drawn up by a Savannah Unionist, was virtually the same as the Georgia Platform.[76]

The preamble urged Georgia to accept the Compromise while warning the North not to mistake such acceptance as weakness. Five resolutions followed, the fourth and the fifth bearing the weight. The fourth declared that should Congress act against slavery where it existed, prohibit territories from admission because of the presence of slavery, prohibit slaves in Utah and New Mexico, or repeal the Fugitive Slave Law, Georgia would resist even if that resulted in disunion. The fifth resolution maintained that the Fugitive Slave Law must be enforced to preserve the Union.[77]

"A more objectionable document . . . was never written in Georgia," declared the *Georgia Telegraph,* reflecting the radical disappointment over losing the state. And an increasingly conservative Alabama lay between South Carolina and Mississippi. Georgia had, in effect, saved the Union by unifying the moderate opinion of the South, but the Democratic party was deeply wounded.[78] The convention resulted in the formation of a Union party, mainly because it had provided the opportunity for caucus and organization. A Southern Rights party also split away—not through positive effort, but because Union Democrats deserted them. Towns lamented that all that had resulted was the opportunity "for designing politicians to agitate and divide the people" with the effect of jeopardizing Southern rights and hence the Union.[79] The Union party movement divided Democrats in Tennessee, Louisiana, Georgia, and Mississippi and was to lose five Democratic Senate seats to the Whigs.[80] By early 1851 Alabama Democrats had separated into Union and states rights groups. In Mississippi, the Union group, formed at Jackson on 18 November, included Old Line Whigs as well as Union Democrats.

While the Georgia Convention had glided toward moderation, South Carolina's legislature, Columbia's "only public amusement," bitterly debated the schedule and method for secession.[81] South Carolina would never completely cool off, but the news of the Georgia Platform sobered some of its angrier citizens. William Gilmore Simms in October had called for either the formation of a Southern confederacy or whatever other measures were necessary to meet the crisis. Now, he tried to quiet the agitation. He did not want another humiliation like that of 1833.[82] The legislature, bombarded with military bills and nonintercourse bills, labored on in debate until a compromise, termed the Omnibus Bill, unrelated to the one presented to the national legislature in July, met general approval. It gave the governor the authority to join other states in setting provisions for a Southern congress. The package also provided for the election and legislative appointment of South Carolina representatives in October 1851. Montgomery was the suggested site and 2 January 1852 was the suggested date. Finally, the prospect of a state convention was left to the governor or the legislature, depending on what the Southern Congress did or did not do. While this only amounted to a postponement, South Carolina at last had tentatively agreed to a course provided by the Georgia Platform, what Georgian Herschel V. Johnson had called "our true policy," which was "to adopt such measures as will prevent all future encroachments upon our rights."[83]

This was intolerable to the fire-eaters, yet at the time they had to settle for it. The impotence of Nashville ignited their frenzied efforts to garner support for their cause, and they had tried to mask their obvious lack of popular support with unrestrained bombast. With Calhoun dead, neither South Carolina nor any other Southern state offered a widely respected replacement. Advocating Southern rights did not always mean promoting disunion, but it was increasingly perceived as doing so. Appearance gradually became reality by the beginning of 1851, one melding with the other, until Southern rights and disunion seemed for Unionists in both the North and South to cavort with treason.[84] Fire-eaters exhausted their voices and much of their credibility arguing for action that nobody wanted. In the bargain, grievous party splits and a general aura of mistrust would confuse Southern politics for the next decade. The people were not ready for secession in 1850. Those residing in prosperous cities could not sympathize with radicals who might appear in Richmond, Charleston, Savannah, Mobile, New Orleans, Natchez, or Memphis with dire warnings. Citizens, enjoying almost unparalleled prosperity, scornfully rejected the alarms. The *Savannah Georgian* complained when the returns for the Georgia Convention were tabulated, "The election was purchased."[85]

"All things seemed calm, so serenely at peace in our lives and home," said Rosalie Quitman, who could not understand her father's worry about the coming conflict being the plight of his children.[86] Quitman understood the minds of his radical colleagues and knew that peace and serenity were fragile commodities when exposed to angry belligerence, justified in fire-eater minds by overcaution at home and sly opportunism in the North. Governor Towns vetoed the inscription "Georgia Convention, December, 1850," which had been voted by the convention for Georgia's contributory stone to the Washington Monument; instead he substituted, "The Constitution as it is, the Union as it was."[87]

And the South Carolina legislature chartered the South Atlantic Steam Navigation Company, ostensibly to foster trade between South Carolina ports and foreign countries, and provided it with a five-year interest-free loan of $125,000 on a stipulation that its vessels be available in case of war. Ominously, the legislature directed that the company acquire at least two within a year. Acts for state defense enlarged militia and stockpiled ordnance. South Carolina planned to finance the build-up share with her share of public-land revenues. The legislature also increased state taxes some 50 percent.[88]

Presumably the legislation was effective, for Frederick Law Olmstead, travelling through Charleston three years later, was to remark upon the "frequent drumming . . . [at] the State military school, the cannon . . . on the parade ground, the citadel, the guard house," suggesting that the city was "in a state of siege or revolution."[89]

In December 1850, ten years almost to the day before the secession of South Carolina, cannon in Columbia and Charleston boomed in honor of the state legislature's Compromise Bills.[90] The echoes of those reports had hardly died away before Robert Barnwell Rhett renewed his assault upon moderation.

CHAPTER FIVE

"Ungrateful, Cowardly, Stupid State"

When Franklin Elmore died a little over a month after Whitemarsh Seabrook appointed him to Calhoun's Senate seat, conservative observers greeted Robert Barnwell's appointment as "no good omen!"[1] Then in December the South Carolina legislature, after achieving an uneasy compromise between the separate state forces and the cooperationists, elected Robert Barnwell Rhett to replace Barnwell. Violent apprehension must have seized the moderates. In less than a year, the venerated Calhoun's place in the national legislature had fallen to Carolina's most vaunted fire-eater.

Rhett would not enjoy his time in Washington. An unpaved, raw interruption of the countryside along the Potomac River, the capital was noted for its propensity for taverns, the better to lubricate the social machinery that coincided with legislative sessions. Rhett, however, did not drink.[2] Boarding houses dominated the side streets, while the two well-established hotels, Brown's and Willard's, served as the gathering places for Southern and Northern legislators, respectively.[3] Rhett could not have expected a warm welcome from the latter group, and he was regarded with suspicion by Southern politicians, many of whom knew him only by a bad reputation for tactless arrogance and radical sentiments. Rhett's wife, Elizabeth, worried about him in the charged, unfriendly atmosphere. "How do you stand the cold without thus far?" she asked, but she also wanted to know how he was holding up against "the heat within, mentally and physically in the Senate."[4]

Some of Rhett's supporters in South Carolina looked upon his mission to Washington as nothing more than an opportunity to vindicate himself. "I hope that some favorable opportunity will occur," one informed him, "when you can with propriety pay Mr. Clay back in his own coin."[5] But Rhett did not agree, and Elizabeth noted, "I am [not] at all surprised at your feeling toward those poor old men [Clay and Webster]"; yet at the same time, despite Rhett's having obtained "so holy a state of mind with regard to them," she hoped that he would "be able to present a dignified & patient course towards them, without stooping as a *Senator* of South Carolina to compliment or conciliate them."[6]

One could have asked if compliments and conciliation were a remote possibility in a body that increasingly eschewed even patience and dignity. The threat of disruption still stalked the Senate, even though Mrs. Roger Pryor later admitted that "our eyes were holden so we could not see."

Reverence for the national legislature persisted. Mrs. Pryor recalled "the visits to the galleries of the House and Senate Chamber, and the honor of pointing out the great men to our friends from rural districts; the long listening to interminable speeches, not clearly understood, but heard with a reverent conviction that all was coming out right in the end, that everybody was really working for the good of the country, and that we belonged to it all and were parts of it all."[7]

With alarming frequency, however, massive disagreements about what constituted the good of the country plagued deliberations. The Senate in the 1850s lost its institutional memory. Calhoun's death, Webster's departure to Millard Fillmore's state department, and Henry Clay's enfeeblement left the way open to men who possessed neither the talent nor the vision to replace the old guard. Henry S. Foote, for example, would not allow the Compromise issue to rest even after its components had passed into law. He insisted that the new Congress pass a resolution reaffirming support for the legislation. This might have been a reasonable design in the hands of another, but Foote's personality compelled him to introduce the resolution in the Senate by impugning the motives and characters of disunionists in South Carolina. Robert Barnwell Rhett came to his feet.

Rhett began by observing that Henry Clay rightly deserved his attention for having called him a traitor in the previous session, but he would let that pass for the time being. "My business now," he said calmly, "will be with the Senator from Mississippi."[8]

Rhett restated his position on how the Compromise wronged the South and pointed out that Foote had helped perpetrate that wrong. He referred to the admission of California under the terms of the Compromise as the clever enactment of the Wilmot Proviso. When Foote tried to break in, Rhett said, "I would prefer not to be interrupted, because the Senator has not a good temper, and mine is not much better." He proceeded with a calm, long speech that offered no apology and made plain his quiet outrage.[9]

If the Senate had expected Rhett to demonstrate only a talent for bombast, this performance showed a facile mind skilled in quiet, deliberate debate that was more than a match for Foote. Yet while many might have chortled over Rhett's besting the unpopular Mississippian, Rhett gained little influence among Southern colleagues anxious to preserve the Compromise and avoid truculent attacks on its terms, especially the Fugitive Slave Law. The Southern demand for a viable method to return runaway slaves aroused bitter opposition among some Northern Senators. Rhett did not court popularity by joining Northern radicals in their attack upon the only pro-Southern part of the Compromise.

He objected to the law as strenuously as any Northerner partly because he did not believe that the North would support it. The prophecy proved true in Boston in February 1851 when free blacks abducted from a deputy marshal a fugitive slave, Shadrach Williams, and transported him to Canada. The incident spurred a lengthy congressional debate irritated by numerous petitions from Northern state legislatures calling for curtailed enforcement of the law.[10]

Economics stimulated Southern demands for a more stringent fugitive slave bill. The price of good field hands rose dramatically throughout the 1850s, and halfway through the decade a healthy slave could be valued at eleven hundred dollars.[11] Such capital investment could run away to seek refuge in Northern states, a fact that distressed the Southern planter, but the fugitive slave himself simply frightened the Southerner. There was something terrifying in the defiance of the runaway, in a thirst for freedom that could cause a fugitive to challenge pursuing hounds with a knife and failing to stand them off, try to cut his own throat.[12] The supposedly docile chattel of the South, capable of taking extraordinary risks and sometimes making the ultimate sacrifice for freedom, became a potential menace of such formidability that custom and tradition, let alone legislation, became meaningless. The fear of slave insurrection haunted all Southerners; the memory of the brutal uprisings in Haiti in 1798 kept apprehensions vibrant. John Randolph had alerted his colleagues in Congress before the War of 1812 that "the nightbell never tolled for fires in Richmond, that the mother does not hug the infant more closely to her bosom." Periodic alarms kept alive the dread.[13]

On Saturday 25 May 1822, Peter, a slave of Colonel John C. Prioleau, strolled by the Fitzsimmons Wharf near the Charleston, South Carolina, Customs House, where he became aware of an extensive slave uprising planned for Charleston and its environs. He alerted his owner.[14] Foremost among revelations in the Denmark Vesey Conspiracy was the influence of antislavery rhetoric occasioned by the Missouri crisis. Indeed, one of the conspirators, Jack Purcell, told how Vesey had shown him a speech that "had been delivered by a Mr. [Rufus] King, on the subject of slavery."[15]

In 1831 Nat Turner's killing spree in Southampton County, Virginia, gruesomely reinforced the gnawing anxiety and prompted a brief debate in the Virginia House of Delegates on the feasibility of emancipation.[16] But the emancipation aberration passed, and Virginia, along with the rest of the South, closed ranks. Southerners believed that any talk hinting at emancipation or challenging the beneficence of slavery encouraged insurrection. Just as George Mason's fifty-year-old antislavery remarks embarrassed his grandson, James M. Mason, Southerners cringed when Robert Barnwell Rhett joined Northerners in objecting to a federal law designed to restore runaways to their masters.[17]

In February 1851, Hannibal Hamlin of Maine introduced a petition from his state calling for a modification of the Fugitive Slave Law. David Rice Atchison of Missouri moved to have the petition tabled, but Ohio's Salmon P. Chase protested. Hamlin pointed out that similar petitions had been referred to the Judiciary Committee, and that this one should be handled no differently. Georgia's John M. Berrien, however, found the petition so objectionable that he wondered how respectable men could have signed it.

This ignited the ire of the document's advocates. John P. Hale of New Hampshire proclaimed that agitation kept free institutions from stagnating and, as if to prove the point, proceeded to excoriate slavery. William J.

Cooper of Pennsylvania tried to calm discussion by assuring that his state would enforce the law as it stood. Rhett then rose to ask if Pennsylvania had yet to repeal those laws it had crafted to frustrate previous fugitive slave legislation, and Cooper had to admit that it had not—but only, he hastily added, because of various local issues that he did not deem worthy of discussion in the national legislature.

Rhett saw his opening. More than likely, he mused, Pennsylvania's mercantile interests supported the law, but the interior of Pennsylvania, as well as that of New York and other Northern states, desired to suppress it. How long would it be, Rhett asked, before the current petitions to modify the legislation became resolutions to destroy it altogether? Referral to the Judiciary Committee failed, and the petition was tabled.[18] But Rhett's observations were by no means oblique for Southern Senators who well remembered that the slave trade in the District of Columbia had been attacked first by petitions, then resolutions, and was ultimately abolished by the Compromise of 1850.

Henry Clay's request that the Fillmore administration provide information about the Williams incident in Boston prompted renewed sectional grumbling among senators. Complaints from Southerners induced John Hale to observe that unpopular laws were impossible to enforce.[19] Rhett's agreement probably surprised Hale as much as anyone. He asserted that the Fugitive Slave Law should be violated because it gave the federal government the power to infringe upon state sovereignty. Federal coercion in Boston to enforce the Fugitive Slave Law provided a precedent for federal intervention in Charleston. Southern self-interest, according to Rhett, had blinded his section's politicians to the fact that the law was as unconstitutional as previous fugitive slave acts had been. The Constitution provided for the return of fugitives from justice, and to elaborate on this only enhanced federal authority. Rhett could not resist reminding Southern senators that he had denounced the legislation the previous summer as a bad bargain that deserted the surer constitutional remedy for the fugitive slave problem.[20]

This was hardly what John Hale had in mind, but he let it pass. However, when Jefferson Davis said, with resignation, that the North clearly had no intention of enforcing the law, Hale gained the floor again to point accusingly at Mississippi. The South was no better, he charged, for Mississippi had frustrated the arrest of John A. Quitman for violating United States neutrality laws. Davis said nothing, leaving it to fellow

Mississippian Henry Foote, who numbered both Davis and Quitman as vile enemies, to defend the state's judicial veracity at the expense of its governor.[21]

John Quitman suffered the kind of political disappointments that embitter. He brooded over losing the vice-presidential nomination at the 1848 Democratic Convention, where Jefferson Davis had advised delegates that the Mississippi Democracy did not prefer Quitman. Typical of the old scholar-soldier's political naiveté was his bewilderment over this slight.[22]

Quitman's wife, Eliza, was happy that he had not gotten the nomination. She had missed him as first the Mexican War and then continuous canvassing took him away from home. Political achievement, she reminded him, would provide only hollow joy if purchased at the expense of domestic pleasures. John's election to the governor's office in Mississippi left her to loneliness and boredom at Monmouth while he was at Jackson, her life illuminated only by a vicarious participation in his concerns. Eliza's sad devotion poignantly increased even as his infrequent letters assumed colder and more impersonal tones that left her begging for details. "Do not forget," she admonished, "that I am your truest and best friend in this world tho' you may not know it."[23]

By the beginning of 1851, Quitman needed friends. He had become involved during 1850 with a filibustering expedition against Spanish authority in Cuba led by the erratic Narciso Lopez. A Venezuelan soldier of Spain, Lopez had lobbied in the United States since 1849 for assistance to achieve Cuban independence. He met with John Calhoun several times and tried unsuccessfully to interest, variously, Jefferson Davis and Robert E. Lee in either funding or leading a campaign of Cuban liberation.[24] In the spring of 1850, Lopez travelled to Jackson, Mississippi, to persuade Governor Quitman to lead the revolt. Prominent Cuban expatriates in New York warned Quitman that Lopez was a fraud, but the governor listened with fascination as Lopez described the revolutionary fervor in Cuba.[25]

In addition to courting Quitman's military aspirations, Lopez manipulated the Mississippian's apprehensions. Quitman feared a British scheme to establish "near us negro or mongrel states" by enforcing emancipation over protectorates snatched from the feeble Spaniards. Wresting Cuba from Spain and placing it in more vigorous hands would preserve slavery in the island for future Southern expansion.[26]

Quitman finally declined a military role in the proposed invasion, explaining that his duties held him to his post in the time of sectional troubles. He could not resist, however, ruminating over a map of Cuba to suggest strategies. He offered Lopez financial help and accompanied him to New Orleans, where he supplied him with the names of officers and men known from the Mexican War.[27] Texan John P. Henderson, who joined the scheme in April 1850, kept Quitman posted on the progress of the Cuban Liberation Movement. Mississippi Supreme Court Justice Cotesworth Pinckney Smith signed bonds of the proposed Cuban Republic for sale to the public at ten cents on the dollar.[28]

The Lopez expedition was an abortion. No support arose in Cuba, and the general was forced back into Key West.[29] Then a legal storm broke over Quitman and his confederates, who faced federal indictments for violating United States neutrality laws. Making matters worse, Lopez reappeared in New Orleans and started planning yet another expedition. Again, rumors connected Quitman to the scheme. He seemed determined to flout Millard Fillmore's insistence on American neutrality. "What will you do about that Cuban affair?" Eliza asked him.[30]

There was little that he could do but bluster that the entire issue was a contrivance to inhibit his role in the sectional controversy of 1850. A Southern statesman, he railed, could not discharge his duties to his country without inviting slander and abuse. If the federal government, operating in an atmosphere of corruption, could threaten a Southern governor, the Southern people could forsake all hope. Quitman did not regard his observations as self-pitying. He was fulfilling his duty, fighting for property, liberty, even life; to do otherwise would leave him degraded. It was his nature, he stated, to voice his opinions. After all, was this not a free country?[31]

When the United States Circuit Court indictment came down from the grand jury in New Orleans, Quitman asked friends what, as governor of Mississippi, he should do. They told him either to resist arrest and test the constitutional limits of federal power over a sovereign executive or to seek vindication by standing trial. If he chose the latter, he should resign. Quitman chose vindication, resigning on 3 February 1851 after an unsuccessful attempt to have his trial waived until the completion of his term. Four days later he appeared before the court in New Orleans and was released on bail of a thousand dollars.[32]

Quitman tried in New Orleans to remain inconspicuous or, at least, maintained a pretense of doing so. Yet serenades, fetes, and praise repeatedly placed him in public view. At a masked ball where New Orleans belles teased him for having to stand trial, Quitman visibly enjoyed the attention, remarking that his Mexican campaigns never matched the vigor of the good-natured banter. One "charming little sylph announced herself a fire eater" and volunteered to fight against Northern aggression.[33]

Quitman had cause for carefree buoyancy. The government's case against him rested on his allegedly having loaned one thousand dollars to friends coincidentally involved with Lopez.[34] John P. Henderson's trial, prosecuted with no better documentation, became the government's test case consequent to the Texan's demand for speedy justice. On 7 March 1851, Henderson's third trial ended, as had the previous two, in a mistrial, and all indictments were dropped. The telegraph sped the happy news to Mississippi, where Quitman supporters dragged out "The Governor," a brass cannon mounted on the state house lawn in Jackson, and fired it repeatedly for Quitman, Henderson, the South, and "'the rest of mankind.'"[35]

Quitman naturally interpreted this and other festive receptions of his exculpation as support for his political positions. He had evidence that even beyond Mississippi, he was regarded as important enough to woo. In New Orleans, John S. Preston and "other distinguished South Carolina gentlemen" invited him to a private dinner. Quitman, happy that his resignation had brought him more fame than his service in the Mexican War, toyed with the idea of not going to the dinner but then decided the affair would be an enjoyable duty. He informed his Southern Rights friends from South Carolina that he would be glad to come to their dinner if they could hold it before he left town.[36]

Quitman's ideas had changed little since the previous autumn when Whitemarsh Seabrook had implored him to initiate Southern secession in Mississippi. The Carolinians at the dinner could not have been pleased that Quitman still held the opinion that South Carolina should begin the withdrawal because "so long as the several aggrieved states wait for one another, their action will be over-cautious and timid."[37]

Quitman's attitude partly influenced events in South Carolina. There, secession sentiment, virtually unanimous as to intent if not method, raged strongly throughout the opening months of 1851 and then rapidly diminished.[38] The issue of pressing concern was the state convention authorized by the legislature in December 1850. Worried that South Carolina might create a Palmetto version of the Georgia Convention, Isaac W. Hayne warned voters to be as aware of delegates' resolve as they were of their opinions. In some cases they would be elected a year before the convention met. The possibility of a wavering group of submissionists loomed ominously for those who wanted secession assured, and calls issued from parishes for concise statements of opinion from prospective delegates.[39] Elections during the first two months of the year revealed that the convention was in trouble. James H. Hammond declined his nomination, as did William Gilmore Simms.[40] And when on Monday, 10 February 1851, torrential rains in Charleston held the number of voters to below two hundred for the entire city, the weather could be only partly blamed. A general apathy resulted because nobody knew when the convention would meet.[41]

For radicals the explanation was simple. Langdon Cheves and Robert Barnwell had induced the indifference, Rhett was informed, by their moderation during the legislative session.[42] Fire-eaters began to regard these leaders with suspicion. Cooperationists transformed the indifference to alarm by predicting that a convention under radical control would take South Carolina alone out of the Union. Separate state action implied an unforgivable arrogance, they argued, for it assumed that only South Carolina could perceive danger. Carolinian delusions about forming a vanguard of states sequentially seceding from the Union courted ruin. "One of the Minority," who was actually Charleston cooperationist J. W. Wilkinson, reminded everyone that the proposed convention was only part of a compromise to reconcile paralyzed divisions in the South Carolina legislature. The idea of the convention, however, had grown monstrous, and radicals described it as having unlimited power. The parts of the Compromise had grown greater than their sum.[43]

In any event, Palmetto moderates declared that the realities revealed in 1832 promised to make this proposed convention only another contemptible humiliation. "The political history of the State, the credit of her people abroad, and their feeling at home forbid the disgrace," Wilkinson admonished. Beyond this, functional problems connected with the convention bothered cooperationists. If the people were ready for secession, why did the legislature defer the scheduling of the convention to a subsequent legislature? The possibility might arise that with delegates already elected, there would be an outstanding convention simultaneous with a sitting legislature whose majority, reflecting the sense of the people, did not want the convention to meet.[44]

Separate state action advocates sought to counter moderate apprehension with Southern Rights Associations. Carolinians took as their guide the actions of such associations in Alabama where visitors from other states and local radicals addressed weekly meetings in large towns. When the Alabama associations called for a general meeting, St. Phillip's and St. Michael's Parishes in Charleston did so as well, offering to host a convention of South Carolina's associations on the first Monday in May.[45]

Aside from Mississippi, Alabama was the only Southern state that South Carolina could depend upon for support. Southern rights extremism in Alabama encouraged Carolina radicals who were either unaware of or refused to see the serious factiousness splintering the Alabama Democracy. Variously termed the "Chivalry" or the "Talent," the Southern Rights wing of the party emerged during the Calhoun era to find itself in 1851 composed of men who were not always talented or chivalrous. The leadership of the group exhibited little coherence, what with the varying and sometimes hostile degrees of immoderation personified by William R. King, Benjamin Fitzpatrick, and William Lowndes Yancey. Prosperity and an influential Alabama Whig party made disruption of the Union by Alabama radicals unlikely even if they had agreed with one another.

Under leaders who could not agree on how much resistance was too much, the Democracy split along separate state and cooperationist lines. When the Whigs in late January put up a strong slate of candidates for August state elections, some Southern Rights groups immediately moderated their rhetoric. Needing a united party, Alabama Democrats planned to bring secessionists in southern Alabama, largely under Yancey's sway, to the table with moderate elements from the north of the state. This was no easy task. Antagonism so hardened the factions that things had been said that never could nor would be forgotten.[46]

Both a desire for conciliation and a compulsion for confrontation directed Democratic efforts in January, resulting in a general convention of Southern Rights Associations in Montgomery on 10 February 1851. The gathering was supposed to settle on a policy and also provide a demonstration of popular support. It failed to do either. Unionists tried to frighten delegates from attending by publishing false accounts of a smallpox epidemic in Montgomery, but the ruse was unnecessary.[47] When the convention opened, only eleven counties, all from the Montgomery and Mobile Districts, had sent a total of ninety-seven delegates. In addition to this crowd's self-flattery in calling itself a convention, there was the problem of pretending to represent Alabama while actually and obviously representing only a minority of the Alabama Democracy. There was not a Whig in sight. Indeed, there were precious few Democrats. As it happened, even these Democrats would be unable to agree with one another.

The smallness of the convention allowed Yancey to dominate the proceedings. His oratorical prowess captivated and cajoled in a way that was all the more amazing because practically no one trusted him anymore. He had spun fine, sticky webs before, as in 1848, when the Alabama Platform had nearly committed the state's Democratic delegation to hopeless renegadery. Then, upon the press of expediency, he had abandoned the position he had proclaimed as unabandonable. The crises of 1850 had seen him stamping and snorting for Alabama's representation at the Nashville Convention, to which then he had refused to go. In July, he had shared the speaker's platform in Macon, Georgia, with Rhett, who was perceived by many Alabamians as little more than a madman, and then he had begun a slow process of temporizing subsequent to his discovery that gleeful extremism abroad excited political contempt at home. Hence, moderate Democrats viewed him as possessing principles dangerous to the Union, while radicals saw him as possessing no principles at all. Upon writing the resolutions at Montgomery, he confirmed the suspicions of both sides. Retreating from separate state action for Alabama, he yet held fast to Alabama's duty to support coerced states. And his attempt to accommodate cooperationists by describing the potential for Alabama's secession as "reduced to that of time and policy only" brought the radical house crashing down around his ears.[48] From the floor, fire-eaters, tired of equivocation, pushed him aside and, with ugly determination, amended the resolution to say that secession in Alabama was a question of "time only."

Yancey lost control of his people—the "corn field boys," as they were known—and consequently lost his claim to the leadership of the Southern Rights Associations, let alone the Alabama Democracy.[49] The Mobile Association repudiated the Montgomery resolutions at the direction of John A. Campbell, who then began a process of divorcing Alabama

Southern rights from extremism. That meant, in part, whipping Yancey into line with political reality. Yet he floundered over the stark alternative of deserting the radicals he had encouraged to placate the moderates he had denounced. He persisted in simplifications that proved unacceptable to all but overly impetuous corn field boys; he attacked economic boycotts as ineffectual and effeminate and continued to speak of secession or submission as the only courses available, all the while quietly, but fervently, hoping that South Carolina's secession would vindicate him by dragging along Alabama in the resulting turmoil.[50]

The chance that South Carolina would secede grew dimmer because of other states' activities. While radicals in Virginia were sure that there was not "the least possibility [of] the Fugitive slave law ever being carried out," moderates were trying to find a middle course by proposing the taxation of Northern goods.[51] Fire-eaters were afraid that a cowardly Virginia legislature would do nothing. Whigs openly supported the Compromise, but the Democrats were divided. Conservatives, led by Thomas Ritchie, were mainly happy with the outcome, but the states rights wing of the party, under the direction of R. M. T. Hunter, caviled. Making no secret of his complaints against the Compromise, James M. Mason nevertheless had to reaffirm his devotion to the Union to save his Senate seat during the legislative session of December 1850. And while M. R. H. Garnett, in the spring of 1851, advised William Henry Trescott of South Carolina that the Palmetto State should lead the way out of the Union and expect defensive help from Virginia against federal coercion, the Virginia legislature passed six resolutions that not only refused South Carolina's invitation to participate in a Southern congress, but also warned against secession and further agitation.[52]

"I think our poor old state disgraced by the late action of her legislature," lamented the younger Edmund Ruffin, who predicted it would only "tend to accelerate disunion by stimulating the activity of the abolitionists." Virginia, he wailed, had "long ago lost all influence with the North, [so] what can she now expect to have in the South?"[53] She was to have absolutely no influence, said angry Carolinians. Simms told Beverley Tucker that Virginia had been "crossed by Yankeedom!" "Tell your Virginia Gentlemen," he spat, "that they have lost all right to counsel S. C."[54]

In Washington, Rhett had painfully obvious evidence of the lack of support for South Carolina. He labored to impress upon his Southern colleagues the need for immediate action against Northern aggression, but they remained unimpressed. Even Andrew Pickens Butler disagreed with Rhett that South Carolina could survive the folly of secession alone. "I have done what duty requires of me," Rhett would finally tell the Senate, "and as other duties call me elsewhere, I shall stay here no longer."[55]

Clearly those other duties beckoning Rhett were the attentions he had to pay to his cause in South Carolina. "Rhett is not a wise man," William Gilmore Simms noted, "but, in the great struggle before us, if rash, he is perhaps right."[56] Simms had no idea how rash Rhett intended to be nor how wrong he was to be.

In an address to the Charleston Southern Rights Association at Hibernian Hall on 7 April, Rhett declared that cooperation between the states of the South was an impossibility. No longer needing to coddle Carolina's neighbors, he vented his indignation on them, especially noting the cowardly retreat of Virginia from its bold stance on the Wilmot Proviso. Mississippi's heart was right, but her geography was not; she was landlocked and could be expected to reject a course that might result in her isolation. South Carolina's coastline afforded her the better advantage outside the Union. He hoped there would be no Southern congress because it was sure to counsel cooperation, and South Carolina would have to ignore such advice; better to go out alone, confident that the North realized that to make war on Carolina was to unite the South. "To reach us," he observed, "the dagger must pass through others."[57]

This extraordinary performance shattered any chance of radical success in South Carolina. Whether born out of Rhett's frustrations in Washington or his angry perceptions of the faithlessness of other Southern states, the naked honesty of his speech implicitly charged that cooperation as a condition for secession was merely a disguise for Unionism—or, as he would have put it, submission. The cooperationists had abided Rhett and his fellows because they seemed to believe that secession by South Carolina would arouse other Southern states to follow suit. Indeed, political comity in South Carolina had rested on the idea that what distinguished a Palmetto radical from a moderate was that the former envisioned cooperation after Carolina's withdrawal while the latter required it before. In his speech, Rhett confirmed cooperationists' darkest suspicions. The radicals recognized that no other state would help in leading the way, but they did not expect any to follow, either. South Carolina would be alone, again. After the evening of 7 April many of South Carolina's most prominent and influential politicians regarded Robert Barnwell Rhett, rather than the North, as the primary threat to the state's welfare.

The Rhett faction did nothing to mollify this opinion when the general meeting of the South Carolina Southern Rights Associations convened in Charleston during the first week of May. Instead, Maxcy Gregg, a Rhett lieutenant, commenced a three-day manhandling of the moderate minority. Radicals brushed aside the admonitions of Langdon Cheves and pretended not to hear the vigorous protests of A. P. Butler, James L. Orr, and Robert W. Barnwell. Ultimately force-fed resolutions calling for separate state action, these men emerged from Military Hall embittered by their treatment and determined to bring the state to its senses.[58]

For their part, radical leaders exuded a smug surety for only a few days. Then a slow sense of alarm began to intrude as they surmised they had gone too far. Governor G. H. Means optimistically predicted to John Quitman "that the next Legislature will call the [South Carolina] convention . . . and when that convention meets the state will secede," but he either was putting up a brave front or was unaware of the political storm about to sweep over his state. Maxcy Gregg made no secret of his apprehension. He urged Quitman to "abandon all temporizing and come out boldly for secession"; or, at the very least, to "for God's sake, let the resistance leaders of Mississippi express no hasty opinion against us."[59]

Quitman's heart was with South Carolina's radicals, but his political sense told him to avoid extremism. Guided by a modicum of political sagacity and encouraged by the cheering approbation from crowds who greeted his return from Louisiana, he nevertheless found the Southern Rights party nervous that his radicalism would fare badly against the Union party's nominee for governor, Henry S. Foote. Some scoffed at Foote's candidacy—"He is now a foot," punned the *Mississippi Free Trader*, "but in less than nine months he won't be SIX INCHES"—but the Southern Rights Convention in June took the bellicose Unionist seriously enough to give Jefferson Davis a decided majority. The persistence of Quitman's supporters and news that Davis was gravely ill secured Quitman the nomination.[60]

The campaign that followed was marred by an ill-conceived plan that had Foote and Quitman appearing together on a tour of the state. Quitman looked dull and uninspired compared to his dynamic opponent, and by July Foote was pronouncing "Quitman and Quitmanism . . . dead in Mississippi forever."[61] As the canvass progressed, Foote's already abrasive manner, coupled with his continual assaults on Quitman's character, heightened the hostility between the two until, in Panola County in mid-

July, Quitman lost his temper and tried to batter Foote's face.[62] Afterward, Quitman followed behind Foote at a safe two-day distance, his performance increasingly desultory. The September elections for the Mississippi Convention, authorized by the previous legislature, delivered a stunning Unionist majority and consequently confirmed what, by then, everyone had suspected. Quitman, meandering toward an electoral disaster foreshadowed by the convention returns, withdrew from the race as gracefully as possible. Jefferson Davis, whose bad health so far had saved him from the embarrassment of campaigning for this losing cause, took up the limp Southern Rights banner, lamely warned of the growth of federal power, avoided even the word secession, and lost the election.[63]

The same fate befell Southern Rights parties wherever they were strong enough to warrant attention. National leaders like Lewis Cass and Thomas Ritchie bemoaned, for example, the splintering of the Georgia Democracy, but Unionist Democrats saw no chance for reconciliation with stubborn colleagues who persisted in purveying what Howell Cobb called "that danger which has so lately threatened the Union."[64] Adversaries of extremism in Georgia coalesced into the Constitutional Union Party, an astonishingly powerful coalition between Democrats following Cobb and Whigs led by Alexander Stephens and Robert Toombs. This invincible combination nominated Cobb for governor and effortlessly proceeded to a massacre of Southern Rights candidate Charles J. McDonald in the fall elections.[65]

Consequent to John A. Campbell's direction of the Alabama Southern Rights party, it was to fare better and effect reconciliation with Democratic regulars more quickly than occurred elsewhere in the Deep South. Yancey, vacillating throughout May between varying degrees of immoderation, had succeeded only in reiterating his Alabama Platform with a "Secession Address" and had manipulated the Montgomery Southern Rights Association into passing resolutions sufficiently radical to alienate the powerful J. J. Seibels, editor of the *Montgomery Advertiser.*[66] Campbell and the Mobile Southern Rights Association, however, dictated the course of the June Southern Rights Convention. Calm resolutions that offered no practical encouragement to South Carolina fire-eaters accompanied an endorsement of the cautious and moderate Henry Collier for reelection to the governor's office. This marked a substantial departure from radical policy. Yancey behaved himself on this occasion and in the subsequent campaign save for one instance when, during a series of debates with Henry W. Hilliard, he lost his temper and disparaged Hilliard's loyalty to the South—a display of pique that drew scoldings even from Yancey's own camp.[67] The summer campaign in Alabama otherwise moved to a quiet conclusion, a Unionist victory, and a thorough disintegration of radical dissent. Yancey, visibly disappointed, announced that he would not assist in the inevitable reorganization of the regular Alabama Democracy, as if anyone wanted him to.[68]

The Rhett faction in South Carolina suffered a growing sense of isolation as these Southern Rights candidates executed daring, though sometimes unsuccessful, retreats from secession advocacy in last-ditch efforts to save their political hides. Charles McDonald proved Alexander Stephens's estimation of him as "an adroit and wily competitor" by distancing himself from the taint of Rhettism. Henry Foote's supporters so gleefully exploited the notion of a secessionist conspiracy organized in the Carolina Low Country that Quitman had to refute charges that he and Rhett were conspiring through the mails.[69]

Rhett's lack of influence was so palpably demonstrated throughout the South that his claim to the majority sentiment in South Carolina likewise waned. Cooperationists and other moderates, lacking any other occasion, directed their attention to securing a triumph in the otherwise meaningless October elections for delegates to the Southern congress that would never convene. Such a victory, while only symbolic, would crush the influence of the Rhett faction and leave the South Carolina Convention to the moderates.[70]

In the face of this challenge, Rhett appeared to remain calm, but the urgency of public appearances that carried him from one end of the state to the other betrayed his worry. The *Charleston Mercury,* the Rhett organ, churned out propaganda in such volume as to send the paper reeling into debt. And the Rhett faction, seeking to purge the Charleston Southern Rights Association of ideological impurities, attempted to oust wavering members, failed to do so, and consequently created an auxiliary association that only widened the rift begun in the spring.[71]

Charlestonians avidly following the twists and turns of this miniature political drama might have found it amusing had the radicals not shown such terrifying imperturbability. Fire-eaters dismissed concerns over a civil war by angrily questioning the courage of the people. When Edward Bellinger blithely expressed disregard for the safety of Charleston should an invasion occur, animus against Rhett and his followers spread through the public. Accused of an ambition that knew no bounds and counted no costs, he was perceived as prepared to stand in the ashes of the city to prove his political point.[72]

Finally, the frustrations of the summer had pushed Rhett to the consideration of a mad scheme that would have had the South Carolina militia strike without warning at federal forces garrisoned in Charleston Harbor. The secret plot to precipitate a civil war never went beyond the planning stage because it horrified Governor Means. From Columbia he goaded Rhett back to rationality. Without any formal warning from state authorities, such action would be treasonous. "I fear my dear Sir," he wrote, "that there is an unnatural state of excitement in your city at this time. I hope that you will use your influence to allay it."[73]

Rhett would have never contemplated such a dire course had he not been acutely aware of the impending disaster his cause faced in October. True, his frenetic pace in August and September suggested to the faithful that by sheer persistence a majority of voters could be persuaded to support immediate secession, but the futility of it all surely contributed to that "severe bilious attack" that removed him, at the close of September, from the political scene. A scant two weeks before the elections, at what should have been a crucial period, Rhett sailed from South Carolina for Europe on what was described as a recuperative journey. Perhaps he was truly ill, but the impression must have lingered that he was running away.[74]

The elections of 13 and 14 October delivered an overwhelming majority to Unionism veiled in the euphemism of cooperation, long a dead issue. Moderates could claim the very large turnout as giving the lie to the lame charges of secessionists that the election was meaningless because, of course, there would never be a Southern congress. But Elizabeth Rhett, untypical because her assessment was so intensely personal, cared nothing for attempts to put a pleasant face on the disaster. South Carolina's repudiation of immediate secession, in her view, mattered little beyond the grave injury that the rejection inflicted on her husband. Heavy with their twelfth child and only eight weeks away from a confinement that would end with her death, she would never have the chance to forgive "this ungrateful, cowardly, stupid State" for what it did to her husband in 1851.[75]

Radicals, less inclined to despair over past mistakes, tried to find any alternative that could keep their cause alive. Some of them—without benefit of their ostensible leader, Rhett, who was still out of the country—took up James Henry Hammond's "A Plan for State Action," which they had haughtily dismissed in the spring. The origins of the plan lay in Hammond's political ambitions following the death of Calhoun.

When John C. Calhoun died, Hammond must have seen at last his opportunity to break away from the scandal to which the Hampton family had so resolutely and sternly chained him. During the long years of his forced retirement, he had brooded at Silver Bluff, cultivating the image of the wronged and misunderstood intellectual. He had purveyed such an image to a select group of Southerners, both in South Carolina and beyond. Although Hammond privately disparaged Beverley Tucker as hapless and pitiful, the Virginian had found Hammond a beacon. Edmund Ruffin, personally acquainted with Hammond since James Henry's days as governor, had had his agricultural and political ego stroked by the Carolinian for years.[76]

William Gilmore Simms, who acted as Hammond's informal political advisor, had never found John Calhoun's ideas attractive nor his tactics admirable, but Hammond's reverential attitude toward the old man had been almost obsequious. When Calhoun died, Hammond quickly placed him in the pantheon of classical Greek thinkers, a position that he would have liked to achieve for himself. If Calhoun's political place could translate into Calhoun's political influence, Hammond imagined himself the only statesman worthy of the opportunity to try. He would later complain that politics had become a "small game played by small men," but he never considered himself a small man. At the Nashville Convention he took pains not only to voice the departed Calhoun's ideas on Southern unity but also to emulate his calm, expository manner. His objections to the Address written by Rhett at the convention—an address with which Hammond basically agreed—perhaps arose not from the desire to avoid divisiveness in a Southern movement, but rather from the earnest wish that Calhoun not be succeeded by anyone except himself, and least of all Rhett, who could pose as a dangerous rival for the old man's place.[77]

Hammond's actions could never be considered without recalling the threat of exposure by the Hamptons. Perhaps he did not attend the second session of the Nashville Convention, for which he had argued, because he did not wish to become so visible as to invite reprisals from that quarter. His public explanation, that the sickness of his family prevented his returning to Tennessee, drew derision from those who judged that, if this were so, it would be "the first time in his life" that he had shown any concern for a family he had estranged, albeit temporarily, by his attention to a pretty mulatto in his household.[78] Actually Simms had advised him not to go, and probably for reasons that Hammond later divulged to Ruffin. "The first [session] was a farce," he explained, "& [I] knew the next would be an abortion."[79]

"You erred in not going to the [second session of the] Convention," Simms told him at the end of January in an extensive analysis of why Rhett had secured Calhoun's Senate seat in the December legislature.[80] This was a small consolation by then, for the postmortem showed a Hammond candidacy strewn with such miscalculations. Invited by the Charleston City Council to deliver a memorial oration for Calhoun in November 1850, he had responded with a lengthy, professorial narrative of Calhoun's achievements. Rhett, however, when Governor Seabrook requested that he address the South Carolina legislature on the same subject, delivered a powerful speech that interpreted Calhoun's warnings on the dangers to the South and how best to meet them. As a campaign document, the latter address was much more effective.[81] And finally Hammond refused to go to Columbia during the session of the legislature in December. Again, this might have been out of a real apprehension that to do so would invite the unpleasant attention of the Hamptons, but also it was the kind of thing that Calhoun would have done. In any event, it was yet another mistake because the legislature could not help but reject a candidate who showed a proficiency only for being indifferent or coy.

Hammond's petulance reached new heights after this disappointment. He commenced a pout that compelled him to write morose lamentations about his political career interspersed with virulent attacks on the legislature. Through the carelessness of his son, these achieved wide currency. "I am Pariah," he wailed to Simms, who, clearly losing patience, told him to keep silent, stop feeling sorry for himself, and await an opportunity. "A Letter, six months hence, on the affairs of the state," Simms calculated, ". . . will not be unadvisable."[82]

In spite of the fact that Hammond felt himself to be a "Girondist" surrounded by "Dantonists" who had "got possession of the state" and would presently resort to the guillotine, the errors of the radicals in the spring and subsequent cooperationist dissent encouraged him.[83] On 2 May, he published "A Plan for State Action," which called for the state to cut all ties with the federal government short of secession. South

Carolina's elected officials in Washington would resign and would not be replaced. This would prevent any "pretext for collision" until other states joined the move.[84] Hammond's authorship of this exotic scheme was an open secret, and radicals on the eve of the ill-fated South Carolina Southern Rights Convention suspected that it was only a ploy whereby he could replace Rhett as the leader of the radical cause. On the other hand, Robert Barnwell and other moderates the plan was supposed to attract found it no better than Rhett's extremism. Rebuked yet again, Hammond wished a plague on both factions' houses.[85]

The radicals' contempt for the plan, however, changed rapidly after the October elections, and persuasive arguments for it appeared with all sorts of designs to keep Hammond's name out of it. "Harmony is the object," he told Ruffin, who from Virginia attempted to smooth over the difference between South Carolina's vanquished radicals and triumphant moderates.[86] Maxcy Gregg, once Rhett's political strongman, even suggested that Rhett should be the first to resign. But when he returned from Europe, Rhett was unwilling to leave, as he surely would have, A. P. Butler alone in the Senate. "It is now thought that Rhett will not resign & some think he will be for following the lead of defeated So Rights Parties in other states & go into the Democratic Convention," Hammond predicted. Highly piqued by his inability to take advantage of his rival's misfortune, Hammond searched for traces of Rhett's hypocrisy. "Nothing from him would surprise me," he continued. "I have long thought he was not sincere in his Revolutionary tactics. They were too wild & insure defeat."[87]

Hammond was both right and wrong. Rhett's tactics did ensure defeat, but he would be following no one in the coming reconciliations. The highly touted South Carolina Convention, meeting in April 1852, provided the moderates the chance to pay back the radicals in their own coin. Langdon Cheves orchestrated the proceedings toward a bland endorsement of the theoretical right of secession with as much disregard for fire-eater objections as Gregg had shown for moderate protests a year before. Silenced and rebuked, a final caucus of the handful of men who still called themselves secessionists decided to seek unity with the cooperationists; and when Gregg suggested that Rhett, who was not a delegate but was in attendance, advise them, the group flatly declared that Rhett did not have anything to say that it wanted to hear.[88]

Not until this final humiliation could Rhett have comprehended the utter completeness of his fall. As he sent his resignation from the Senate to Governor Means, his mind must have whirled under the cumulative effect of ruin upon disaster. He had heard the cheers of the faithful thousands turn into the silent rejection of fewer than twenty disoriented, disenchanted politicians scampering for cover. Quitman, Yancey, McDonald, and others less conspicuous had endured, in their own way, such humiliation, but they had not buried a devoted and adored wife. They had not taken the great and, it seemed, final gamble. Perhaps like all men who fail so completely, Rhett puzzled repeatedly over the mistakes and misjudgments that had led him to defeat. If so, he would have the time during his "profound retirement" from an arena he professed no longer interested him to mull over exactly what had gone wrong.[89]

In any event, he knew—perhaps as early as April 1851, certainly after April 1851—who the enemy was. Quitman and Yancey and the rest who had tied their political aspirations to the falling star of disunion also knew. For the fire-eater, if any good could be unearthed from the crushing blows of 1851, it was a better awareness of purpose, a redefinition of objective, a doubling of the burden, unspoken among them and to which they would each react and respond differently but nevertheless perceive similarly, rising from their defeat. If given another chance, each would have the task of saving his state not only from the North, but from itself as well.

CHAPTER SIX

"*The Sympathy of Angels*"

It was too good to be true. For the first time in five years the country enjoyed relief from harrowing disturbances over slavery. As the dust settled and things returned to normal, even those events that before might have caused superstitious alarm now occasioned only ordinary concern. Late in December 1851 a fire had consumed the Library of Congress and briefly threatened the Capitol. "The destruction of that building would be a startling omen," the correspondent for the *Charleston Mercury* had written, but by then no singular, dark prophecy was attached to the event. It had just been a fire, albeit a costly and distracting one, that had, much like the sectional fervor of the South, gone out.[1]

Most Southerners finally asserted themselves, even if only as Georgian John M. Berrien had. He agreed with neither the Compromise of 1850 nor the Georgia Platform, and he quit politics rather than carry the Whig banner in the 1850 elections. Yet Berrien had not grumbled in disagreement. He simply stated that he was "opposed to any renewal of the agitation of the slavery question" and that he would "acquiesce in the legislation of Congress on the subject."[2]

Berrien's attitude was typical. The problems of 1850 and 1851 had not so much renewed patriotic regard for the Union as they had fatigued most Southerners. In the aftermath, they would shy away from old, troublesome issues to languidly suffer new, calmer ones.[3]

Rhett's anger, although unabated, no longer enjoyed a popular forum; nor would it—save for a few pseudonymous attempts—for more than seven years. Deeply religious, not given to physical outbursts, a teetotaller, Rhett usually remained calm, sustained perhaps by the belief that he had been and was still in fact right. Former supporters would not call him from his profound retirement, as would Yancey's, to capitalize on a glowing oratorical talent.[4] Nor would anyone immediately beckon the return of James Henry Hammond, for whom time was a heavier weight than for Rhett. Hammond kept to himself in gloomy isolation and talked of dying. He abandoned temporarily the South Carolina he no longer judged worthy of him, moving to Georgia where he grew fat even as he complained, from beneath fifty new pounds, that he was wasting away. "I can't last long," he warned Ruffin, sixteen years before he died.[5]

It was much the same for many radicals. Hopkins L. Turney, defeated in the Tennessee Unionist-Disunionist combat of 1851, professed that he had no regrets except being from a state that was too timid to protect its own rights.[6] But that kind of talk sounded as empty as it was hollow. Edmund Ruffin, his bilious colic growing worse as he neared his six-tieth year, turned his straight-mouthed, humorless face away from politi-cal tinkering while yet vowing "to express my opinions" valiantly and without regard to cost. He, at least, had the chance to express those opin-ions as a preeminent agricultural reformer. As president of the Virginia Agricultural Society, he spoke all along the Eastern Seaboard. He could lambast Northern corruption, exalt Southern nationalism, and laud the beneficence of slavery to audiences willing to endure his stilted style and eccentric declamations in order to find out how to replenish their farmlands. Such attention offered a high consolation for Ruffin and, despite all else, for a few years it thoroughly occupied and equally grati-fied him.[7]

Quitman, occupied as well, pursued his frustrating dream of Cuban liberation with a near obsessiveness in the coming years as bitterness sat deep within him. When Jefferson Davis took up Quitman's doomed can-didacy in 1851, he had announced, "If any man charges me with being a Disunionist, I will answer him in monosyllables." Quitman scorned him. "I carry my State-Rights views to the citadel," said the old general, "you stop at the outworks."[8]

The citadel—if that meant the fortress of the electorate—ultimately proved no less cruel to Henry S. Foote, the ostensible victor in the great Mississippi struggle of 1851. Foote was disgusted by the advent of the Pierce administration largely because of the selection of Jefferson Davis to head Pierce's War Department, and after a failed bid for the Senate in

1853, he huffily resigned his governorship on 7 January 1854, five days before the inaugural of states righter John H. McCrea. Many Mississippians must have thought that Foote, departing for California, at last was bound for where he belonged.[9]

In Mississippi the only real winner in the turmoil of 1851 had emerged. Earlier than any other radical, Albert Gallatin Brown had felt the cold breath of public opinion signalling disaster. He always monitored the mood of northern Mississippi, unquestionably moderate in 1851.[10] So in February 1851, Brown backed away from radicalism so completely, so stunningly, that he left those who might have charged him with inconsistency thoroughly bewildered until after the elections. "I am not, and never have been for disunion or secession," he proclaimed, then added, "I may *submit.*"[11] After this astonishing announcement, Brown kissed more babies and charmed more mothers than did his opponent, A. B. Dawson, also a Democrat. He could support Quitman while deprecating Quitmanism and could revere the Constitution while vilifying Fillmore's administration. His allegiance to the glorious Union, he promised, only matched his loyalty to his constituents. This masterful, if graceless performance assured his reelection to the United States House.[12]

Yancey's shift was almost as spectacular as Brown's. The Alabamian also softened out of necessity, subordinating his radicalism to John Campbell's moderation, but with personally unhappy results. His vacillation hurt him with moderates and fire-eaters alike, so in January 1852 he joined with forty-eight compatriots, all from Black Belt counties, to call yet another Southern Rights Convention. It met in Montgomery in March. By then, his change completed, he argued for the Georgia Platform before a startled audience that should have predicted Yancey's unpredictability. Clearly confident in his resiliency, Yancey quashed separate nominations for the coming presidential contest and got appointed chairman of a standing committee—the duties of which were decidedly unclear—composed of J. G. Gilchrist, John A. Elmore, Jefferson Buford, and Percy Walker, radicals all. Yet persistent discontent amounted to little more than the aftershocks of the previous turbulence, annoying yet not too alarming. The Southern Rights diehards could nominate George M. Troup and John A. Quitman to run for the presidency, and Mississippi might threaten to send radical delegates to join with Free Soilers in denouncing the Compromise of 1850 at the Democratic Convention in Baltimore, but almost everyone dismissed these performances as aberrant. Georgia Democrats squabbled all the way into September, but Henry Benning signalled the beginning of reticent, yet inevitable reconciliation upon the emergence of Franklin Pierce. Albert Gallatin Brown thought Pierce "as reliable as Calhoun himself," and South Carolinian Milledge L. Bonham confided to the candidate from New Hampshire that nobody could have expected "a nomination so favorable to the South."[13]

Predictions that the presidential canvass would heal Democratic wounds proved true. Looking across the aisle from the Whig side of the House, Alexander Stephens expressed astonishment at the Democracy's reconciliation "without any regard to principles or the past" where "a man may be a disunionist and a good Democrat, and an Abolitionist and still a good Democrat."[14]

Equally dumbfounded radicals felt a real fear rise among them. The cheerful demonstrations of renewed congeniality in the National Democracy foreboded a dramatic change in the traditional political forms of the Old South, most dramatically in South Carolina, where an entrenched aristocracy maintained the oldest traditions of elitism. The election of the governor and presidential electors by the legislature was only the most obvious example of this. Local government control almost did not exist because the legislature exercised extravagant power in the state. A twin formula of population *and* taxation determined representation in the lower house, while the upper house provided for one senator from each parish or district, regardless of population. This arcane method placed oligarchical control into the hands of a small group of families from the less-populated Low Country parishes.[15]

The parishes jealously guarded their dominance throughout the Jacksonian period, when great shifts of political power marked the transformation elsewhere of tightly controlled republicanism to manipulable democracy. Alabama revealed the dangers in such trends. Taking to heart the slogans that hailed the Democracy as the political haven of the common man, Democrats controlling the Alabama legislature in the late 1830s and early 1840s had abolished the three-fifths rule for congressional elections and gerrymandered the Black Belt Whig counties to reduce about 40 percent of the population to political insignificance. Little wonder then, according to the Southern traditionalist, that white trash like W. R. W. Cobb could defeat Jeremiah Clemens for Congress in 1849 by singing songs that began, "Uncle Sam is rich enough to give us all a farm!"[16]

Calhoun assiduously kept South Carolina aloof from national party affairs to protect both the system and his hold over it. That system was not his creation, but the traditional one that had existed from colonial times. Youthful J. Motte Alston, only eleven years old during the Nullification crisis but aware of the excitement, remembered his grandmother pinning a "blue rosette" to his chest and explaining that because his father was a Nullifier, he was one too. "That settled it forever," remarked Alston some sixty years later. "This was my first lesson in political life."[17]

Often political schooling remained just that simple and simplistic. Calhoun's dictatorial control denied ambitious young men in the state a place in the national sun, the better to exert his own will without significant challenge. Those who rose in Carolina politics did so as Calhoun's protegés or not at all. Others simply left the state for greener political pastures. Yancey went to Alabama and Louis Wigfall to Texas, both coincidentally having been South Carolina Unionists under the tutelage of B. F. Perry. Using their talents, both managed to master the popular politics of the Jacksonian age, although they occasionally exhibited old South Carolina habits. Yancey was sometimes haughty toward his colleagues, and Wigfall was carelessly contemptuous of their social background. Standing outside the Texas House chamber in 1859 on the morn of his election to the United States Senate, he could not resist commenting loudly on the members of the legislature as "cooperas breeched hayseeds" who had no right "to be vested with the power of electing a gentleman."[18]

Politicians who stayed in South Carolina lived in an insular environment that yielded little real experience inside the state and almost none beyond its borders. Rhett had been in pubic life more than twenty years before he addressed a popular assemblage outside of South Carolina. So both Rhett and Hammond demonstrated a high degree of parochialism in all of their political maneuvers. The mistakes that both of them made resulted, on one level, from nothing more than sheer inexperience. Neither could control a system that Calhoun, at the time of his death, found increasingly difficult to manage. Armed with a bad issue, Rhett shattered it in only a year.

Out of the turmoil of 1851 that ended with the April 1852 convention, James Lawrence Orr emerged as the leading politician in the state. He was also a thoroughgoing National Democrat determined to break the old Calhoun habit of mere coexistence with the national party. Known as "Larry," easygoing and amiable, Orr suggested more Henry Clay (writ small) than John Calhoun. He possessed ordinary oratorical talents and his political capabilities rested mainly on a unique knack for reading Northern opinion and understanding it. His greatest strength lay in his being a loyal party man who played by the rules. Orr was ordinary when people were weary of flamboyance.[19]

He wished to break Low Country control of the state, seen as the main obstacle to the democratization of politics. During the Calhoun era, Orr, like the rest of his generation, walked the edge of the periphery that the old man set up. Then, in the vacuum created by the rejection of Rhett, he surveyed a marvelous opportunity. What were previously Orr's flaws suddenly became strengths, the main one of which being that he never had really stood for anything. He had opposed Rhett's Bluffton Movement in the 1840s yet insisted on the right of secession. In Congress he voted against the Compromise of 1850 but then organized the South Carolina Democracy against Rhett's faction in 1851. It was a tribute to Larry Orr's congeniality and invisibility that he could, throughout all of this, maintain friendships with those who, by all rights, should have been his bitterest enemies. However, many radicals could not abide him, and they accused him of vile self-interest because they saw his program of democratization as merely a device to fix his own political ascendancy.[20]

Actually Orr was less opportunistic than he was fortunate, for he happened to find himself leading an Up Country surge at the same time that the Low Country was discredited by its stand on disunion. The democratization of state politics, however, was not merely a reaction against the slavocracy. The Up Country in many cases had large populations of slaves. Moreover, it was a cultural issue. After 1851 the districts and Charleston merchants flexed muscles long bound by the parishes and began to institute a series of political reforms. New men with names unfamiliar to the drawing rooms of Low Country society began to aspire to and achieve office.[21]

While the *Charleston Mercury* sniped at Orr's nationalism, calling it little better than groveling at the altar of Unionism, Orr's movement, aimed at taking South Carolina into a Democratic national convention for the first time ever, attracted many influential men. Benjamin F. Perry, Christopher G. Memminger, Robert W. Barnwell, and John Manning agreed with Orr that South Carolina's participation in national politics was the surest way for the South to protect its interests in the nation.

Preston S. Brooks, giving his complete loyalty to the new order, stood before the Thirty-third Congress and proclaimed that "the time has been when I was sectional, and it has passed."[22]

Discredited fire-eaters could only sullenly look on, occasionally grousing about the corruption of federal patronage buying the loyalty of Southerners. Others interested in pursuing political careers had to compromise. Lawrence M. Keitt, representing the Low Country Third Congressional District, was youthful enough—twenty-nine in 1853—and amiable enough—Preston Brooks was a close friend—to make do under an uncomfortable situation.[23]

No such amity marked the course of Mississippi's Democratic reconciliation. The schism of the party saw two conventions send separate delegations to the Baltimore Convention in 1852, and although both would declare for the Pierce-King ticket, such unity only thinly veiled grim differences. Albert Gallatin Brown's protestations that his wing of the party had never embraced disunion so angered Mississippi Congressman John A. Wilcox that he confronted Brown in March 1852 and called him a liar. Brown slapped Wilcox. Wilcox smashed his fist into Brown's face. Mutual friends stopped the planned duel, but Brown would spend the next two years living down his 1850 radicalism, all the while evincing a growing hostility to Pierce's administration. His anger had concrete causes—disagreements over the acquisition of Cuba, for example—but mainly proceeded from the open social contempt Brown suffered in Washington from aristocrats like the Jefferson Davises and other Southerners. Brown's elevation to the Senate in 1854 augured ill for the fortunes of Northern and Southern Democratic amity, although no one could have foreseen it then. The states rights wing of the Mississippi Democracy was again ascendant and could take pleasure in the vindication of its candidates, if not its stand of 1851. Brown, after all, had survived only by deserting Southern rights for nationalism. That had been how he had combated "Footeism," but he also had to cope with Jefferson Davis who, in Pierce's cabinet, was as much a nationalist and more attractive to the regular party.[24] As Davis grew more moderate and attempted to align the party with the national organization, Brown, obversely, ate more fire. This personal and political feud developed into a struggle for dominance of the state party and would have stunning effects at the end of the decade.[25]

The Virginia Democracy also saw the development of a political feud within its ranks after 1852. Southern rights had little to do with the struggle until it reemerged as a factional weapon in 1856. Thomas Ritchie's retreat from public life concluded the breakdown of the Richmond Junto, traditionally the controlling force of the party. Into this vacuum moved Senator R. M. T. Hunter, ostensible leader of the Southern Rights wing and who wanted to be president. Hunter would clash frequently with the influential, opportunistic, and distrusted Henry A. Wise, whose command of a large following in the western part of the state made him impossible to ignore. Before 1857, when the Hunter-Wise contest for control of the party became quite bitter, the Virginia Democracy maintained a persistent moderation that angered radicals like the Ruffin family as much as it chagrined extremists like James A. Seddon, himself replaced in 1851 by a conservative.[26]

More important for Virginia's traditionalists than this political calm was the state's constitutional convention held during the controversies of 1850. Somewhat ignored then as to its long-term implications for traditional forms of state government, the convention did alarm some radicals. Ruffin's son noted that everyone seemed to "forget entirely that this is a struggle between the East & West for power." That power would derive from extending the franchise from the established Tidewater to beyond the Piedmont, a change that gave Wise a western constituency whose enhanced electoral voice would challenge the orthodox authority of the Virginia Democracy.[27] Confronted by the potential equality of the western part of the state, traditional elements would finally polarize into radicalism, but at first the challenge had the salutary effect of checking impetuous fire-eaters.

The emergence of popular reform in Virginia moved Beverley Tucker to insist that "South Carolina alone can act, because she is the only state in which the gentleman retains his place and influence, and in which the statesman had not been degraded from his post." Yet Tucker warned, "You are fast coming to that hopeless and irreclaimable condition; and then all hope of action is gone."[28] With the fall of Rhett's faction in South Carolina, "mobocracy" indeed seemed the logical conclusion to political reforms aggressively pursued by Up Country leaders following Orr.

Not only in South Carolina, but all across the South, many men and women who rebuked the fire-eaters could not agree with political changes that heralded social egalitarianism. The government would fall prey to corrupt, insincere men, went the reasoning, who would place their own interests before those of the people. Testifying to the power of a Low Country mentality beyond the parishes of South Carolina, large reforms were never to take hold. For example, traditionalists fretting over the advent of chaotic mob rule continually stalled attempts to reorganize the overlarge Pendleton District. Neither encouraged nationalists nor apprehensive radicals saw that the main strength of Orr's nationalism did not spring from popular sympathy with its programs. People merely had grown weary with the principal opposition to Orrism, the failed radicals.[29]

For years, radicals had dreamed of reorganizing Southern politics. In 1851 G. W. Gayle, an Alabama fire-eater from Cahawba, suggested to Rhett methods to obliterate Whig and Democratic delineations and reconstitute a Southern party even as Gayle watched, with considerable distress, Yancey desert the cause.[30] But the radicals, who had always played the outsiders, now found themselves functionally banished, incapable of blocking the dreaded changes that promised to lock them out of politics forever. Calhoun had heard Rhett described as "a rash and ultra man" who was "contemptuous of all about him, with neither tact [n]or discretion and without sympathy or popularity with the great mass of men."[31] All else being equal, Rhett on his best day could not have defeated backslapping Larry Orr in a popular election. Yet protecting proud lineages of diminished circumstances, the aristocratic Rhetts had to preserve their place in politics. Ruffin and Hammond, who had both amassed wealth but had not been born into it, aspired to this tradition and fell prey to its pitfalls. Rhett needed only to peruse the October 1851 election returns to see that when districts bested parishes, it signalled the defeat of his brand of Southern rights. There must have been a chilling urgency in the discovery that parish control of the state, accosted by Orrism, was the only hope for his political future.[32]

So both practically and philosophically the true radical deplored the changes brought by reform. Henry A. Wise argued for free education in the South, but so did, on occasion, Albert Gallatin Brown and William Lowndes Yancey. It did not matter that the advocacy of state-supported education arose from a desire to rid the need for Southerners to go North or Northerners to come South. In spite of the sectional motives, education reform appealed to neither Rhett nor Ruffin because it threatened their society's existing order. One thereby engaged in the fiction of protecting a way of life by destroying its characteristics.[33]

What had happened to national party politics after the Kansas-

Nebraska Act unwittingly encouraged Democratic unity. The agitations of 1851 had hurt the Democracy, but not nearly so much as they had Southern Whigs beset by the taint of the Seward wing's behavior in the North. Alexander Stephens and Robert Toombs had to desert the Whig party for Constitutional Unionism to save themselves in Georgia.[34] But the wholesale disintegration of the National Whigs after the Kansas-Nebraska Act dwarfed the problems of 1851. Democrats celebrated the destruction of the Whig Party, but they should have paused. A party without an organized enemy will find enemies within its own ranks. As it happened, the Democracy did face a new nationally organized party. The budding Republicans (or, as they had styled themselves earlier, the Anti-Nebraska party) could not pose the same kind of threat as the Native American party, familiarly called the Know-Nothings. In April 1854 this new party carried traditional Democratic strongholds in the North, including New Hampshire, Pierce's home state. In the South, it became a haven for many Whigs.[35]

It was at best a desperate movement in the South that attracted anxious men bewildered by the loss of their political home. Not all Whigs could bring themselves to accept Know-Nothingism. Robert Toombs rebuked it and was voting with the Democrats in the Senate regularly by 1854. Stephens, though with more reluctance, ultimately gravitated to the Democrats.[36] But other Whigs joined the party out of a love for the Union that found the Democracy unacceptable but bigotry tolerable. That intelligent men like Henry A. Hilliard could affiliate with a group that spoke of Mary as "the Whore of Rome" described an emotional turmoil groping for a way to save the Union and the South at the same time, that attempted to diminish the importance of slavery by exploiting national concern. For a time, before the Know-Nothings themselves split over the slavery issue, some believed that baiting foreigners was a small price to pay for the elimination of sectionally squabbling traditional parties. The raucous denunciations of Stephen Douglas by Northern Democrats for his role in the Kansas-Nebraska business inspired more than a few Southern Democrats to swell Native American ranks as well. Jeremiah Clemens, Reuben Chapman, and Percy Walker joined Hilliard in Alabama, Walker actually defeating Democrat James A. Stallworth in his Mobile district in a Southern Rights contest. The nationally oriented Stallworth could not compete with a freewheeling radical carrying the Know-Nothing banner.[37]

In Arkansas, Albert J. Pike found his way into the party. Richard K. Call of Florida, Benjamin H. Hill of Georgia, John J. Crittenden of Kentucky, George Eustis of Louisiana, John Minor Botts of Virginia, and Sam Houston of Texas either flirted with or openly joined the organization, sometimes for starkly different reasons. The anti-immigration stand of the party appealed to Southern nationalists, for example, since they believed that immigrants increased the potential power of abolitionism.[38] Consequently the radicals' attraction to the Know-Nothing party amounted to a sentimental rationale and a realignment of purpose. Some fire-eaters exchanged disunion for bigotry, entering a bizarre alliance with former Whigs to oppose the National Democracy. The party claimed Yancey for a while, but he showed shrewd calculation in denying any affiliation, although with equal shrewdness he expressed sympathy with some of its philosophy.[39]

More to the point, Lewis E. Harvie of Virginia believed that sooner or later there was going to be "a row with the North" and that "to get the South straight Know-Nothingism must be overcome."[40] Rhett in South Carolina branded the party as no better than its Democratic adversary, although John Cunningham, editor of the *Charleston Evening News,* disassociated himself from national Native Americans to attempt the construction of a Southern party on Know-Nothing ideals. In South Carolina the party attracted eccentrics like the conservative Colleton planter David Gavin who railed against both the "mob-o-cratic" party of Orr and the Democracy's Southern Rights wing that had levied high property taxes to fund the state's defenses.[41]

The party was never really powerful, but it seemed to be and hence excited the ire of strong enemies. Orr, Brooks, Perry, and Pickens finally persuaded usually hostile radicals like Lawrence Keitt, John McQueen, and William Boyce to join a coalition to crush the threat to South Carolina's political structure. Ironically, it was just this temporary unity that allowed for the National Democratic surge in South Carolina that realized Orr's dream of taking the state into the Cincinnati Convention of 1856.[42]

The Know-Nothings ultimately worked a great mischief on the chances for a continued Union, for although their operations appeared to help the regular forces of Democratic nationalism, only the Republican party and the Southern fire-eater would benefit. The Know-Nothings broke down traditional ties between Southern Whigs who otherwise might have formed an institutional resistance to the Democratic Party.

Befuddled and adrift after the failure of the Know-Nothings, Whigs instead entered the Democracy. The South then became a one-party section. Northern Democrats, facing in their section a growing Republican presence, found Southern positions gradually more obnoxious.[43] The Native American party, in addition, made the careers of men who, without the focus of Know-Nothingism to fight, might have never come to prominence within a Democracy controlled by responsible forces. The spectacular rise of Louis Trezevant Wigfall in Texas offers a stunning example of this.

Out of South Carolina College after a rambunctious student career, Lewis T. Wigfall (he changed the spelling of his given name when he left South Carolina) settled in Edgefield District in 1837 and commenced adulthood as a dilettante, spendthrift, and carouser. He passed the bar in 1839, became a practicing attorney, and earned a good reputation with his dazzling courtroom manner. But Wigfall was restless and erratic, and he spent his energies in efforts to enter politics. He began by plugging for John P. Richardson against James H. Hammond in the gubernatorial contest of 1840, and soon he was trading insults with the influential Brooks family, supporters of Hammond. The result was a series of duels in which Wigfall fatally shot Thomas Bird, nephew of patriarch Whitelaw Brooks; met Whitelaw's brother-in-law, J. P. Carroll, in a harmless encounter; and finally wounded in the hip Preston Brooks, his former roommate at South Carolina College. Wigfall himself took a bullet in this last foray, forcing a recuperation that virtually destroyed his law practice, already suffering because of his belligerent political activities. Although he married Charlotte Cross, a Trezevant cousin from a wealthy Rhode Island family, his debts mounted as his political fortunes declined. After considering for a couple of years departure from South Carolina, he moved to Texas in 1846 where his Carolina lineage and natural aggressiveness pushed him to prominence in the largely unorganized Texas Democracy. Wigfall acted as the chairman of the Resolutions Committee of the Galveston County Democracy, using his position to foster decidedly radical views in the controversy of 1850. Already he was developing a technique of political expression that would have him sometimes perceived as aberrantly unique. Perhaps Wigfall was a bit mad. Edmund Ruffin, encountering him ten years later in Washington, found him disconcerting and "was much am[used at his] oddity of speech & opinions, & their extravagance of [express]ion."[44]

Politicians could achieve prominence in Texas in one of two ways: they could accept Sam Houston as a mentor or make of him an enemy. Typical of Wigfall, he chose the latter course, supporting Peter Bell in the 1849 governor's race. Bell defeated Houston's man, George T. Wood, and Wigfall continued to berate Houston for a variety of sins against the South. It was a risky display of gall because Houston was popular. But Marshall, Texas, and Harrison County radicalism placed Wigfall in the lower house of the Texas legislature where he consistently attacked Houston, although with little effect.[45]

All manner of Texans adored Houston, who had learned the artifices of Jacksonian popularity firsthand. He finely tuned his affectations to the circumstance, whether it was the leopard-skin vest he wore to the Senate or his practice of calmly whittling while listening to debates.[46] Having tweaked his state's Southern sympathies repeatedly and having remained unscathed in the bargain, he apparently felt himself invincible. The Kansas-Nebraska Act and the advent of the Native American party in Texas changed all that. He miscalculated badly when he allowed his anger with the Democracy over the Nebraska question to prompt his open denunciation of the party. Wigfall pounced on Houston's stand and led the successful effort in the Texas legislature to censure him. Although Houston had five years remaining on his Senate term, these events gravely wounded him within his own party. Anti-Houston fever spread across Democratic meetings in the counties goaded by Wigfall's constant assaults upon the "Hero of San Jacinto."[47]

Under normal circumstances, Houston probably could have withered the pesky Carolinian transplant by merely covering him with a long shadow. But these were not normal times. Houston instead punch-drunkenly lashed out at Wigfall and the Texas Democracy. Since the party of Jackson had become the party of Calhoun, Houston drifted toward the Know-Nothings, never allying with them but endorsing them to gain their support. The Democracy, viewing Texas Know-Nothings as a larger threat than the Whigs had been or the Republicans could ever be, gradually elevated Wigfall, noted for years as a marginally successful Houston fighter, to higher posts of influence.[48] Big enemies make big men—this Wigfall knew better than most. He helped reorganize the Texas Democracy along more rigid lines, and the party rewarded him for his loyalty and service in 1859 by placing him in the Senate. Houston, losing the governor's race of 1857 to Southern Rights candidate H. R. Runnels, bounced back to capture the governorship in 1859. But the damage had already been done because the failure of Houston's Native American alliance diminished him as a symbol of nationalism when the Union most needed him.[49]

Surviving the threat of Native Americanism, the National Democracy emerged ostensibly stronger than ever. Orr's leadership in South Carolina martialled hostile, disparate forces to crush the Know-Nothings; it also took a state delegation to the national party convention in Cincinnati in 1856, basked in the Dred Scott decision, saw Francis W. Pickens appointed minister to Russia, and participated in the successive lowering of tariff schedules.[50] Rhett sat, like Grendel in his cave, amidst the clutter of the *Mercury* office, and squinted out at a Charleston changing before his eyes. When William Henry Trescott went to Congress from South Carolina, radical William Porcher Miles, a professor at the College of Charleston, warned him to keep silent about disunion lest he violate the oath of his office. Rhett marvelled that men warped the definition of honor to muzzle truth and compel Unionism. There were no secessionist leaders anymore, he told Ruffin, who was visiting Charleston in 1857; federal office seduced the best men, and others had given up.[51]

"Well, if we have done our duty," Rhett was told in 1854, "we can rightfully claim the sympathy of angels." Yet even if heaven did smile upon his purposes, he also knew that Jacksonian politics would never let him succeed without the sympathy of men. He could taunt nationalists in the *Mercury*'s columns and pretend to be impervious to the damage that such demonstrations did to his popularity. Ruffin was "willing to risk the odium of opinions so unpopular still with many." But in truth they had become only perennial malcontents.[52]

Having no other place to spend their energies, radicals began to participate in annual Southern Commercial Conventions. Their involvement in these affairs was disingenuous at best, and practically motivated at the very least. "Though these conventions have been of no *direct* use," Ruffin noted on the eve of the thunderous Montgomery gathering of 1858, "they may be of indirect benefit." He made no secret that he attended the conventions in order "to meet & exchange views with men of the south" and privately to lobby for "secession from the northern states."[53] Thus, the conventions did keep the idea of secession alive because they brought together those most interested in it. At the

Exchange Hotel in Montgomery, Ruffin visited with Rhett and Yancey, and he stayed in a room with Lewis Harvie and Roger A. Pryor. Little wonder that moderates looked upon these gatherings as "a humbug."[54]

The Southern Commercial Convention was not a new event. Four such conventions had met in Augusta, Georgia, between 1837 and 1839 in efforts to secure direct trade with Europe. These first conventions virtually ignored political questions. Then two conventions in Memphis, one in 1845 and another in 1849, concerned themselves with internal improvements and remarkably insisted that the federal government assist the South in the work. Commercial self-interest continued to characterize the convention movement when in 1852 delegates to New Orleans argued over designs to link Atlantic and Gulf ports and more importantly, secure the transcontinental railroad for Southern states.[55]

Nothing particularly sinister moved the *Mississippian,* based in Jackson and edited by radical Ethelbert Barksdale, to call for the revival of such conventions in 1850. Radicals and many Southern Rights Associations wanted economic independence from the North as a means of redress.[56] But beginning in 1854, under the press of the Kansas-Nebraska controversy and the subsequent birth of the Republican party, the conventions each year became increasingly militant. At Charleston in 1854, Thomas Hart Benton stalked out of the convention hall after denouncing the meeting as disunionist. He was reacting to a harangue delivered by Arkansan Albert J. Pike, who had exploded at the federal government's refusal to finance a Southern railroad route to the Pacific. Pike, a large man with a full beard and half-closed eyes, was a noted eccentric, his most curious habit being his hunting of prairie chickens with a six-pound artillery piece. The Whigs had read him out of the party in 1851 for refusing to brand Democrat Robert W. Johnson a disunionist, and in 1854 he was on the verge of a brief affair with the Know-Nothings. In Charleston, anger and apprehension over the growth of federal power absorbed him. He reiterated his attack in New Orleans the following year and further condemned the North for failing to enforce the Fugitive Slave Law. Pike did not endorse secession (he was to become a Calhounite seven years after the old man's death), but in Savannah in 1856 he warned that secession was inevitable if matters did not improve. Testifying to the growing radicalism of the conventions, Pike was a moderate compared to others. In 1857 at Knoxville, the mood against the North was so hostile that Virginian W. C. Flournoy shouted to the delegates that he "hated the North . . . and . . . hated everybody who did not hate [the North]."[57]

The primary success of these conventions was in nurturing radical sectionalism, because they certainly failed to achieve their alleged goals. James Dunwoody Brownson DeBow, an ardent convention advocate, complained that any resolves the conventions promulgated were "never followed by sustained efforts" after adjournment. Beginning in 1854, the conventions became nothing more than forums for fire-eaters. Radicals could dominate the gatherings because frustrated, commercially minded delegates gradually discerned the conventions as impotent.[58]

The notion of the South as the victim of economic exploitation by the North served as attractive propaganda for both nationalists and sectionalists alike, who used and abused a wide array of statistics accordingly. When reformers published estimates of Southern expenditures in the North to encourage Southern industrialism, they often aroused only sectional resentment without stemming the tide of dollars northward.[59]

Moreover, a somewhat pathetic inferiority colored Southern calls for commercial reform that, despite their plaintiveness, contained an ominous tint. Persuasive arguments advised young men to attend Southern colleges, vacationers to patronize Southern spas, and readers to peruse Southern literature. Yet these efforts met with little success. Southern students stayed in their Northern schools even after John Brown's raid in October 1859; and though White Sulphur Springs, Virginia, enjoyed a marginal increase in patronage, the most popular watering place for Southerners, Saratoga, New York, continued to draw Southern visitors even in the face of hostility made real by occasional slave stealing. Southerners continued to purchase from Northern firms and visit Northern cities throughout the decade. In the autumn of 1860, DeBow took his bride to New York and Philadelphia for the wedding trip.[60]

In spite of calls for egocentric sectionalism, a national ideal persisted. Clearly Southerners liked the amenities of the North, and this placed advocates of Southern commercial reform in a strangely ambiguous position. DeBow served as a good example of this. Born in Charleston and graduated from the College of Charleston in 1843, DeBow had studied law and passed the bar but chose instead to write for his living. In January 1846 he began to publish *The Commercial Review of the South and the Southwest* in New Orleans. DeBow's *Review* served the South as its only publication of national prestige, attracting noted Southern authors and claiming a wide Southern readership. DeBow labored over the publication with tireless diligence, wasting his eyesight into near blindness and dunning his subscribers for delinquent fees. His business methods and commercial positions did not always earn him the high regard of fellow Southerners. Ruffin thought him to be "a crafty & mean Yankee in conduct and principle." But DeBow fought in his own way for an improved South. Because his attitude was reformist and his influence palpable, he and others gave the impression that the South was changing economically as well as politically.[61]

The South was a rural land capillaried by a magnificent river system. Wealthy members of its population endured a consistently low level of liquid capital since most assets rested in land and slaves. Hamstrung capital discouraged investment and naturally retarded Southern commercial growth. Against this situation, DeBow argued that a program of industrial and urban expansion could eradicate many of the South's sectional problems. With industry and transportation, the South could challenge the North's monopoly of the lucrative Western trade, much of which had been diverted by the railroad from the Mississippi to the Northeast since 1848. An economic offensive could place the South on a more competitive footing with the North, and from this healthy contest would grow nationalism spurred by incentive, rather than sectionalism irritated by victimization. In the 1850s there were promising signs. Virginia enjoyed an industrial expansion that had Willoughby Newton, former Congressman and future fire-eater, insisting that the Old Dominion, with the proper protective tariffs, could become a textile producer rivaling Massachusetts. As Southern shipping interests increased, he said, so would European dependence on cotton. Georgia's close second to Virginia's success prompted Robert Toombs to propose to the Savannah Commercial Convention of 1857 a Southern protective tariff. William Gregg of Graniteville, South Carolina, and Edwin Holt of Alamance, North Carolina, not only expounded on the virtues of cotton manufacturing but built factories to prove the point. Southern railroad mileage, although meager relative to that of the North in 1850, quadrupled by 1860.[62]

In spite of this good start, the movement for Southern commercial reform foundered on the ambiguity of the reformist impulse. DeBow and George Fitzhugh wanted cities to grow so the South could assert economic independence from the North; too easily the call for economic independence became a call for political independence from the North. Willoughby Newton wanted Virginia to industrialize so it could impoverish Northern textile mills, not compete with them. Edmund Ruffin supported Toombs's idea of a Southern protective tariff because the competition for tariffs between Northern and Southern manufacturers would, he thought, turn the sections against each other. Moreover, when the Southern Pacific Railroad Company was formed to build the transcontinental route, this was the first agitated attention given the issue by the South. "A railroad to the Pacific," a Texas legislator was told in 1858, "has become a *sectional* question and will henceforth assume all the importance and sectional rivalry which belongs to the Kansas question." Slave labor would build a Southern route, whereas the Northern route would employ "white labor and secure to the northern states a vast territory and a lasting preponderance in the country."[63]

The fire-eaters' constant insinuation of sectional rhetoric did not sabotage these Southern efforts at commercial and industrial expansion. The fire-eater did not have the influence to wreck a popular movement, and traditionally conservative planters and merchants, unable to place their commerce on a competitive level with that of the North, did not turn to secession to rid themselves of burdensome debt to Northern capitalists. The South did not change to an industrialized economy because it did not want to. While there were many things about the North that the Southerner liked, the Southerner did not want his section to be like the North. He was made uneasy by those proponents who maintained that for the Southerner to combat the North, he must emulate the Northerner. When the fire-eater, not by design but from a deeper vein, protested that the South was more virtuous than the North, that the North was decadent and corrupt, and that the North's representatives merely reflected unstable constituencies composed of immigrants and other undesirables, he was touching Southern chords that reverberated back as far as the American Revolution, when colonists had sneered at the machinations of British politics stained by graft and corruption. Ruffin echoed the patriot fathers when he said, "This alone would be sufficient reason for our separation."[64]

The fire-eater was outside the political establishment, but he was in the mainstream of Southern traditionalism. As a social traditionalist, he stood the best chance of arousing the deepest fears of a dormant, though potentially powerful constituency. It is altogether too tempting to assume an overpoliticization of the Southerner in the 1850s. To take the preoccupations of Rhett, Ruffin, Yancey, Wigfall, Brown, Orr, Toombs, Cobb, Stephens, and indeed all other politicians and extend them to the antebellum Southerner is surely to entertain a great myth. At the beginning of 1860, three months after John Brown's raid and only three months before the Democratic Convention in Charleston, in what should have been a time of great agitation, Alexander Stephens, away from public life for the first time in over fifteen years, noted that "there is really not the least excitement in the public mind upon public affairs."[65]

Most Southerners were not politically radical at all, but they were philosophically so conservative that challenges to their fundamental beliefs would cause them to lash out. Apprehensive over change, but dimly aware of its ineluctability, this largest and calmest segment of the population seethed and rumbled when barraged by Northern assaults upon slavery that seemed patently unfair. When pressed for political, social, and economic reform by neighbors little understood and gradually mistrusted, most Southerners resisted. Willoughby Newton and George Fitzhugh typified a Southern attitude that discarded Jeffersonian ideals of equality for the rights of property as the basis of society. Fitzhugh determined that antislavery was godless and communistic and that only by subordinating commercial interests to the keystone of slavery could the South continue to serve as a bastion of stability in an increasingly *radical* world.[66] A strong morality tinged with evangelical fervor permeated the proslavery movement as only a part of an agrarian idea. Not solely for the planter but for the yeoman farmer, the artisan, and the merchant as well, the system of slavery and class subordination combined with an agricultural tradition as psychologically captivating as it was physically changeless. Agricultural addresses in the 1820s and 1830s had striven to show the virtue in sameness to render more substantial security and stability in the sweeping flow of Jacksonian politics. Faced with soil exhaustion and the westward migrations that cotton planting compelled, agricultural reform to restore fertility assumed a profound meaning. Edmund Ruffin's advocacy of marl enculturation to refurbish Tidewater soil could also save Tidewater political influence.[67]

The sectional crises of the 1850s and the requirements of controlling slaves heightened the appeal of agrarianism. Consequently, unanimity among the white community became the greatest imperative. Class differences were best submerged by an indisputable attachment to this agricultural denominator. To maintain community values, proslavery became wedded in other than radical minds to a society untainted by commercialization and democratization. Southerners did not revile Hinton Helper because he proved slavery stultifying and inefficient. Rather, he threatened the unanimity of Southern attitudes on slavery and consequently subverted the agrarianism that was the universal bond of Southern society. The system had to be defended, even glorified, and never criticized. In 1841 James Henry Hammond counseled against further cotton planting; seventeen years later, he proclaimed cotton as king.[68]

From such a vantage, the politically moderate forces of reform ultimately appeared radical, while the politically radical advocates of secession seemed to propose a reasonable way to protect the system. The government could fall sway to the enemies of slavery who were, in turn, the enemies of the Southern way of life. On the other hand, a Southern confederacy could offer political and economic benefits within a traditional, secure order.[69] When the former fear became intense enough to compel the ordinary Southerner to the latter solution, the fire-eater would have much more than the sympathy of angels. Previously perceived as a monomaniac, he would then be exalted as a prophet.

CHAPTER SEVEN

"Glory Enough for One Day"

As early as September 1852, Henry L. Benning, bowing to the inevitable reconciliation of Georgia Democrats, made a prophecy to Howell Cobb. He predicted that a victorious Democracy in 1852 would break up the Whig party. Northern Whigs, moving into an antislavery faction, would be defeatable in 1856 but would prove invincible thereafter. Cobb dismissed Benning's prediction—he was wrong only about the cause and time of the Whig split—because it seemed impossible in the quiet of the times. Yet four years later William Gilmore Simms made a similar prophecy, this one for the Democracy. Simms believed that the Democratic party, even in victory, could no longer protect the South. The South was potentially powerful, but only if united under a strong leader who would direct Southern political strength away from the distractions of national party politics. Simms told Orr that he could be that leader, but only if he dropped his nationalism to join the extreme Southern Rights wing of the party. Quite simply, Simms declared, "All existing organizations must perish under the strife of sections."[1]

Orr dismissed Simms's grim warnings as easily as Cobb had Benning's. The National Democracy in the 1850s seemed impervious to the subversive schemes of radical sectionalism from both the North and the South. Nationalists in the party labored strenuously to placate the concerns of Southerners, while local struggles unique to each Southern state defused potential radical designs. Brown opposed Davis in Mississippi, Wigfall challenged Houston in Texas, and Hunter contended with Wise in Virginia, to name just the most prominent contests.

Also, during the decade neither the staunchest fire-eaters, like Rhett or Ruffin, nor any of the radicals who had presumably deserted disunion, knew exactly what to do. Some had a vague notion that the National Democracy was the dragon to be slain, an idea that had existed since Yancey's lonely and impractical advocacy of the Alabama Platform at Baltimore in 1848. But always the greatest problem was how to insure Southern unity while splintering away the Northern wing of the party. It was an old problem, as aged as Calhoun's efforts, that had begun in the late 1840s. Impractical then, those efforts seemed impossible as the years wore on.

Slavery was central to the problem. Slavery made the South unique and was the only issue upon which all Southerners had to agree. Fire-eaters tried to exploit Northern evasions of the Fugitive Slave Law, but they quickly gave up the hope of arousing Southern anger because the widely accepted Georgia Platform made protests impotent unless the federal government repealed the legislation. The next radical strategy tried to use the issue of the African slave trade to free Southern sentiment from Northern contamination.

Leonidas W. Spratt, editor of the *Charleston Daily Standard,* apparently had no ulterior motive when in 1853 he proposed reopening the African slave trade. The issue, however, like everything else in the stormy 1850s, became involved with the Kansas question and hence attracted a wider range of support than it should have. DeBow in Louisiana, Wigfall in Texas, Yancey in Alabama, Ruffin in Virginia, and Governor John H. Adams and Maxcy Gregg in South Carolina noisily threw in with the idea by the end of 1854.[2] Yet, proposals to reopen the trade created all manner of controversy in both the North and South because they sought to repeal the constitutionally authorized prohibition of 1807. Northerners saw this as invidious, and many Southerners viewed it as inconsistent. It ran counter to the elaborate compromise of the Convention of 1787, supposedly held sacrosanct by Southern Rights advocates who insisted that their rights proceeded from constitutional scruples of long standing.

Because Southern legislatures consistently dismissed resolutions that called for the reopening of the trade, inevitably lobbying for the trade would invade the only forum remaining for radical voices, the Southern Commercial Convention. In Savannah in 1856 a failed resolution to reopen the trade presaged a series of bitter discussions at Knoxville in 1857. In Montgomery in 1858 the issue exploded.[3]

The Montgomery Commercial Convention turned out to be the high-water mark for both the slave-trade debate and the convention movement. The slave-trade issue helped kill the convention movement, but by 1858 both the issue and the commercial convention had outlived their usefulness to the radicals. Nevertheless, the slave-trade issue yet had some damage to do to Southern unity, as Montgomery would show. Meeting in a balmy Alabama spring, the convention opened on 10 May in a roofless cotton warehouse. Yancey here would show he had learned absolutely nothing about political reality in the previous decade. On the following day the mood turned chilly under the warm Alabama sun when a resolution to remove the ban of 1807 renewed Knoxville's tense debate. Yancey dominated the discussion, explaining that more Negroes would reduce prohibitively high prices and allow a wider participation in slave ownership. Correspondingly, he said, more slaves would encourage Southern expansion into the territories, specifically beleaguered Kansas. The argument had precisely tied Kansas peculiarly to this bad issue.

Ruffin agreed with Yancey, but he was the only Virginian who did. Roger Pryor took the floor to denounce the proposal as confirming the worst Northern charges of Southern perfidy and self-interest. When Pryor finished, Yancey again pushed to the rostrum to level accusations at Pryor's state. Virginia was being selfish, he shouted, by opposing the trade so that Virginian slave-breeding would continue to enjoy high prices within the domestic trade. Ruffin listened with increasing outrage. He admitted that the speech was "eloquent and powerful," but it was also "too wordy & too long," and the "censure improperly cast upon Virginia" forced him to the rostrum to rebuke the Alabamian.[4]

The convention, now rumbling toward disruption, nervously tabled the offensive resolution and did not meet the following day so that tempers could cool. When it reconvened on 13 May, Yancey, who had numbed his temper by dousing it with alcohol, delivered a drunken, slurred speech that, according to Ruffin, was "suitable to his condition," but attempted to mend the damage done by his previous performance.[5]

Rhett showed an uncustomary shrewdness regarding the slave-trade controversy, certainly more than Yancey, usually the more sagacious of the two. Rhett saw the danger in aggravating Northerners while dividing Southerners. So he refused to tie secession to the foreign slave trade as Gregg and Spratt persisted in doing. Governor Adams's support of the trade ran him afoul of the electorate, proving Rhett right in believing radical advocacy for this bad cause merely strengthened an already powerful National Democracy.[6]

Elsewhere politicians deserted the slave trade issue with alacrity when it became politically inexpedient. Texas editor Hamilton Stuart ardently supported the renewal of the trade until the 1859 elections. To its great detriment, H. R. Runnels's Southern Rights wing of the Texas Democracy attempted to rally behind the slave trade. Stuart, the customs collector in Galveston, did not want his party broken, so he supported Houston and unblushingly rushed to an anti-slave-trade argument. On the other hand, Wigfall and John H. Reagan also deserted the issue without a blink to oppose Sam Houston.[7]

By the summer of 1859, the slave-trade argument had all but killed the commercial convention. In Vicksburg, Unionism was rampant with only eight states attending. Virginia, still smarting over its treatment the previous year, did not send a delegation. The issue lingered, however, because of the stubborn Spratt, who kept the debate alive long after even most Carolinians had dismissed it as hopeless and dangerous. Such foolish persistence worried Virginia into 1860, when conservative Virginians argued against secession by predicting that a Southern confederacy would reopen the slave trade and hence harm one of their state's most profitable enterprises.[8] The issue became anathema, and smart politicians avoided it.

Yancey, usually crafty, showed a remarkable stupidity about the slave trade. He had accomplished his return to prominence in the Alabama Democracy with customary opportunism cloaked in lofty, facile oratory. In January 1856, a contingent of homeless Whigs attended the Democratic state convention in Montgomery to register opposition to the Know-Nothings. The convention asked Yancey, there only as a spectator, to speak. He did so creditably, calling for a fusion between disaffected Whigs and the Democracy. This good performance, warmly greeted, actually presaged his hidden yet unswerving design to gain control of the party—an attempt he again undertook with such brash confidence and artful dissimulation that the May nominating convention revealed his work on the county level at every turn. The conservative Montgomery Regency headed by Seibels and Benjamin Fitzpatrick would provide no moderation here. A group of young delegates arranged Yancey's appointment to the chairmanship of the resolutions committee without a dissenting vote. Yancey then brought the Alabama Platform out of retirement.[9]

Yet he remained cautious and watchful, apparently careful to avoid the pitfalls of the 1851 debacle. Even without the restraining influence of John A. Campbell, whom Pierce had appointed to the Supreme Court, Yancey behaved himself in the 1856 campaign. He worked within the regular Democracy to destroy the Native American–Whig threat in the state. The success of this effort and Buchanan's victory made Alabama a one-party state. As a participant in the National Democratic organization and under irresponsible direction, the Alabama Democracy could destroy the party. Yancey already had something like this in mind. When administration operatives offered him a patronage reward for his work on Buchanan's behalf—perhaps he would like a cabinet post, went the suggestion—he disingenuously insisted that he wanted Buchanan to "be disembarrassed of all considerations respecting me." He went on to explain, in words loaded with meaning, "I feel even now, crippled with uselessness, if ever we shall be forced to act against Mr. B[uchanan]."[10]

Yancey was not crippled with uselessness at all. He was biding his time, awaiting the opportunity to boldly seize the state party and use it to create a Southern party. He was, moreover, awaiting an issue of sufficient importance to bind together the South against the North, or more specifically the Northern Democracy. He was dimly aware, as his actions show, that the Kansas-Nebraska Act had already provided him with such an issue, but he was not altogether sure what it was nor how to use it. In his confusion, he had much company. Most politicians spun in the ill wind that the Kansas-Nebraska Act had raised.

When it passed in 1854, removing the Missouri Compromise line as a restriction to the expansion of slavery, Alexander Stephens saw the Kansas-Nebraska Act as a vindication of Southern institutions. He exulted, "Is not this glory enough for one day?"[11] But other Southerners were not so sure. Edmund Ruffin thought the whole idea ill-advised. While 36°30' had kept slavery out of the upper part of the Louisiana Purchase, Ruffin could see how the principle, in extended application, had kept abolitionism out of the Southwest.[12]

In the North, the Kansas-Nebraska Act did just what Stephen A. Douglas thought that it would—raise a hell of a storm. Douglas also believed that the bill, once passed, would recede from controversy and that the storm would pass. Much to his dismay, he was wrong. At first the North vilified him for selling out Northern ideals for Southern support. He then took positions sure to alienate the South so he could regain the grudging approbation of the North. Ultimately, most Southerners came to loathe him. One Southern belle referred to the Little Giant as nothing more than "a drunken demagogue."[13]

The issue was not worth it, and that a few politicians initiated it for commercial and political advantage made it seem even more pointless. Neither the great commercial gain—the northern route for the transcontinental railroad—nor the political capital ever materialized. The tainted specter of opportunism would follow Douglas, in one form or another, for the rest of his life. Franklin Pierce, already embarrassed by misinterpreted moves to acquire Cuba, plodded through the two turbulent years remaining to his botched presidency. And David Rice Atchison, the Missouri senator who had acted as one of the principal architects of the deal that had done away with 36°30', participated in the business, said cynics, with an eye to the vice-presidential nomination on the 1856 ticket.[14]

Rice Atchison said, within months of the bill's passage, that "I know that Union as it exists is in the other scale, but I am willing to take the holy land." Further, he confided that "the game must be played boldly." To secure Kansas under the competitive auspices of popular sovereignty meant the chance to carry slavery to the Pacific. To fail surely meant the loss of the territories and possibly of Missouri, Arkansas, and Texas.[15] Yet the game became too quickly for too many a deadly serious business. To counter the New England Emigrant Aid Society, Alabamian Jefferson Buford's celebrated expedition to fight antislavery in the Kansas Territory attracted wide vocal support from Old Line Whigs and Know-Nothings as well as moderate and radical Democrats.

Ominously for the Southern cause, however, it attracted little else. With sparse funding and consisting mainly of poor men who wanted to go West for the land rather than the assertion of Southern principles, the expedition got lost in the controversy of "Bleeding Kansas."[16] "After the base calculating treason of 1850," wrote one Virginian, "I gave up all hope that the Southern states could ever secure an acre of the public domain over which to extend their institution."[17]

The controversy became immortal, the destroyer of political careers, and anyone interested in a political future tried to stay away from it.[18] But even the ablest of men with the best of intentions could not stay clear altogether.

Preston Brooks, friend of Orr and a professed moderate, was so much a nationalist in 1856 that fire-eaters occasionally castigated him for failing to defend South Carolina and the South. Moreover, most of his colleagues liked and admired him, so his beating of Charles Sumner was all the more tragic. His actions on the morning of 22 May 1856 were as understandable as they were uncharacteristic. Three days before, Senator Charles Sumner of Massachusetts had levelled a searing blast at Douglas, Atchison, and especially A. P. Butler, Brooks's second cousin. Sumner titled his effort "The Crime Against Kansas," and so viciously phrased and delivered it that Douglas, who knew that Sumner had rehearsed the speech for weeks before a mirror, remarked during Sumner's performance that "that damned fool will get himself killed by some other damned fool."[19] Sumner's speech ostensibly responded to Douglas's challenge to lay the Kansas controversy before the people in the upcoming fall elections, but Sumner actually used the occasion to settle old scores. He reserved special venom for Butler, accusing the old gentleman of making the "harlot" slavery his mistress. The unjustified attack on Butler, who was absent because of illness, had nothing to do with Kansas. Butler's greatest crime was being from South Carolina and having, two years before, criticized Sumner's offensive debating technique. Now, Sumner cruelly ridiculed Butler's speech impediment—the Carolinian's tongue was too large for his mouth—by sneering at "the loose expectoration of his speech."[20]

Brooks, who had not heard the speech, obtained a copy and spent the next two days brooding over it while plying himself with brandy. He confronted a great crisis in his life. He did not believe in dueling. His only bout with violence had been with Louis Wigfall in 1841 when only twenty-two years old.[21] But then, as now, the dispute had concerned family honor, so Brooks felt compelled to avenge his kinsman's character. He sought out Sumner to teach him a lesson in manners, and found him at his desk in the Senate chamber. After announcing his intention, Brooks splintered a gold-headed gutta-percha cane over Sumner's head in repeated blows of chastisement.[22]

Sumner suffered enough physical injury—or psychological trauma, no one has ever been sure which—to require a three-year convalescence that kept him away from the Senate. Meanwhile Northern reaction prompted a strong Southern support for Brooks's actions. A week after the event, Lawrence Keitt described Washington as permeated with "wild and fierce" feelings. The city would flow "with blood" if any Northerner tried anything.[23] "Sumner deserved what he got," was not a lonely cry from South Carolina. North Carolinian Thomas Jefferson Green's support for Brooks typified Southern sentiment. Green observed that "the whole north are [*sic*] mostly abolitionist," a fact proven for him by Northerners becoming excited "because a public man who had greatly provoked was flogged with a gutta percha the size of one's finger."[24] One could overlook the fine of $300 for the assault, but not the possibility of Brooks's expulsion from the House of Representatives. "Something should be done [even] if it dissolves the Union."[25]

Brooks contracted tuberculosis within a year and died in Larry Orr's arms at Brown's Hotel. He had spent the remaining few months of his life regretting his action but never the spirit behind it. The House tried to expel him but could not, so he paid his fine for battery and resigned his seat, but constituents in his district immediately reelected him. Overnight he exhibited a thorough redirection in his political outlook. Even before the canes sent from all over the South began arriving in Washington to replace the one he had broken, he was calling South Carolina to the colors of Southern nationalism, explaining, "I have been a disunionist from the time that I could think." Thus he implied that he had not had any thoughts at all until he beat Sumner about the head. By October he was talking about tearing the Constitution to "fragments."[26]

No sooner had the Brooks-Sumner incident receded from the forefront than a new controversy concerning Kansas emerged. James Buchanan, fresh from his inauguration, appointed Robert J. Walker to replace General John W. Geary, whom Pierce had sent to pacify the territory with good effect. Southerners could have regarded Walker, a native of Pennsylvania who had come to prominence in Mississippi politics, a good choice for this sensitive job. Quitman liked him and Buchanan had heard him recommended for other tasks.[27]

Perhaps Southerners had forgotten that in the 1856 campaign, Walker had declared that he did not think that Kansas would become a slave state. He reminded them upon his arrival in the territory in June 1857. His inaugural address indiscreetly implied that the territory was destined for free-state status. "His 'isothermal' and 'thermometrical' arguments and follies," noted Robert Toombs regarding Walker's scientific arguments,

"I suppose simply means [*sic*] that Kansas is too cold for 'niggers.'"[28] Worse, Walker's behavior outdid his oratory. He associated with free-state advocates in Topeka, even attending church with them.[29]

Southerners heaped plenty of invective on Walker, but they saved their main abuse for Buchanan. Howell Cobb, serving as Buchanan's secretary of the treasury, loyally explained that Walker was carrying out the president's plan to salve "the other side" while assuring that Kansas would become a slave state. Many of Cobb's fellow Georgians, however, could only see that "Buchanan has turned traitor."[30] In June, the Georgia Democratic Convention passed resolutions demanding that Buchanan remove Walker immediately, and by autumn the party was once again dividing into National and Southern factions. Self-serving Joseph E. Brown, recently elected governor and claiming a volatile, adoring piney woods constituency, led the Southern faction. Yet Brown moved cautiously, especially when Cobb warned that the governor and legislature, growing truculent, "should remember the fate of Gov. Towns and the democratic party in 1851."[31]

Yancey certainly remembered what his neighbors to the east might have forgotten. In a 27 June meeting of Alabama Democratic leaders in Montgomery, he took the minority side to insist that no evidence suggested that Walker and Buchanan were conspiring to undermine the rights of the South. Only after such evidence emerged, he said, could the Alabama party justify deserting Buchanan. Fellow radicals criticized Yancey for his moderate stand, which was understandable because much of the South was up in arms.[32] Old Buck "will stand by Walker with the pertinacity of Old Hickory," DeBow told South Carolinian William Porcher Miles. "Therefore let the South trust in God & keep her powder dry."[33] Carolina Representative Lawrence Keitt believed that Buchanan treacherously planned to save the Northern Democracy by allowing Kansas in as a free state.[34] John Quitman agreed but could see no treachery, only a surprisingly vigorous project by the president to protect the party in the North at the expense of the South.[35]

When Buchanan chose to back the monstrosity known as the Lecompton Constitution, he alienated the Northerners the South had accused him of courting. Drafted by an unrepresentative, proslavery convention boycotted by free-staters, the document mocked popular sovereignty by providing only the illusion of a referendum to determine the constitution's fate. Buchanan did not care. He wanted the territory in the

Union as a sovereign state to rid himself of the Kansas problem. However, Stephen A. Douglas, who could no longer disregard Northern sensibilities, could not abide the pro-Southern Lecompton Constitution. Of course, Southerners wanted the Lecompton Constitution. South Carolinians like Barnwell Rhett and Benjamin F. Perry had not agreed on anything for years, but they agreed on the necessity of supporting Lecompton.

Many who supported the document doubted the territory would ever enter the Union as a slave state, proving that the issue had less to do with Kansas's fate and much more to do with a Southern desire to test the reliability of Douglas Democrats. Also the old political tocsins, so long silenced, again began to sound. "If we could make it the rock upon which to split the Union," one Southerner wrote, "I confess it would suit me precisely."[36] Joe Brown mused that congressional rejection of the Lecompton Constitution would violate the Georgia Platform; if this were so, he would have to call a convention and instruct the Georgia delegation to withdraw from the national legislature. Alexander Stephens, who was helping William H. English draft a compromise bill to break the deadlock, told Brown that nobody was violating anything and to calm down, much to the governor's relief.[37]

The Lecompton Constitution could not guarantee concrete advantage to the South, and Buchanan's support of it could not preserve the uneasy comity between increasingly tense factions of the Democratic party. Despite earlier moderation regarding Robert Walker, Yancey felt that the time had arrived for his move. The Walker controversy combined with Douglas's behavior over the Lecompton Constitution convinced him. He planned to create a Southern organization called the League of United Southerners, the charter of which was innocuous enough—no more compromise on Southern rights in party platforms or state legislatures. While the League would not nominate candidates for any office, members would exert influence within the Democratic party to promote Southern Rights men from the South[38]

In June 1858, Yancey revealed the real purpose of the League in a letter to Alabamian James Slaughter. He contended that "no national party can save us" and "no sectional party can ever do it [either]." He envisioned the League as a Southern network of Committees of Public Safety that would "at the proper moment, by one organized, concerted action . . . precipitate the cotton states into revolution."[39]

He was fortunate that this letter did not come to light until two years later. Even then, in 1860, his flattering credit to Ruffin for instigating the League would make the conspiratorial language seem more ominous because it gave the appearance of a widespread plot aimed at revolution. Actually, in 1858, the collaboration was slight, but so were the true intentions of the League deliberately shrouded. Otherwise, it would not have stood even a poor chance of success.[40]

Yancey hatched the scheme in May after the Montgomery Commercial Convention. Differences over Virginia's stand on the slave-trade issue did not mean differences about the larger areas of politics, and Ruffin bore no hard feelings toward Yancey for his abrasive manner during the convention. The day after the meeting adjourned, he went to a party at Yancey's home to enjoy "a superb cold collation."[41]

Ruffin would charter the organization in Virginia. His gadabout activities had kept him busy since 1851, but Ruffin eagerly entered this new enterprise. In the autumn of 1857 he was suffering from severe psychological depression. At his plantation, Marlbourne, he brooded over mortality while battling insomnia. Writer's block worsened his self-torture. The death of son Edmund's wife, Mary, catalyzed the depression, but there was more to it than that. Occasionally—it would occur more frequently in coming years—his erratic memory panicked him. He could not remember writing works he saw published under his name, and his diary revealed that often he went for days unaware of the date. Convinced that absentmindedness heralded mental decay, he virtually surrendered to depression. In time, he would soar out of such states—he always had before—but prior to the recovery he suffered awfully, crippled by tormenting doubts.[42] In one sense, Yancey's League became Edmund Ruffin's therapy. It gave him something to do.

Ruffin returned to Virginia and enlisted the help of Willoughby Newton to form branches of the organization. Almost immediately editorials denouncing the idea appeared in *The South,* a newspaper Roger Pryor edited for the Hunter faction in Virginia. Pryor's opposition not only shocked Ruffin, it hurt his feelings. Following the election of 1856, when asked by his young friend to contribute a piece for the *Richmond Enquirer,* Ruffin had written "On the Consequences of Abolition and of the Separation of the Union." Published in December 1856, Ruffin's essay described Buchanan's recent victory as insignificant when compared to the strong showing of the "Black Republicans." Ruffin predicted that in 1860 the Republicans would win and begin constitutional perversions aimed at emancipation. The South would have to secede to save itself.[43]

Pryor had accepted the essay without reservation. But what sounded good in 1856 was unacceptable in 1858 because it threatened the plans of the Hunter wing of the Virginia Democracy. John Letcher joined Hunter in attempts to quiet the slavery debate for fear that a revivification of it would shatter a precarious coalition of states rights constituents in the east and Unionists in the west, a coalition carefully fashioned with an eye toward Hunter's chances for the presidential nomination in 1860. In a deadlocked convention, so went the reasoning, Northern and Southern Democrats would find in Hunter a compromise candidate untainted by the slavery question. Henry Wise had shifted toward radicalism to keep alive the slavery debate because it served as the best means with which to sunder Hunter's coalition: if Wise could push Hunter toward Southern rights, he would lose the western counties, and if Hunter moved the other way, he would alienate the east.

There were already too many distractions in Virginia to admit another. So Pryor rebuked the League as pointless as long as the Democracy controlled the government.[44] Most Virginians agreed, and Newton's efforts to form a chapter in Westmoreland County drew heavy criticism that threatened his own political position. Ruffin sadly agreed that the idea was dead. Even James H. Hammond counseled him that the South's best protection lay in Union. So Ruffin dropped his advocacy of the League, but he remained unconvinced and unforgiving. He broke off his friendship with Pryor. It would not be the last casualty of the old man's radicalism.[45]

Rhett, who also heard the plan for the League at Montgomery, either dismissed it or declined to enter it. He would not have proven a valuable promoter for it in South Carolina anyway, for he was still much out of favor there. Attempts to end his retirement began again seriously in 1856 and ended in abject failure. After he, like Ruffin, lashed out at Buchanan's victory as offering only a numbing security, he published a letter to Governor Adams in the *Mercury*. The people, Rhett said, had to be reawakened to the danger, and he offered to assume the leadership of the task, perhaps as governor. The *Charleston Courier* attacked him for inventing issues, and the December session of the legislature did not even regard him as a candidate.[46]

Worse even than this humiliation had been the fatal consequences of the campaign for William Aiken's House seat. The seat represented the Charleston Congressional District, a moderate enclave for years, so it was foolish for the nascent Rhett faction to attempt a disunion campaign by running Rhett's son, Edmund. The nationalists, headquartered at the business center of the city on Broad Street, nominated Andrew Gordon McGrath and consequently revived Rhett-McGrath animosity that stretched back to the bitter quarrels of 1851. It ended when A. G.'s son, Edward, challenged William R. Taber, Rhett's nephew and junior editor of the *Mercury,* to a duel and killed him. Everyone was horrified, especially the elder McGrath, who withdrew from the race. Who could still doubt that where there was a Rhett, there was sure to be trouble?[47]

When A. P. Butler died in May 1857, the South Carolina legislature met in the fall to choose a replacement. Candidates included Rhett, Francis W. Pickens, John Smith Preston, James Chesnut, Jr., and James Henry Hammond. Never in serious contention, Rhett had to endure watching Hammond, the clear favorite, play the political coquette. As late as October, Hammond professed no interest in serving the state, even if the legislature chose him. However, both nationalists and radicals found Hammond acceptable, the nationalists because his fourteen-year absence from office left him untouched by the sectional crises, the radicals because they saw him as a Carolina traditionalist. Ironically, in the course of the three ballots it took to award him the prize, Hammond benefited from the state's new egalitarianism. When the old family scandal threatened to reemerge, many regarded it as nothing more than a pointless persecution, something fashioned by the nearly dead Wade Hampton for reasons many could no longer recall.[48]

Rhett had tried to use the Kansas controversy to his advantage and had failed. Every move he made against Orr's Carolina Democracy only strengthened it, so in the fall of 1857 the *Mercury,* threatened by economic catastrophe, bowed to the pressure and announced itself as moderate, indicating a major retrenchment. The preoccupation of the Rhett family then became the task of saving the newspaper from bankruptcy. The Rhetts planned to buy out John Heart's interest in the publication because Heart, a Hammond supporter, had gotten into the habit of quarrelling with Barnwell Rhett, Jr. Hammond's people, working through Heart, toyed with the idea of buying the paper but were put off by its tottering finances. They could more easily pluck it from the hands of the receivers, anyway. In a bold and risky move, however, the Rhetts absorbed the *Charleston Standard,* a cooperationist daily created in 1851, to bolster the *Mercury*'s account books. The calming of the paper's editorial voice also had a felicitous effect, even as it raised the howls of radicals deprived suddenly of their forum. Maxcy Gregg exploded when the *Mercury*'s new policy closed it to his appeals against Orrism. "Such treatment," he wailed, "is not what is due to me."[49]

The League of United Southerners got lost in the welter of these local concerns. Only six chapters were ever formed, all of them in Alabama.[50] Even this minor success was due not to the efforts of Yancey, but rather to William F. Samford, the so-called "Penman of Secession." Samford, a native of Russell County in Alabama, had an intellectual bent—he had taught English literature at Emory College in Oxford, Georgia—and held principled positions. Predictably against Northern emigrant aid societies, he also opposed the Lecompton Constitution because he insisted it was a fraud.[51] Samford attracted a small clique of Southern Rights men who did not always understand his positions but were willing to trust him in office. He declined to run for governor of Alabama in 1857, stepping aside for Albert B. Moore, but in 1859 he declared from Auburn that he would "run against the politicians" who wallowed in "partyism" to the detriment of the South.[52]

Paradoxically, this "Penman of Secession" opposed Alabama's secession until after the election of Lincoln, and then supported the state's withdrawal from the Union only as a cooperationist. Before that, in 1858, writing under the pseudonym "Zeno" in the *Montgomery Advertiser,* Samford had killed the League of United Southerners, which he supported. With the best of intentions, he described the League as the forerunner of a new political party to replace the Democracy. The revelation completely dispelled any doubts Democrats had about Yancey's purpose. J. J. Seibels, by then supporting Douglas, denounced the League as a means to destroy the National Democracy for the advantage of William Lowndes Yancey. Yancey protested with an elaborate lie, as though he could convince the people with words while they disregarded his actions.[53]

Yancey ran for the Senate in 1858 against Benjamin Fitzpatrick. He had the support of Noah B. Cloud and John Gill Shorter of the radical Eufaula Regency. They had just purchased the *Montgomery Advertiser,* and they placed the newspaper in the Yancey camp, plugging for him while attacking Fitzpatrick. But Yancey shattered his chances by adding to a series of unforgivable indiscretions. In May he delivered his drunken speech to the Montgomery Commercial Convention, alienating Virginia and arguing for the morally indefensible slave trade. Then he entertained filibusterer William Walker in his home and announced support for Walker's adventurism in Latin America. Even under its new radical owners, the *Advertiser* began to have second thoughts about supporting Yancey. He lost the election to Fitzpatrick while renewing the distrust of moderates and reinvigorating the animosity of Seibels' Montgomery Regency.[54]

Thus far Yancey had acted like a marplot in every radical scheme he advanced. He likely would have faltered on indefinitely, ruining one plan after another. But even as Yancey battered an apparently invulnerable wall of nationalism, Stephen A. Douglas unwittingly shattered that wall's principal mortise. Because of his opposition to the Lecompton Constitution, Douglas had to fight for his political life in the Illinois Senate contest of 1858. Pitted against a wily Republican organization sponsoring Abraham Lincoln, Douglas also had to fight the Buchanan administration. Buchanan had become so angry over Douglas's opposition in the Lecompton fight that he plotted the Little Giant's destruction at all cost. Lincoln cleverly adopted the argument that the Dred Scott decision, in which the Supreme Court just months before had declared the Missouri Compromise line unconstitutional, rendered Douglas's popular sovereignty moot. Douglas responded at the Freeport, Illinois, debate by declaring that slavery could not exist where local laws did not support it. Thus the Illinois Democrat carelessly tossed the so-called Freeport Doctrine to the ground. Fire-eaters would take it up like a bludgeon.

To label what Douglas said at Freeport a doctrine misses the point. Four years earlier, in the congressional caucuses crafting the repeal of 36°30', Douglas stated the same principle to the agreement of, for one, Albert Gallatin Brown.[55] Also, a year before his appearance at Freeport, in the Hall of Representatives at Springfield, Illinois, Douglas reiterated the position in an extemporaneous explanation of the Dred Scott decision.[56] Douglas's statement at Freeport did not cause all of his problems with the Southern Democrats. The substance of his statement was at least four years old when he offered it at Freeport in the debate with Lincoln.

The fire-eaters seized upon this Freeport Doctrine as if it were a newly revealed reason to oppose Douglas in 1860. Yet, in truth, the fire-eaters did not oppose Douglas in 1860. They wanted to shatter the National Democracy, and the party had designated Douglas as early as 1857 as the nominee for 1860. In fact, many of the Southern politicians who would abet his vilification liked Douglas, a charming man with a reputation for unforced congeniality. Douglas's position on the Lecompton Constitution annoyed Albert Gallatin Brown, but he supported Douglas against Lincoln and cheered when he won.[57] Ironically then, Douglas's problems would start with the volatile Brown, who drew a bead on the Little Giant actually to take aim at Jefferson Davis.[58]

The Brown-Davis feud in the Mississippi Democracy had dictated party matters there for five years. In November 1855 in an attempt to pacify Brown, Democrats in the Mississippi legislature placed John A. Quitman in the Senate. Quitman remained unreconciled to the National Democracy, but the party feared that Brown's irritation over Davis's control of the party would cause his disaffection. Brown suspected that Davis had supported Quitman hoping that any ensuing rivalries would help Davis.[59] Perhaps this was so, for Davis, who had opposed Quitman's vice-presidential bid in 1848 and who probably had a hand in the general's similar disappointment in 1856, apparently liked neither Quitman nor his positions.[60] Brown, however, was delighted, though occasionally unsettled, by his new colleague because Quitman had more reason to ally with Brown than Davis. But Quitman died in July 1858, and Jefferson Davis replaced him. The contest for the state party then became brutal with neither side taking prisoners.

Brown won election to the United States House and subsequently to the Senate by disowning his radicalism of 1850 and 1851. Yet John C. Frémont's strong showing in 1856 and the rhetoric of belligerent abolitionism in the national legislature made radicalism again palatable if not altogether popular. Soon Brown viciously denounced Northern antislavery proponents to the predictable applause of Southern Rights men, but also he gained the cautious approval of Unionists like William Sharkey. By September 1858, he resumed the radicalism he had deserted seven years before. At Hazelhurst, Mississippi, he assessed disagreements between the sections as irreconcilable and described secession as inevitable. His deft sensitivity to the subtly shifting mood of his constituents shaped part of his performance. Moreover, he wanted to draw a sharp definition between himself and Jefferson Davis. So thoroughly aligned with the National Democracy himself that he had to support the party's heir, Davis must have winced when William Seward delivered a speech a few weeks later envisioning an "irrepressible conflict." The New York senator had dovetailed, from a Northern perspective, all of Brown's arguments.[61]

The opening session of the Thirty-sixth Congress saw another angry contest for the speakership, and Brown used the turmoil to narrow his attack on Douglas as he widened its choleric nature. In February 1859 he attacked the Little Giant's opposition to a congressional slave code for the territories by insisting that a slave code was the least the South could settle for. He demanded, with phrases purposely designed to offend Northerners, that the United States acquire Cuba. And while he privately expressed to Douglas his "highest regard . . . politically in all things save *niggers*," he warned Mississippi audiences of the dangers of continuing in the Union.[62]

Brown's increasingly acerbic threats about destroying the Union greatly influenced the Mississippi State Democratic Convention, which assembled on 5 July 1859. Reflecting the anger stirred by Brown, fire-eaters controlled the convention. They appointed ardent secessionist Ethelbert Barksdale, publisher of the *Mississippian,* to the chairmanship of the platform committee. Jefferson Davis's futile attempts to moderate proceedings confirmed that the party had spun away from his influence. The convention passed resolutions declaring that if a Republican won in 1860, Mississippi should secede. On 6 July it nominated fire-eater John J. Pettus for governor. The kind of sectional rhetoric that had doomed Quitman in 1851 paled in comparison to the wild declarations of Pettus during the subsequent campaign. He shouted that a Republican triumph in 1860 would cleave the Union and launch a war. The coalition of Union Democrats and Whigs that Henry Foote had used to smash Southern rights eight years before was only a timid shadow in the summer of 1859. Calling itself cryptically the Opposition—apparently it did not dare to mention Unionism—the coalition attempted to revive the fear of radicalism that had worked so well before, but Mississippi's voters remained unconvinced. On the first Monday and Tuesday of October, the fire-eating Mississippi Democracy smashed the Opposition in all offices with a better than three-to-one margin.[63] The party was in the hands of the zealots.

Robert Barnwell Rhett viewed these events with growing interest. The controversies that Brown stirred in Washington and Mississippi ended

Rhett's retirement. Uninterested at first, he slowly realized that here were issues with which he could destroy Orr's National Democracy.[64] In April 1859 six citizens of Grahamville, South Carolina, invited him to offer "opinions on public affairs" at a Fourth-of-July festivity.[65] He eagerly accepted and on the appointed day appeared before an audience for the first time in eight years. The sizeable crowd was thoroughly Low Country, for Grahamville sat amidst the wealthy rice plantations of Beaufort Parish. Rhett's statement began with familiar arguments about Southern rights, but soon he displayed some remarkable changes in his thinking. He no longer demanded South Carolina's separate secession. The man who in April 1851 had declared cooperation an impossibility now called for Southern unity.[66]

Four days later in Columbia, South Carolina, Yancey made a speech urging Carolina's attendance at the upcoming Democratic Convention in Charleston. He called upon Carolinians to join all true Southerners to stop Stephen A. Douglas and his hateful doctrine by demanding a platform based on the Dred Scott decision. If denied such a platform, the South should withdraw from the party; and if a Republican won in November, it should secede from the Union.[67] It was a brash and paradoxical speech to make in the land of James L. Orr, for it stepped across the lines of faction in South Carolina to encourage attendance at a national convention (which appealed to Orr's followers but repelled radicals) in order to press a radical program or disrupt the party (which was repugnant to nationalists but appealing to fire-eaters).[68]

Across the South, Old Line Whigs, still untethered to any political party, and moderate Democrats disdainfully shook their heads at Yancey in Columbia. They had heard it all before, and true enough, the entire Yancey plan was nearly identical to the one he had haplessly launched in 1848. But now there was one major difference: this plan was going to work.

CHAPTER EIGHT

"One of the Most Aristocratic Cities of the Union"

In some ways, Robert Barnwell Rhett and William Lowndes Yancey were much alike. Each was a bad politician in his own way, and both were too incautious and indiscreet. But these two men in most respects could not have been more different. Yancey cajoled and charmed, while Rhett posited and lectured. The Alabamian held the platform as a peerless orator; the Carolinian depended on his words rather than a style of delivery to carry forcefully his message. Hence, Yancey, striving for simplicity of diction made powerful by his voice, drew men from miles to hear him speak. Rhett, sometimes stumbling over fervid, sophomoric declamations tangled in mixed imagery, attracted only those interested in what he would say, not in how he would say it. Yancey moved easily in society, always ready for a drink and a flirtatious encounter. Rhett felt comfortable only with his family and observed a stiff formality with women. Yancey resiliently rebounded from failure, while Rhett brooded over it.

The dissimilar responses each had to the sectional crises at the end of the 1850s reflected these differences in personality. Like a bad penny, the Alabama Platform had appeared again, made shinier by the polish of the slavery controversy in the territories. First in Columbia and then in the *Charleston Mercury,* Yancey sang the praises of this plan designed to force the National Democracy into line with Southern rights.[1] He presented the idea as a point-by-point program: go into the convention and secure a platform based on Dred Scott or, failing that, withdraw to nominate a Southern candidate. Should a Republican triumph in November, secede from the Union.

It all seemed so simple and neat, but it was really too simple and too neat to suit Barnwell Rhett. Rhett decried Carolina's participation in national party conventions, and about the only substantial faction he could count himself a member of agreed. Reflecting Low Country suspicion of democracy, the anti-Conventionists caviled at Orr's integration of the state party into the national organization and muttered and moaned when South Carolina's delegation departed for Cincinnati in 1856. Indeed, the National Democracy, realizing the measure of Carolina attendance at Cincinnati, chose Charleston as the site of the 1860 convention both to reward and encourage Palmetto nationalists. For Rhett, this was precisely the point. The Charleston Convention, he was sure, would only provide "every opportunity for patching up hollow truces" between National Democrats and Southern Rights men.[2]

So he did not believe that Yancey's plan would work, and the John Brown raid convinced Rhett no other issue was needed anyway. South Carolina should refuse to participate at Charleston, the *Mercury* declared. Instead, the state should arm itself against abolitionism and reject Douglas.[3] Sounding too much like Rhett's old calls for separate state action, the advice fell on the deaf ears of the legislature. The lower house ignored it, and the Senate slapped down Edmund Rhett's efforts to have the body act on it.[4] But the moderate nationalists' dismissal of Rhett's counsel did not mean they could ignore what had happened at Harpers Ferry. Governor William Henry Gist, a blatant secessionist as it turned out, had muted his radical sentiments to gain election in 1858, but after the Brown raid he told the legislature that South Carolina should contact Virginia's General Assembly. Stunned by the advent of violent abolitionism, the Carolina legislature paralyzed itself in debate.[5]

For so many years the nationalists had derided the radicals for sounding alarms where no dangers existed. At the end of 1859, they now encountered a very real danger indeed. It did not matter that Northern Democrats tried to prove their outrage over Brown's exploit. More visible to Southern eyes was, for instance, John A. Andrew's election as governor of Massachusetts after he had publicly stated his sympathy for Brown's purpose. After Brown's execution, demonstrations from New York to Chicago to Lawrence, Kansas, and back to the Town House in Concord, Massachusetts, revealed an astounding breadth of support for abolitionism. It was by no means the typical Northern response, but it seemed so to the Southerner. Actually, the affair at Harpers Ferry simply was seen by most people, North and South, as dangerous and deplorable, foreboding badly for the future. It changed many opinions about the inevitability of a coming conflict.[6]

The Carolina legislature finally agreed on a compromise. It would call for yet another Southern congress and send Christopher G. Memminger to Richmond to propose Virginia's cooperation in the move.[7] The compromise could not have pleased reemerging radicals very much, but at least it moved away from the implacable nationalism that moderates had pursued for most of the decade. For their part, the moderates, accustomed to compromise, took the first step toward compromising that nationalism.

Memminger was a good choice to send to Virginia. An immigrant boy who had grown up in the Low Country of South Carolina, he had distinguished himself by graduating from South Carolina College in 1819 at the age of sixteen. Admitted to the bar in 1825, he enjoyed a long career in Carolina politics, serving in the state legislature from 1836 onward with only a brief interruption in 1853. He had opposed Nullification and had grudgingly accepted the Compromise of 1850, so there was nothing to suggest Palmetto radicalism in the person of Christopher Memminger. Fifty-six years old in 1859 and with a reputation as a moderate Southerner and confirmed Unionist, he was the picture of brilliance tempered with discretion.[8]

Even before Memminger's visit to Virginia was planned, it appeared as though the disruption of the Union would occur because of events in Congress. Republicans nominated John Sherman of Ohio for Speaker of the House. That Sherman was a Republican was only part of the cause for the Southern outburst. After all, Southerners after a two-month fight had unhappily consented to Massachusetts Republican Nathaniel Banks in 1856.[9] But Sherman had been one of sixty-eight Republicans to endorse Hinton Helper's *The Impending Crisis and How to Meet It,* a book that Southerners judged would excite class resentment among nonslaveholding Southern farmers. At the beginning of another two-month ordeal that by mid-December already had everyone on edge, speech after Southern speech condemned Sherman as unacceptable. Only Georgian Alfred Iverson openly justified secession, but a few South Carolinians had a dire response in mind. William Porcher Miles and Lawrence M. Keitt kept in touch with Gist in Columbia, and the governor told them to withdraw if Sherman became Speaker and other states withdrew. Gist briefly considered sending troops to Washington, but that was only silly bluster. Ultimately both he and Barnwell Rhett, Jr., counseled moderation as the House moved toward the election of New Jersey's William Pennington, a conservative Republican. The crisis became quite serious when Miles suggested that Southerners could stop Sherman's assumption of the chair by force, but Gist got over his version of such a fantasy and vetoed the plan.[10]

From the setting of this controversy, Miles provided Memminger, about to set out for Richmond, with some lusty advice. Woo the Old Dominion, he told Memminger, to "urge our Carolina view in such a manner as to imbue Virginia with it—(and at present she is in the best condition to be impregnated)—[and] we may soon hope to see the fruit of your addresses in the sturdy and healthy offspring of whose birth we would be so greatly proud—a Southern confederacy." Miles contended that "this would indeed be a worthy heir . . . to spring from the loins of the Palmetto State."[11]

By the time Memminger arrived in Richmond, the chances of his mission bearing fruit had already passed. Even Miles observed from Washington that Virginia was "rapidly cooling down" and that there was "little prospect of uniting the South in any *practical* and effectual *actions*."[12] Memminger had already heard the reservations of North Carolina governor William H. Thomas, who complained about South Carolina and Virginia planning anything without consulting their neighbors.[13] So although a committee of the General Assembly warmly received him at the train station, Memminger must have known by then that he was on a fool's errand. Yet he completed it. Governor John Letcher, new to the office recently vacated by Henry A. Wise, prepared the way for Memminger's address to both houses of the legislature and the judges of the state.

Edmund Ruffin, eager to hear what Memminger had to say, knew that the legislature would dismiss suggestions to follow Carolina's lead in dissolving the Union.[14] Immediately following the John Brown raid, Virginia had sat dazed and incredulous. "We don't yet know enough about it to take any definite position," Lewis Harvie had admitted, although he did muse, "We may have to take [an] extreme position. Let us wait for developments."[15] Further, he had written to Robert Hunter, "We do not desire nor design that this outbreak should be used to subserve the selfish purposes or schemes of profligate and unprincipled politicians." In other words, Henry A. Wise should not benefit from any panic by using such fears to Hunter's detriment.[16] Soon enough, however, Harvie's awaited developments emerged, and when they did, no politician's machinations inspired the people's extreme position. James M. Mason discovered Brown's involvement with Northern abolitionists—though the extent was and would remain ominously unclear—and quickly a reactionary fear spread beyond Virginia throughout the whole South. Vigilance committees sprouted in every state from South Carolina to Texas. Charged to prowl the countryside to weed out terrorist abolitionism, the committees themselves often perpetrated a rough terror of their own, ignoring the distinctions between allegation and proof and attracting the kind of men who needed little excuse for vigilante justice.[17]

Meanwhile, Henry A. Wise moved with considerable dispatch both to capitalize on and calm the passion Brown's raid aroused. As governor Wise had carefully adjusted an erratic radicalism to suit his rivalry with Hunter. By the end of December Wise had Brown brought to an unquestionably fair trial that insisted upon the old fanatic's dubious sanity so the affair could end with an execution and become a memory. Yet it also remained a weapon he could use against Hunter's moderate nationalism. Southern Rights Associations boycotted Northern goods, and homespun clubs appeared. The legislature enlarged the Virginia militia and even talked of a Southern convention.[18]

Ruffin, who rushed around a great deal, gathered as many of the pikes as he could that old Brown had brought to Harpers Ferry—he planned to send one to every Southern governor—and finally was outside Charlestown to watch Brown hang.[19] At the end of the year he recorded that "never had there been such an opportunity for secession," but he was attending the flaring mood of the people. The politicians already had different ideas.[20] Wise stated, for his own trimming reasons, that the South should fight within the Union. Northerners, he said, were trying to force Southern secession, so Southerners should disappoint them. The idea, Miles snorted, was "the most puerile folly and nonsensical stuff that ever was written." By January, however,when Memminger appeared before the General Assembly, Wise's solution had obtained, with Virginians at least, a rough attractiveness.[21]

Memminger went through the motions. South Carolina admired and respected Virginia, he told the legislators. He then warned about the

Republican menace, of which John Brown was only the most startling exemplar. Leaving the legislature with a series of dire predictions, he retired to await its response to the suggested initiation of a Southern congress. After three weeks, he had the hard evidence in the General Assembly's silence that he was wasting his time, and he was angry about it. Yet Memminger pondered the chance that petulance and impetuosity would allow alarmists to quash moderation and Southern unity, ever the goal of men like Memminger. He already heard Porcher Miles contemptuously dismiss Virginian vacillation by declaring that "We, farther South, must act, and 'drag her along.'" Memminger knew that such radicalism, if only expressed, let alone applied, would be deadly. So he carefully drafted a letter to Governor Letcher expressing South Carolina's sympathy and solidarity with the Old Dominion and requesting that when the legislature got around to deciding something, it advise Governor Gist. Then he quietly headed back to South Carolina, where he reported to Gist, whose possible actions apparently worried him, that "the diversity of sentiment which yet prevails among [Virginia's] people as to proper remedies, may impair her unity and promptness of action." He was sure "that Virginia will assuredly take her place in the United Councils of the South."[22] This best face, however, could not mask that Virginia had tacitly rejected Carolina's overtures. Fire-eaters would have made more of this rejection had not their attention now focused on the promising activities of fellow radicals in Alabama and Mississippi.

The Harpers Ferry raid jarred the resolve of Alabama nationalists while making the fire-eater message more attractive to the people. The Perry County meeting of the Democracy on 17 October 1859 was typical. Resolutions both denounced Douglas and pledged to defeat him. The delegates also determined to abandon any nominee unwilling to advocate congressional protection of slavery in the territories.[23] The fine hand of Yancey, so evident here, similarly aroused a swelling tide of radicalism from the southern Alabama counties that on 11 January 1860 propelled the state party convention to his purpose. Francis S. Lyon, elected chairman of the convention under the guise of compromise, quickly proved himself a Yancey man. He skillfully directed maneuvers that declared Douglas delegates irregular, thus excluding Seibels' Montgomery Regency and Mobile moderates formerly under John Campbell. It was then remarkably easy to bind the thirty-six delegates headed for

Charleston to the Alabama Platform and to provide them with instructions to quit the convention if it were rejected. Yancey confidently depicted the delegation's position as that of the state, but J. J. Seibels branded this as pure fiction and told Stephen Douglas so.[24] Both Yancey and Seibels were partly correct—probably Seibels more than Yancey—but then, of course, that meant that neither was wholly wrong; paradoxically, from the latter perspective, Yancey was probably less wrong than was Seibels, because Yancey had ostensible control of the part of Alabama that would really count in April—the delegation. Neither Douglas nor his managers, pulling their chins and counting heads, were ever able to weigh the confused tangle of this paradox and derive from it a notion of the dangerous degree of risk involved in manipulating this particular convention. For just as Yancey had a plan, so did the Little Giant.

Douglas planned to purge the convention of Yanceyites, and in having his supporters work toward that end, he unwittingly collaborated with Yancey's design to disrupt the gathering. The Illinoisan's frustrations by 1860 had come to control his thinking, always a dangerous state for a politician, even in the quietest of times. The roiling controversy over Kansas-Nebraska, the brutish behavior of radical Republicans, the glaring acrimony of Southern fire-eaters, and the enmity of an administration for which he had labored in 1856 all combined to form yet only part of the circumstances that hurled Douglas toward the disaster of April 1860. Back of everything else there was, in his memory at least, his stepping aside in 1852 and then again in 1856, taking the role of loyal party man, always striving for harmony, cheerfully supporting the other man, waiting for "next time," so that by 1858, he had determined that the next time, by God, would be his time. If anybody, whether Lowndes Yancey or Old Buck or anyone else said otherwise, then Douglas would kick in the naysayer's teeth or, at the very least, ride him out of the party.

For Douglas, in this frame of mind, it was felicitous that Yancey arrived in Charleston pledging to leave the convention if it did not meet his demands. The Little Giant was not sure he could capture the nomination (or worse, that it would be worth anything) with Yancey tearing about.[25] Yancey's intentions meant that he would not have to be purged from the party but would leave it himself. In a meeting with Republicans in 1857, Douglas had suggested the tactic that would be the thrust of his strategy in Charleston in 1860. He had planned then in the Lecompton fight to put the radicals "in the position of insurgents, instead of letting them create a situation, as they wish to do, in which we must revolt. We will let them be the rebels."[26]

It sounded easier than it was to be. Henry B. Payne of Ohio declared privately that if Yancey's demands were met in Charleston, the Ohio delegation would withdraw, and seven other Northwestern delegations probably would follow.[27] Douglas could not allow that to happen, since without the Northwest, he would lose any chance for the nomination. But perhaps more fearful to him was the prospect of securing the nomination before the adoption of the platform and then having radicals saddle him with the Yancey platform, driving away the Northwest and making his candidacy worthless. In short, there were several ways things could go completely wrong if everything did not go completely right. The game his managers would play was fraught with complications that would require efficient and coordinated moves, but at base the objectives distilled to pure simplicity: have the platform written first and make sure that the convention rejected Alabama's demands. Thus Douglas would have a platform he could run on, and the provoked purge would insure his nomination.[28]

Getting the platform written first would prove easy. Radical Southerners also wanted the platform first and might have been a little surprised that Douglas's managers consented to it. Then the dangerous part would begin: any hint of the Alabama Platform would have to be thoroughly rejected and the Cincinnati Platform embraced to hold moderate Southerners and beleaguered Northerners in the party. That would require the Douglas people to know exactly how each man in each delegation would vote. The Yanceyites would then withdraw—or would they? Douglas himself understood his fire-eating foes better than did most Northern Democrats because he knew that they usually meant what they said. But there was always the chance that they would remain in the convention to make trouble over the nomination, deadlocking the balloting and providing the opportunity for a compromise candidate to take the prize.

The apprehension was plausible because of R. M. T. Hunter's popularity. His acceptability to Northern Democrats encouraged the Virginian's hopes.[29] James Seddon, undoubtedly biased but no less observant, told his friend at the end of 1859 that it would be best for Douglas to renounce his candidacy and support Hunter, "for how could either he or Wise be nominated without plain ruin to the party."[30] The Virginia

Democracy's state convention agreed and appointed a pro-Hunter delegation to attend Charleston. Wise, already a victim of one vacillating shift too many, declared for Douglas and for no better reason than to oppose an apparently irresistible Hunter in Virginia.[31] Hunter had the tentative support not only of Cobb and Toombs in Georgia but also of Levi Woodbury of Massachusetts and even George Fisher of Illinois, because these men reflected Buchanan's hostility to Douglas. Given the right developments, he could also count on the support of the entire Deep South. But as a potential compromise alternative to Douglas, Hunter required exactly the right set of circumstances to capture the Northwestern delegations as well. In fact, he needed to have the nominee chosen before any vote on the platform because the acceptance of the radical platform would drive off the Northwest, and a platform vote the other way, causing the radicals to bolt, would remove the opportunity for a paralyzed convention seeking a "dark horse" compromise.[32]

Douglas's people were up to this challenge and the potential complications it posed. Talented William A. Richardson organized for Douglas the efforts of fellow Illinoisans John A. Logan and John A. McClernand as well as those of amiable George E. Pugh of Ohio and unscrupulous George Sanders of New York.[33] These men were well equipped variously by temperament, disposition, and loyalty to cajole and shove, charm and threaten, promise and equivocate, and even purchase, according to the circumstances. And if the business called for getting nasty, or for shaming out the Yanceyite troublemakers, Douglas had a troublemaker of his own in Michigan Democrat Charles E. Stuart, known for an acerbic style he usually directed at Southern Rights brethren.[34]

Douglas expected to get roughed up, but provided with only what the Little Giant and his managers could see, there was no reason to believe that he would not ultimately secure the nomination of an essentially united Democracy. In fact, this is what should have happened. Yancey's scheme was, by the obvious evidence, as feckless in 1860 as it had been in 1848. The Deep South delegations upon which he depended did not appear promising. In January Albert Gallatin Brown introduced resolutions in the Senate calling for a congressional slave code, a move obviously designed to embarrass Jefferson Davis. Brown had batted Davis around for almost a year and a half on this issue, and Davis had heard enough. The two had muted their hostility, but now it broke out into open belligerence. The rival resolutions Davis introduced, after an

unprecedented chastisement of the radicalism of his fellow Mississippian, only presaged a quieter, more methodical Davis plan to regain
the Mississippi Democracy. Davis's resolutions, bowing to the realities of
Mississippi passions, were only a little less radical than Brown's, but in
not calling for a national slave code they catered to Douglas Democrats,
which was the whole point. Brown found Alfred Iverson of Georgia,
Clement Clay of Alabama, James Mason of Virginia, and even rambunctious Texan Louis Wigfall against him, and he discovered soon afterward that the Mississippi Democracy in convention was not his to
command. Barksdale's *Mississippian* had slinked back into the Davis
camp, and the *Free Trader,* Brown's staunchest organ, had abandoned
Brown's recklessness. Pettus was suddenly hedging, and it became
apparent that Brown had gone at last too far; the Charleston Convention
would be a serious affair, and Davis had his say in directing the choice
of the delegation to it.[35]

Likewise, the power in Georgia delivered a moderate delegation in
spite of the presence of Henry Benning, who, after all, had been quiet
for some years. Robert Toombs typified the sentiment. He did not support
Douglas, but he also opposed any move that would disrupt the party.[36] In
Texas, Sam Houston's gubernatorial victory and the muting of Louis
Wigfall's sectionalism, especially about the slave trade, indicated that the
state party was in line with the National Democracy.[37] In addition, North
Carolina sent a moderate delegation to Charleston that contained only
two radicals, Waightstill Avery and Thomas J. Green, the latter the more
fiery and yet strangely the more cautious. Douglas Democrats could take
heart that Green declined to join Yancey's committee of Southerners to
fashion a Yanceyite platform because the moderate North Carolina delegation did not agree with his views.[38]

South Carolina's delegation was the picture of moderation. For a
variety of reasons, some of them starkly different, the Orr majority
attracted elements not previously for South Carolina's participation in the
Democratic Convention. Only a tiny minority wanted to be in the convention to break it. Orr presided over the state convention, which offered
no support for Alabama and left its moderate delegates unencumbered
with instructions. At most, some had the vague notion of pushing Orr as
Douglas's running mate.[39]

Douglas's managers, however, seriously miscalculated the strength
Yancey could wield at Charleston. On the eve of the convention, Yancey

brought together a caucus of Deep South delegations from Alabama, Georgia, Mississippi, Louisiana, Florida, Arkansas, and Texas. All more or less agreed that they had to stop Douglas. The last phrase—stop Douglas—was the master stroke of the Yancey scheme because, in focusing discontent on the Little Giant, radicals stood to pick up support from the Buchanan administration, still angry over Douglas's defiance in the Lecompton controversy. Without the administration's enmity, Douglas probably would not have faced much of a threat from the radicals, but the administration's operatives at Charleston had come to the position of the man who wishes to rid his house of a rodent and does so by burning it down. Consequently, not only did Louisianan John Slidell, who had blocked Yancey in the platform committee in 1848, agree to stop Douglas by foisting a platform intolerable to him on the National Democracy, but so did Jesse D. Bright of Indiana and William Bigler of Pennsylvania.[40] Not everyone was blind to the great danger in this course. Jefferson Davis, for instance, wanted to emulate the Whigs of 1840 and dispense with the platform altogether, merely settling on an agreeable candidate. But in the main, most Democrats, not wanting a disruption in the party, did not think it would happen or, if it did, that it would signal anything worse than an inconvenience. James Henry Hammond came very close to the mark when he later observed that "Douglas occupies his present position solely because his opponents were so afraid of him that instead of allowing him to kill himself, they must kill him also."[41]

The other great mistake that Douglas's managers made was not taking into account the effect the site of the convention would have on the attitude of Southern delegations. A few years earlier, a first-time visitor described Charleston as joining "all the advantages of a northern and southern city. It is probably one of the most aristocratic cities of the Union . . . [with] a fine society, happily blending sincerity of manner with independence and high minded feeling."[42] Yet Charleston, while quaint, was not metropolitan. Pastel stucco, cobbled streets, high church steeples, lush courtyards bright with bursting flowers—that was Charleston in the springtime. Strolling up Church Street, one could see through the shivering Spanish moss that veiled St. Philip's churchyard the large marble slab that merely said CALHOUN and nothing more. Because it did not have to say anything more was, in a way, a reflection of this city that honored greatness with powerful simplicity. There was an attitude both peculiar and unique among Charlestonians. They were generously cordial to strangers, but they always preserved an ineffable aloofness because strangers were, after all, strangers, meaning that they were from someplace else not quite as good as Charleston.

God had worked a charming miracle on the little neck of land between the mouths of the Ashley and Cooper Rivers, but it was an exceedingly small miracle, too little to accommodate the strangers the Democracy brought crashing into its cloistered world in April. The Mills House and the Charleston Hotel, the only hotels of note in the city, were quickly filled with delegates who each paid ten dollars a day, double the standard rate, for places in rooms already overfull. Citizens opened private homes and merchants turned warehouses into dormitories to let for exorbitant rates. The sheer numbers strained the city's capacity to meet the most elemental needs. Food was bad when it was available. Delegates who had neither slept nor eaten very well withered in steamy heat that after a rain became damp cold, and they collected in Institute Hall, where everything was a little too close and noisy. Yancey had the streets around the building muffled with straw, but no such remedy could subdue the behavior of the galleries. Citizens grew weary of this convention that had outstayed its welcome even before the opening gavel, its members having "rendered theirselves [*sic*] unpalatable to the quiet people of Charleston." Delegates undoubtedly felt the same way, especially since the quiet people of the city obviously were not the hooting and jeering observers in Institute Hall.[43]

The convention opened on Monday, 23 April to tentative sparring between Douglas and administration men, who had successfully appointed Caleb Cushing to preside. Douglas forces balanced the defeat by steering the Committee on Organization away from its original commitment to the rules of 1856 (which required delegates to vote with the will of their delegation's majority), to recommendations that would allow Douglas to reap votes in unfriendly delegations. There was a slight tumult when the South urged the adoption of the platform before the nomination of the candidate, but it probably was more show than actual, and the convention agreed to write the platform first.[44]

It was a good day, strangely for everybody, because each faction, working for exclusive advantage, did so by using roughly the same tactics. But on Tuesday in the platform committee meetings the neat schematics of the Douglas plan began to fall apart. By Thursday some delegates sensed that the convention was moving inexorably toward disruption, only the scope of which was in doubt. Rumors bred of habit falsely accused the South Carolina delegation of stirring up the trouble, and there was speculation that a large withdrawal—perhaps the Alabama, Mississippi, Texas, Louisiana, and Arkansas delegations—would attract national moderates to Douglas in sufficient strength to give him the nomination.[45] But Douglas's managers could not have been so sure that the chance they had confidently taken on Monday was by Friday such a good idea. The platform committee produced three reports. The first, essentially the Alabama Platform, called for congressional protection of slavery in the territories and dismissed popular sovereignty. The second, the Douglas position, augmented the Cincinnati Platform of four years earlier by declaring faith in the Supreme Court's authority to settle disputes over property, which was to say that the Democracy would abide by the Dred Scott decision. The third, proposed by Benjamin F. Butler, consisted of only a reiteration of the Cincinnati Platform, a policy that was at once the most sensible and most unrealistic of the three, because too many men had decided to make the Democracy stand for something. The Douglas men expected all of this up to a point, but what could not have failed to disturb them was that the Alabama Platform, supported by fifteen Southerners and California and Oregon, was the majority report of the committee.[46]

When Yancey came to the rostrum on Friday afternoon to argue for the majority report, the galleries exploded into a thunderous ovation that went on and on and reluctantly fell silent only to erupt again and again during his speech. Never again would he be this popular, and the enthusiasm he inspired might have surprised even him. His manner was determination itself; his message was simplicity crystallized: if protecting the South meant destroying the Democracy, then there was nothing left to be said. There was more to say, of course, and Yancey said it, chiding the North for complaining about Republican challengers it sought to beat by subverting the rights of the South. By the time Yancey was through, the convention and the galleries were in an uproar, and George Pugh betrayed the outrage and incredulity of the Douglas men over the way the convention had virtually gotten away from them. Expressing amazement that any Southerner could expect Northern politicians to commit political suicide to prove their loyalty to Southern slavery, he fell to ranting.

"Gentlemen of the South," he shouted, "you mistake us—you mistake us! We will not do it."[47]

When Saturday only produced heightening tension and passion with delegates making unforgettable and unforgivable declarations, the Douglas men used Sunday to good purpose, lining up the necessary support for the minority report. On Monday the convention accepted it in a nerve-racking, close vote of 165 to 138. The vote was so close, in fact, that Douglas's managers had to sweeten the pill with modifications that declared for the protection of slavery where it existed and that resolved to acquire Cuba. Too many Southerners had edged too far toward single-mindedness on the platform, and they sat ominously silent, sullen and brooding during the polling on the additions.[48]

Every eye must have glanced furtively, hopefully, or nervously toward the Alabama delegation during the voting, expecting at any moment for it to rise and leave Institute Hall. But the delegation did not move. Perhaps it had been a bluff after all, and the troublemakers now intended to block Douglas's nomination, perhaps to fight for Hunter. The scene had the look of Slidell and the administration's trickery about it; so with the high confidence of men who have just won a close contest, the Douglas forces turned loose Charles Stuart to finish the job.[49]

The reasons for Alabama's inactivity were complex, and they made the reasons for its eventual bolt labyrinthine. Over the weekend, Yancey changed his mind about leaving the convention and argued accordingly in a caucus of the Alabama delegation prior to Monday's polling. Perhaps he changed because administration men James A. Bayard, Slidell, and Bright, needing the Deep South for the Hunter candidacy, had made at last a successful plea for harmony. Also, Douglas operative George Sanders had informally approached Yancey with an interesting proposition. Sanders, a navy agent in New York, worked tirelessly, if unscrupulously, for the Little Giant's candidacy, usually by dispensing promises of position in exchange for support. In December 1859 during the beginning of the John Sherman controversy, he had offered William Porcher Miles help in a possible attempt to secure the House speakership, doing so with words opaque enough to be safe, yet clear enough to be meaningful.

In Charleston he was indefatigable, full of guile and evidently, if the Douglas forces are to be believed, working outside the regular Douglas machinery. Sanders offered Francis W. Pickens the vice-presidential nomination, and he offered Yancey the same thing. He further told the

Alabamian that Douglas would be dead within a half year after the election, something he could not have known but in which he strangely proved inaccurate by only a month.[50]

Whatever the truth or fiction of these machinations, by 29 April Yancey obviously decided to keep his personal options open. He had predicated his disruptive scheme on the belief that the Democracy, closed to him, would have to be destroyed. Then the two great powers of the party approached him, betraying weaknesses and providing openings. As Yancey counseled the delegation to ignore its instructions, former governor John A. Winston suddenly insisted that delegates had to follow those instructions. Winston's advocacy of withdrawal confused an already confused situation because he was one of the few Alabamians in Charleston who supported Stephen A. Douglas. At the January state convention he had denounced the Alabama Platform, but his subsequent activities provided evidence for the motives behind his advice in Charleston. Privately, Winston counseled young Anthony W. Dillard, an Alabama delegate relieved at the prospect of disregarding the delegation's instructions, to quit the convention for Douglas's sake. Upon his return to Alabama, Winston broke from the new state convention to sponsor the Douglas delegation to Baltimore.[51]

Winston did not, however, lead the Alabama delegation out of Institute Hall, and neither did Yancey. Stuart of Michigan successfully provoked Leroy P. Walker into the shouting match that ended with Walker and his delegation stalking out to the streets of Charleston. The Mississippi, Louisiana, South Carolina, Florida, Texas, Arkansas, and Georgia delegations followed, leaving some of their members behind. The moderate South Carolina delegation, which never had any intention of leaving the convention, followed Louisiana with a quiet, grim air of inevitability. The taunts and hisses from the galleries drove the followers of Orr out, and as Barnwell Rhett, Jr., later remarked, "If they had not retired, they would have been mobbed, I believe." Moreover, if this large exodus did not signal cooperation, always the prerequisite for the moderate South Carolinian, what did?[52]

The bolters gathered in St. Andrew's Hall, hastily declared themselves the Constitutional Democracy, improvised the adoption of the majority report, and then waited for the regular party to call them back. A few Southern stragglers came, but there was no peace offering because the remainder of the party in Institute Hall struggled on for a few hours and finally adjourned to try again in Baltimore on 18 June. In a day already too full of stunning developments, this last one shattered the illusion of Southern unity at St. Andrew's Hall. The members of the new Constitutional Democracy disintegrated into angry recrimination directed more or less at Yancey for having brought them to ruin. The entire affair began to resemble a debacle, and radicals blamed Yancey for that, too. Barnwell Rhett, Jr., watching the event with his father, scorned the Alabamian's want of "nerve" and "leadership." "Yancey is not capable in that way," he concluded, "however great an orator and debater."[53]

The best and most the gathering could do was agree to go to Richmond after seeking the sense of their respective state party organizations. As it happened, the delegates returning home would have some answering to do. Moderate opinion held that the best way to accomplish the election of a "Black Republican" was to persist in Southern withdrawal from the Democracy, and most of the South was none too happy about it. The Democracy was rightly seen as the only party capable of holding the Union together, and suspicions about the fealty of Northern party brethren diminished now under scrutiny. Northerners did not object to the ideas of the South, became the wide thinking, but rather to Southern methods to protect those ideas. The radicals were seen as pressing the issue needlessly, and moderates, after having time to reflect, wanted no part of a Richmond gathering. As Georgian Thomas Butler King remarked, "I am of the opinion that it will be wise to send delegates to . . . the convention in Baltimore and postpone the movement to Richmond."[54]

In Georgia, in fact, rather serious divisions marked by angry accusation crowded the county meetings of the Democracy wherein locals squinted at explanations of the delegation's behavior at Charleston.[55] Howell Cobb said the unacceptable platform justified the walkout. Toombs agreed, stating, "Our greatest danger today is that the Union will survive the Constitution," which was beside the point, as Alexander Stephens implied when he quietly thought the bolt, though perhaps justified, was nevertheless stupid.[56] It did not help that Cobb's and Toombs's position, bearing too much the stamp of Buchanan's animus against Douglas, resembled that of the radicals. Many Georgians perceived the fire-eaters as only "ambitious politicians . . . trying to gain notoriety for themselves."[57]

The recalled state convention invigorated the argument. Gathered at Milledgeville on 4 June, it approved the withdrawal and returned the original delegation with instructions to again withdraw if the platform left slavery unprotected in the territories. Moderates led by Herschel V. Johnson broke from this convention to send a Douglas delegation to Baltimore.[58]

Mississippi under the guidance of John Pettus made an elaborate show of accelerating a program of military preparedness as plans progressed for sending a delegation to Baltimore. The state convention on 30 May displayed a considerably muted belligerence. An attempt sponsored by Wiley P. Harris, a stalwart supporter of Gallatin Brown, to bind the delegation to Richmond first and Baltimore only on its own discretion failed in a compromise put forward by the Davis forces. Delegates would attend Baltimore and then proceed to Richmond only if the regular party suffered another disruption.[59]

Yancey in Alabama fared no better but no worse. Support unified behind him in the southern part of the state, but north Alabama Unionists finally roused themselves. The state convention on 4 June resisted his attempts to prescribe attendance only at Richmond, and the best he could do was have the delegation accredited to both. Simultaneously, conservatives, having first tried at Selma, met in Montgomery under the leadership of a resurgent Montgomery Regency that, combined with Old Line Whigs, would send to Baltimore an uninstructed delegation expected to support Douglas.[60]

Although Alabama led the walkout, many still saw South Carolina as the firebrand, the rabble-rouser, although this was not a true estimation of the nature of the state. Visiting Columbia in May, Edmund Ruffin found little enthusiasm for immediate secession.[61] Many South Carolinians believed the highest priority was to unite disparate party elements to meet the coming ordeal. Surprisingly, the Rhett faction did not present an obstacle to unity, and Rhett himself withdrew a *Mercury* editorial calling for a public meeting. Instead he agreed with the idea of another general convention. To make sure that he would not have the chance to clog any conciliatory initiative, however, moderates sought to exclude him from the convention.[62]

The Democratic central committee did call for the convention to include even anticonvention party members, especially after they had promised to behave. Charleston did not want Rhett in Columbia for the meeting, but St. John's Colleton Parish obliged him. Two months before, James Henry Hammond had gloated that the Rhetts were politically dead in Carolina. At the June convention, however, Rhett was at the head of the St. John's Colleton delegation, and son Barnwell Rhett, Jr., was there from Charleston and brother Edmund was there from St. Helens, all of them very much alive and designing to capture the party. Orr, on the other hand, was not there.[63]

Convention proponents swiftly grabbed control of the meeting but just as quickly lost it over a technical point that allowed state electoral districts rather than federal congressional districts to choose at-large delegates. Low Country parishes thereafter dictated the choices for the delegation, and when they elected Rhett over Isaac W. Hayne, the convention broke wide open. Names were called, fists shaken, and finally the nationalists stormed out of the meeting. Rhett—obviously his blood congealed over the similarities to the dreadful error of 1851—called after them with cajoling reassurances that he would strive for reconciliation and that he knew if secession occurred that the Union would be reconstructed, though this obviously was not very encouraging to anyone. None of the Charleston delegation would go to Richmond, nor would the new delegation go to Baltimore. The nationalists quickly descended into bewildered disorganization as they whined and complained then washed their hands of an affair that was actually a hollow victory for Rhett. By June 1860, most Carolinians did not consider it a question of policy, but of men, and Rhett's unpopularity with the Up Country and the rest of the South was exactly what everyone wanted to avoid. Secession sentiment was not pervasive, and withdrawal from the Democracy was not yet tantamount to disunion. Rhett was told to keep his mouth shut.[64]

"I do not think," wrote John Letcher, "that any party can survive the leadership of two such politicians as Rhett and Yancey." Having discerned their purpose as the destruction of the Democracy, Letcher expected cooler heads to unite against them.[65] Perhaps that would be Virginia's role, although Edmund Ruffin, meeting with James Seddon on the eve of the Richmond Convention, expressed mutual disgust over the Old Dominion's refusal to withdraw from the Charleston Convention. A Carolina friend, the Reverend John Bachman, goaded Ruffin with taunting questions. He asked about Abraham Lincoln's nomination, "Will old Virginia nestle under the wing of that black buzzard? Are all her great statesmen dead?"[66] Surveying the landscape, Ruffin rather had to say they were, and for a time he considered transplanting his family southward, perhaps to Florida. It must have galled him, but finally he told Alabama and South Carolina delegates arriving in Richmond that they should support Hunter's nomination to court Virginia's support. Visiting Yancey, Ruffin was discouraged by the Alabamian's reluctance to talk and noted that rumors painted him as a trimmer, holding his tongue to keep from impetuously charting his course.[67] Better, to Ruffin's thinking, was James Mason's prediction of "the end of the government" and Lawrence Keitt's promise that Lincoln's election assured South Carolina's secession. Ruffin warranted that the Palmetto State "would not be alone long."[68]

South Carolina was nearly alone in Richmond after a brief 11 June meeting of the bolters accomplished only a temporary organization and then adjourned on the following day so that all of the delegations, except South Carolina's and Florida's, could go to Baltimore. So Rhett and the Carolina delegation waited with other isolated renegades in Richmond while the National Democracy in Baltimore completed the last, torturous stages of its self-destruction. When the full South—Virginia included—reappeared in Richmond on 26 June, it was to affirm rather than accomplish the nominations of John Breckinridge and Joseph Lane. The Southern Democrats had withdrawn from the Democracy again, this time over a dispute about the original Georgia delegation's credentials, and had rushed to Maryland's Institute Hall to choose their champions and adopt the majority platform of Charleston.[69]

For Rhett it was both provident and humiliating that the final split and nomination of Breckinridge and Lane occurred this way. He probably could not have survived the renunciation of a still careful South Carolina had he taken any direct part in these affairs. On the other hand, his absurd unimportance in Richmond demonstrated his insignifance. He returned to South Carolina chastened and refrained from making any disunion speeches. Even the *Mercury* quieted down.[70]

It was a wise yet not altogether successful course. The potential harm of his support made even his calmest statements objects of suspicion. Hammond, always on the watch for threats to his coveted Senate seat, warned that the worst that could happen to Breckinridge would be exuberant support from Rhett and the *Mercury.* When Rhett made a noncommittal speech for the Constitutional Democracy's candidate, Hammond observed that from anyone else it would have been effective, "but with [Rhett's] name there is besides just enough Rhettism in it to make it useless out of So. Ca."[71] Actually, it was equally useless in the Palmetto State, where moderates and radicals alike, for different reasons, wanted nothing to do with Rhett or his harmful influence. Hammond observed these apprehensions and warned that Orr remained too strong for radicals to think him powerless. "I would not taunt him into doing wrong," Hammond counseled the radicals; rather, they should meet him firmly and fairly without automatic and useless charges of "Orrism."[72]

The ground moved beneath the feet of most Southerners after the disruption of the Democracy. Hammond, never too sure of his footing anyway, characterized the confusion of those who realized that something momentously dreadful was occurring yet clung to the illusion that the campaign of 1860 was only a more complicated version of politics-as-usual. Hammond was the clearest example of the antebellum Southern habit of accommodation within ambiguous boundaries, a habit manifested by men saying only half of what they believed and believing only half of what they said. Hammond developed the practice into an art while portraying it as statesmanship. In 1858, he said that Southern expansion into Kansas was a deluded contest with the North that the South could not win; and on 4 March 1858, eight years to the day after Calhoun's famous swan song against the Compromise of 1850, he delivered his supreme bid for the old man's place in words and manner calculated to deliver him the prize. To all appearances, Hammond's "Cotton is King" speech accomplished the goal because, as the *Mercury* noted, with "one bold stroke of Senatorial eloquence" he had leaped "into the almost inaccessible niche occupied by Calhoun."[73]

But Hammond was not Calhoun, nor could he occupy his place, because Hammond did not believe in anything except himself. He had reversed his attitudes on too many questions. After trying to isolate his slaves from pernicious outside influences in the 1840s, he finally gave up while claiming that such influences did no harm anyway. He first railed against the Wilmot Proviso, then declared it a nonissue. His stand on the Kansas question bore the stamp of this habit because by the late 1850s, one had to insist that the system and indeed the forces of change so clearly aligned against traditional Southern institutions could do those interests no harm.[74] He therefore watched with unfeigned disgust, but also with petulant alarm, the momentum of that movement that insisted otherwise, and he castigated it, with some justification, as a reflection of its instigators' ambition. Gallatin Brown's slave code resolutions, Hammond muttered, were the stalking horse for the Mississippian's presidential ambitions. Yancey, wishing to control the Alabama Democracy, concocted a plan to destroy his nemesis, the national party, then went to Unionism again, skulking into Baltimore, all for personal gain.[75]

And while these observations were true, they overlooked that the Douglas blaze designed to drive pesky radicals away had been ignited with a frightening unawareness of how much combustible material lay around the National Democracy. The conflagration that resulted was larger than moderates and radicals in both the North and the South, and the half-light of it cast distorted shadows across ill-illuminated opportunism in both camps. Men became less concerned about putting out the fire and more obsessed with what to do when it was over.

And in that massive heat, Hammond and the rest of the South felt the ground move beneath their feet. Having stood for very little for so long, true moderates and nationalists and opportunists alike, compromised to their earlobes, found themselves unable to stand at all in the summer of 1860. They would not regain their feet until the nation had been broken.

CHAPTER NINE

"Instruments in the Hands of God"

Only one surety existed in the presidential campaign of 1860. A Republican victory would compel the South, or part of it, to secede from the Union. More than four years' worth of radical propaganda had pounded the idea into the public mind. In 1856 men who had previously scorned disunion saw the Republican party as an actual, vivified attack.[1] If Frémont were in the White House, the reasoning had gone, free-state fanaticism would be in the Senate as well, the unlimited admission of free states would follow, and abolitionists appointed to the Supreme Court would uphold abolitionist laws enacted by the legislature and enforced by a federal army "mostly commanded by northern officers."[2]

That Southern nightmare became real in 1860. By the end of July, many in the South, anxiously expecting Lincoln's triumph, began advocating a Southern confederacy.[3] Moderate James Chesnut, Jr., who helped fight Rhett's extremism in 1851 and who won his place in the U.S. Senate in 1858 because of his nationalism, now believed that Lincoln's election would require secession.[4] Also, Orr's statements that Lincoln's election would require secession marked a serious shift in his position, if not his reflexively Southern thinking.[5] In Georgia, Howell Cobb's younger brother, Thomas R. R., a confirmed Unionist, became so disillusioned by autumn that he admitted his error in accusing fire-eaters of bad faith. Moderates without principles, he charged, would allow the Republicans to destroy slavery and Southern society. With evangelical zeal he embraced the cause of Georgia's secession as though it were a moral crusade.[6] A mass meeting in Charlotte, North Carolina, in late September saw old Bedford Brown, nearly seventy years old, "still vigorous in intellect, and full of fire and zeal for a righteous cause." That cause was the disunion he had so vehemently protested ten years before.[7]

In Mississippi, Governor Pettus gradually increased the caliber of his fiery barrages until he declared that the telegraph wires bringing news of Lincoln's victory would send out a call for a special session of the Mississippi legislature. Under similarly responsible auspices elsewhere in the South, demagoguery in all camps reached uncontrollable vehemence. Even John Bell's Constitutional Union candidacy, which was a sad third- or really, fourth-party attempt to calm the waters with a platform that consisted of only the Constitution and called for the enforcement of the laws, was painted with the same brush that tarred the Republicans. Southerners scorned Bell's position as nothing more than "a show of glittering generalities, hiding much sin and old fogeyism."[8] But Douglas rated the main vilification. John Slidell said that Douglas's "object now is very plainly to break down the Democratic Party, elect Lincoln, and place himself at the head of the Anti-Slavery Party in 1864."[9]

With more justification, both Constitutional Unionists and Douglas Democrats charged that the Breckinridge candidacy wanted to elect Abraham Lincoln. In Virginia, the fearlessly nasty John Minor Botts, so despised by Ruffin and other radicals, came very close to the truth with these charges.[10] The radicals did desire Lincoln's election to force an issue already well forced by the campaign. Breckinridge men who dreamily insisted that his candidacy represented something other than a stalking horse for radical secessionists turned upon the radicals and denounced them, too. Lawrence O'Bryan Branch, a North Carolina Congressman and a Breckinridge man, saw the disunion issue sticking to Breckinridge only because of Rhett's and Yancey's "machinations." "When I speak on the stump," he said, "I feel inclined to repudiate entirely Rhett & Yancey and their doctrines."[11]

Amidst the swirl of denunciation and countercondemnation, Lincoln seemed largely ignored, but only because he was so great an evil it did not need explication. Albert Gallatin Brown, in mild disfavor again consequent to the resurgence of the Davis wing of the party in Mississippi, played it safe by reviling Lincoln. But he neither thoroughly castigated Douglas nor endorsed Breckinridge.[12] And, of course, Brown's hedging only made the surreal confusion of the campaign in the South appear more foolish to the North. The *Atlantic Monthly* mused that Yancey's "throwing a solitary somerset will hardly turn the continent head over heels."[13] Such Northern disdain obviously born of ignorance could not have alarmed Henry Hilliard more. The North apparently did not realize that Yancey and Rhett had become dangerously influential. But Stephen Douglas did, and he travelled excessively, especially in the South, not so much campaigning for anything or anyone as arguing against the dreaded wave of secession he knew would greet Lincoln's victory. On election eve, he was in Montgomery to give a confused speech in a hoarse voice to a crowd so aroused by hatred that it pelted him with rotten food. Douglas knew exactly how dangerous radicals were.[14]

But the agitation flowed not only from radicals. The Association of 1860 originated in Charleston to sponsor propaganda designed to guarantee secession in the wake of Lincoln's election. Of course, it attracted radicals like Edmund Ruffin, who happily distributed the numerous pamphlets, but its founders were influential, prominent men heretofore distinguished by their moderation. John Townsend, a planter on Edisto Island, had been a Unionist in all of Carolina's previous sectional crises, but in 1860, he cooperated in calls for secession with the noisiest radicals.[15]

Rumors of Negro insurrections, both impending and actual, helped spur the formation of propaganda associations. Johnson J. Hooper, an editor of a Know-Nothing newspaper in Montgomery, Alabama, told Ruffin that slaves all over the South had cached strychnine and plotted murder and mayhem. Ruffin grimly hoped that any uprisings would occur in "the dull spirit & lethargic body" of Georgia to spur it to disunion.[16] Yet it was in Texas that a mysterious series of fires that bore sinister evidence of arson hurt Unionism in the northern part of the state. The fires resurrected the specter of John Brown and so doomed attempts to fuse Union support against Breckinridge. Further, when fires in Dallas, Denton, and Pilot Point raged into the second week in July, lynchings and vigilante justice marked a white vengeance that sent Northerners, blamed for it all, fleeing from the state. George Bickley, a blustering fanatic whose annexationist dreams envisioned the creation "of a great Democratic monarchy . . . which shall vie in grandeur with the Old Roman Empire," formed the Knights of the Golden Circle ostensibly to guard against abolition plots. In South Carolina, calmer and more responsible men did the same, forming "Minute Men" militia to maintain vigilance against insurrection and prepare for the coercion that would challenge secession.[17]

Such disturbances and the reactions they prompted profited the fire-eaters. Radicals were in the enviable position of getting what they wanted whatever they did. They could support Breckinridge and do him damage, or they could be silent while others divided and alarmed Southern sentiment. Both circumstances helped Abraham Lincoln, whose election assured an irresistible move for secession. So unique local concerns had more to do with each fire-eater's activities. Rhett remained silent, Gallatin Brown hedged, and Wigfall blustered. Yancey, however, took an entirely different course. He toured the nation.

The only similarity Yancey could claim to Stephen Douglas, who was a candidate attempting at this late hour to unfurl the banner of statesmanship, was that they both travelled the North and South in the fall of 1860. Yancey was not a candidate. He was, at least in the North, a curiosity, and there was nothing statesmanlike in his equivocal speeches that were fashioned to fit whatever situation he encountered. He said he undertook the tour to disabuse Northerners of the notion that Southerners wanted Lincoln elected so they could secede. In 1858 he delivered a wild address at New York's Cooper Institute that only alienated his audience. It seemed in 1860 that he would accomplish little more. He began in the South, which would have been a problem—as Douglas discovered—if consistency had been a point of pride for Yancey. He first went to Memphis, where he spoke for four hours in spite of threats against his life, then to Kingston, Georgia, and Knoxville, Tennessee. In Knoxville the formidable Unionist Parson W. G. Brownlow confronted Yancey with a simple question: what will you do if Lincoln wins? Yancey eluded the question by asking Brownlow whom he supported. The Tennessean stated he was for Bell and the Constitution, and he continued, "When the secessionists go to Washington to dethrone Lincoln, I am for seizing a bayonet and forming an army to resist such an attack, and they shall walk over my dead body on their way." The response provoked Yancey, and he showed it. He would follow Alabama, he shouted, and if Brownlow got in the way then he could be obliged as to the dead body.[18]

This was not a good start, but Yancey learned from it. In New York on 10 October, he refused to speculate on the chance of secession in the event of Lincoln's election; and his apparent candor at Faneuil Hall in

Boston won him respectful attention similar to that given him at Albany, Syracuse, Rochester, and Cincinnati. Back in the South again on the eve of the election, he basked in the glow of high acclaim. Edmund Ruffin lauded him on his inimitable eloquence, calling him the new Patrick Henry.[19]

Some who completely opposed secession before Lincoln's election became avid supporters of it afterward. An expectant mother talked proudly of having her child in a Southern republic rather than "the detestable Union."[20] But there was still a residue of confusion from the campaign. David Gavin wailed before the election, "God alone is our hope! I write it with a full sense of our helplessness." R. M. T. Hunter, only ten days before South Carolina seceded, calmly remarked how presidential elections would "break down the government at no distant day, if something cannot be done to quiet them."[21]

Actually then, for a substantial number of Southerners, especially those with influence, the election only increased the uncertainty. "It will not do to wait on the politicians," one observer wrote. "They are very good judges of the weather, but very bad shelters in a storm."[22] As if to prove this, South Carolina's governor, William Henry Gist, sent a series of letters to six fellow Southern governors in late October and early November. Like Whitemarsh Seabrook ten years before, Gist wished to assess the possible actions of Carolina's neighbors if Lincoln won, especially whether they would follow Carolina's secession. The answers were not encouraging. Governor Thomas E. Moore of Louisiana said no to Gist's appeal, and Governor John W. Ellis of North Carolina was anxious over even the arrival of Gist's letter. "It is the desire of South Carolina," Gist had written, "that some other State should take the lead or at least move simultaneously with her." Senators Thomas L. Clingman and Thomas Bragg had already advised Ellis that nothing would happen after Lincoln's election and that everyone would submit. Now here was Gist saying that "if a single state secedes, [South Carolina] will follow her." He had to admit, however, that the Palmetto State would not go out alone without assurances of cooperation before or after the fact.[23] Joseph E. Brown, meanwhile, declared that Georgia would wait for Republicans to pursue an aggressive policy. Governors Perry of Florida, Moore of Alabama, and Pettus of Mississippi said their states would follow another's lead.[24]

It was the great uncertainty of Southern unity and cooperation again,

just as always it had been before. Yet a few things, not all of them immediately evident, had changed. Barnwell Rhett, for one, no longer worried
over the attitude of the Upper South. He believed that Virginia and her
neighbors would not act until forced to do so, and he was sure they would
then choose the South.[25]

The Carolina public had reflected caution in the midst of turmoil by
electing a conservative legislature, but Lincoln's election also changed
this. The legislature met calmly but tensely, its moderate majority grimly
aware that events would require decisive action sooner or later. Nobody
talked about a Southern confederacy, but Gist assured that Carolina acting alone would spur others to action too. And A. P. Aldrich, head of the
House Committee on Federal Relations, reported that each hour the telegraph brought more encouragement for action.[26]

Indeed it did. Confused for only a moment, the legislature had its
example the day after Lincoln's victory when Judge Andrew G. McGrath
of the Federal District Court resigned. His was the first of a flood of with-
drawals from national service that included James Connor, United States
attorney for the district of South Carolina, and Charleston port collector
William F. Colcock.[27] All were from Charleston, but there were others
as well, and not only from South Carolina.

James Chesnut resigned his Senate seat; so did Georgian Robert
Toombs. Finally, James Henry Hammond joined the tide, including himself among those "great asses" who, like the Japanese, "when insulted rip
open their own bowels."[28] It was a difficult move for Hammond. Holding
to his nationalism for too long a time, he could not now claim ascendancy in a movement he had so long resisted. His effort to play Calhoun
had failed. "I cannot doubt," Hammond had ventured an opinion on Calhoun's moderation in 1844, "that at this moment he is endeavoring to
sacrifice the South . . . on the altar of his ambition."[29] Those words must
have served as a haunting epitaph for Hammond's own career in November 1860.

Hammond could take some immediate if cold comfort that his misfortune did not signal Rhett's great advantage. While Rhett would enjoy
the people's approbation during the ensuing tumult, even his own camp
tried to exclude him from participating in calls for secession now that
the moment had arrived.[30] When the legislature on 9 November, goaded
by those federal resignations of prominent Carolinians, called for a sovereign convention, crowds lauded and cheered Rhett as they raised the
Palmetto flag over the offices of the *South Carolinian* in Columbia. On

Ruffin's suggestion a crescent flag to represent the whole South soon replaced the banner. Although it carried only one star to signify Carolina, Ruffin hoped that "others may soon be added."[31]

This hope and the appearance of the old dispute in the legislature over separate state action versus cooperation led the radicals to promote harmony. The legislature scheduled the convention to meet later than the radicals wanted with elections on 8 January and the convention one week later. Ruffin crowed over "the inauguration of Disunion," or at least the independence "of S. C. if of no other state," and that flag fluttering over the newspaper office seemed to indicate the truth of this. However, disturbing signs of caution from one quarter and of impetuosity from another did not look good for fire-eater fortunes.[32]

"They will find it much easier to destroy a government than to make one," Gavin wryly observed from his Colleton plantation.[33] In Charleston, those involved in commerce, as evidenced by businessman Henry Gourdin, reconsidered precipitous action and gradually began to protest a headlong rush into secession.[34] Much of the Up Country believed that if Carolina acted alone, all would end in failure.[35] Meanwhile, excitable popular reaction flared, especially in Charleston. When Major Robert Anderson, commander of the federal garrison at Fort Moultrie in the harbor, tried to remove the stores from the United States arsenal in Charleston, angry Carolina militia stopped him. "I am very sorry for this occurrence," noted Ruffin, who worried that such belligerence would illegally dissolve the Union before the convention could do so legitimately with an ordinance.[36]

The fragile unanimity of the legislature's call for a convention confirmed radical fears over the Rhett problem. Rhett's haughtiness and the *Mercury*'s attempts to force immediate secession damaged efforts to fuse previously conflicting separate-state and cooperationist advocates. When the newspaper demanded secession pledges from convention candidates, conservatives instantly reacted. Led mainly by Memminger, moderates sponsored a proliferation of tickets for Charleston.

William Porcher Miles evinced the disarray this wrought on the radical camp. Lincoln's election disgusted him, and he urged abandoning the farcical "blusters and threats and manifestoes and 'Resolutions.'" Miles believed what Rhett had warned: the North did not think that the South could be even "Kicked into disunion."[37] But in the ensuing weeks, Miles became uncomfortable that many considered him as nothing more that a cipher within the Rhett faction. He said that if Rhett's people believed this, they could remove him from consideration for the convention. Already departed from Washington, Miles found an urgent telegram from Rhett awaiting him in Columbia. "Don't allow your name to be withdrawn from the ticket," it begged. "There is no reason for it & it will do you irreparable injury."[38]

Thus Rhett's influence faded before stable men like A. G. McGrath, Memminger, Orr, and Chesnut. Charleston's vote for delegates to the secession convention dropped Rhett to seventh place, far behind front-runner McGrath. The legislature in regular session compounded the rebuke by placing him a distant third in the gubernatorial contest behind the victor, Francis W. Pickens. Ruffin described Pickens as "an empty boaster" and a bad choice because Carolina needed "at this time one of her best men to fill the place of Governor."[39] But Barnwell Rhett was not to be that man. It did not necessarily have anything to do with Rhett's views. Pickens, too, had declared for immediate secession, pointing up more than ever that Rhett's fate was a personal reproach.

Rhett's importance was already questionable as well. Circumstances surrounding the legislature's moving the dates for the Carolina Convention three weeks before serve as an example. After it settled on the January dates, the legislature received word from Milledgeville that Governor Brown had recommended calling a Georgia Convention; then came the news of Robert Toombs's resignation. The legislature, stunned by a parade of events moving entirely too fast, finally succumbed to an agitated Charleston delegation's demand for an early convention. A large celebration between Charlestonians and visiting Savannahns to commemorate the opening of a coastal railroad stimulated those demands because by 10:30 P.M. on 9 November the revelry of this festivity had been reported to the city's delegation in Columbia as representing much more than commercial amity. So the legislature changed the dates to have the vote on 6 December and the convention on 17 December.[40] Rhett had virtually nothing to do with this radical success.

He also had nothing to do with the convention ultimately meeting in Charleston rather than Columbia. A smallpox scare forced its removal on 18 December to Charleston, where a martial spirit had taken hold; cannon boomed from the battery and cadets marched amidst a general mood of anxious gaiety.[41]

By the second week in December, Jefferson Davis, R. M. T. Hunter, and David Yulee endorsed Carolina's immediate secession. James

Buchanan wrote Pickens, "Whilst any hope remains that this [the secession of South Carolina] may be prevented or even retarded, . . . it is my duty to exert all the means in my power to avert so dread a catastrophe." He was sending Caleb Cushing, he said, to confer with leaders of the state.[42]

Buchanan's attempt to stall the dread catastrophe was futile. Carolina's conduct was set even beyond the power of Rhett or Orr, let alone Cushing. The convention met at noon on 20 December and took less than an hour to approve unanimously an ordinance of secession; then it adjourned until 7:00 P.M. When it regathered in Secession Hall—renamed by delegates that day—members of the Senate and the House sat on either side of the floor, and spectators packed the galleries. The old Lutheran clergyman, John Bachman, forty-five years a Charlestonian but still bearing a trace of his New York accent, opened with a prayer. Then General David F. Jamison, lawyer and planter, close friend of Gilmore Simms, organized the signing. It took more than two hours, during which cheers and applause, prompted by nervous anticipation, sporadically punctuated the event. Finally Jamison held the document up and bellowed that the sovereign state of South Carolina was free and independent. The gathering exploded. Men's hats rocketed high in the air to fall among other men waving theirs amidst a lacy bustle of ladies' handkerchiefs. Outside parades began, and bands competed with muttering cannon from far-off batteries. Bonfires reached skyward while rockets zoomed up through the dark and fireworks cracked across cobblestones. Cushing had arrived that afternoon to counsel patience, but by the time these raucous celebrations occurred he had already quit this impatient, foreign country. He had taken the next train North.[43]

Two rival papers from the convention explained the causes for secession. Christopher Memminger's *Declaration* hinged on recent developments that included the Brown raid and the election of Lincoln, but Barnwell Rhett instead offered an *Address to the Slave-Holding States* that urged the creation of a Southern confederacy. The constitutional experiment failed, he insisted, because Northern perfidy employed a tyrannical majority. In short, the issue was whether or not the South had the right to govern itself, and Rhett framed his argument to invite as close a comparison as possible between Carolina secession and the American Revolution.[44]

Meanwhile, practical matters occupied the convention. It elected in secret session Robert Barnwell, former Governor (and slave-trade advocate) James H. Adams, and James L. Orr to travel to Washington to discuss terms of separation from the federal government. Significantly, Adams was the closest thing to a radical in this moderate group.[45] Rhett was not even considered.

The news spread. Lawrence Keitt, attending a social for Buchanan, jumped up and down while shouting "Thank God!" as he waved the telegram that had brought the news.[46] Others in Carolina itself were not so ebullient. In Society Hill, aged John Nicholas Williams, son of former Governor David R. Williams, became so incensed by firearm salutes outside his door that he grabbed a fowling piece and discharged it in the direction of the shooters.[47] But there could be no doubt that events shaping the popular will forced secession. The fire-eaters and recent converts to their cause—the Association of 1860 being an example—only contributed to the impetuous, precipitous speed of the decision. As James Henry Hammond later observed, the Rhetts and their followers "were instruments in the hands of God (as Judas was)—though it was denied me to see it then."[48]

South Carolina after the momentous declaration of secession became curiously quiescent, as though suffering from anticlimax. The federal post office still delivered the mail, for instance, making the state seem "neither flesh nor fish, neither in nor out of the Union."[49] A visitor to Charleston, finding it peculiarly quiet, suspected that New York City was more agitated about Carolina's secession. While quiet, however, Carolinians were very determined, especially in the face of faint rumors of war.[50]

Moderate Southern feeling even outside of Carolina adopted an attitude of resignation that placed more confidence now in providence than in men. In North Carolina, Platt Dickinson noted that Southerners at last were united in the idea that Lincoln's election would be the last great injustice the North would perpetrate on them. There had to be a compromise proffered, he thought; there always had been one before. When no feasible compromise appeared, bewildered moderates in the South gradually turned toward the fire-eaters.[51] From Louisiana young William H. Tunnard wrote in amazement that the North could affect such ignorance about the cause for the crisis. He prepared to cut himself off from all his relations in the North, and he was sorry that his diploma, earned in 1856, had come from Kenyon College in Ohio.[52]

Tunnard wrote from Baton Rouge a little over a month after Louisiana's secession. He described the making of cartridges and knapsacks, and the militia's four hours of daily drill. In fact, amid the springtime fragrance of the Louisiana countryside, he described the preparations for a war that too many Southerners had come to see as inevitable.[53] The time had been when talk of war alarmed most of the South into caution, but that too had changed by the beginning of 1861. North Carolinian Thomas Jefferson Green drafted a rambling, angry letter to Buchanan that mocked, snarled at, and counseled against the president's attempting to coerce seceded states back to his "octonegnairian [*sic*] authority."[54] Of course, the aged and weary Pennsylvanian intended to do no such thing, at least overtly; but he also did nothing to reassure that the national government would remain idle. Green was dismayed that Buchanan allowed Robert Anderson, a mere major, to remain in command after evacuating Fort Moultrie for Sumter in Charleston Harbor.[55]

Charleston, the site of the disrupted Democratic Convention in April 1860, a year later would stage the opening act of the American Civil War. As early as June 1860 Edmund Ruffin had concerned himself with Charleston's fortifications. He thought they should consist "of small batteries of a few heavy cannon, behind temporary earth works . . . to oppose attacking or passing ships of war."[56] Ruffin happened to be on a steamer departing Charleston on 26 December, the night Anderson quit Moultrie for Sumter. Four miles past Moultrie the old Virginian heard two loud cannon reports following quick upon each other. He thought it "must have been a signal for something."[57]

Actually, it signalled the kind of crisis for which the fire-eaters had been hoping. The radicals lived with the dreadful apprehension, even as the tide of secession swept across the Gulf States, that some compromise would bring it all to naught, that the hollow truces and empty promises Rhett had envisioned occurring at the Democratic Convention in Charleston would once again emerge to effect reconciliation. Rhett loathed the thought and wanted something to happen to remove it from consideration. Miles also "had some nervous anxiety" over the prospect's gaining momentum. In early April an alarmed Ruffin heard that the convention meeting in Montgomery, Alabama, to form a Confederate government had worked under the burdensome knowledge that no state except South Carolina wanted to dissolve the Union and that a general referendum would favor reconciliation. He grimly noted that something would have to happen soon. Miles already had the advice from Alabama Congressman James L. Pugh: start a war; then matters will have gone too far.[58]

"I fear if S.C. takes Fort Sumter by force and fires the first shot," Ruffin's daughter in Kentucky wrote him, "then the *South* will commence the war, and if there is a war, I want the North to have all the blame."[59] From his eldest son, Ruffin heard that it would be best not to do anything "hasty" and that it would be better to "try negotiations first; it may save a bloody civil war." Yet young Ruffin admitted that bloodshed would "unite the whole South." For the fire-eaters, this was precisely the point.[60]

The impetuosity that marked South Carolina's secession spilled over in this crisis and contributed to it. "Revolutions do not admit of long pauses," wrote North Carolina Governor John Ellis. Governor Pickens in South Carolina agreed. He especially wanted a Confederate government formed that would take over the touchy military situation in Charleston Harbor, a situation that every day pointed more toward an outbreak of hostilities.[61]

"We might feel the devastating hand of war," Carolinian Armistead Burt proclaimed to the Mississippi Secession Convention. "We might endure privations—but, [with] the South united, no power on earth can conquer it. Our enemies may burn down every house, and kill every man and the very women will defend it."[62] That was exactly what was worrying Governor Pettus. The vision of women manning smoldering barricades that were littered with the corpses of husbands and fathers surely sobered him. Bold as he acted in public, Pettus was not foolhardy. After Lincoln's election he called the Mississippi congressional delegation together on 22 November to advise him. Senators Davis and Brown, still hardly on speaking terms, and Representatives L. Q. C. Lamar, Reuben Davis, Ortho R. Singleton, and William Barksdale agreed that a convention should meet, but then the group divided. Separate state action was another matter, and Jefferson Davis, Brown, and Lamar wanted to await concerted action by the South. But Reuben Davis, Singleton, Barksdale, and Pettus carried the majority, and the radical line came out of the caucus. The cautious senators and "Moody" Lamar consented with trepidation.[63]

Jefferson Davis's march toward secession was a slow, deliberate one. At first he counseled South Carolinians to be patient, an unpopular position with the radicals.[64] Brown, on the other hand, back in the Senate, took new heart while watching Louis Wigfall taunt Douglas, and he reversed the position he had taken at the Pettus meeting. In a caucus of Southern senators, he joined Slidell's call for immediate secession. Davis still resisted, wanting to wait at least until March before taking any action. Then the failure of the compromise proposals in Congress—especially that of the Committee of Thirteen upon which he had reluctantly agreed to serve—convinced him that secession was the only course. He was perhaps the closest thing the South had to another Calhoun amidst a field of pretenders to that vacant throne; at least many Northerners and quite a few Southerners, Davis among them, thought so. Rather like Calhoun, he came to his position slowly, but once there, he was stolid. Never a fire-eater, Davis by 5 January 1861 was nonetheless indistinguishable in his position from radical secessionists.[65]

In spite of Davis's resolve, some fire-eaters in Mississippi, principally Governor Pettus, began to have second thoughts. If Louisiana and Alabama did not secede, Mississippi could be landlocked. Pettus sent commissioners to both states to report on possibilities as well as cajole, bolster, and persuade. Otherwise the governor was slowing down, largely because Buchanan had not delayed at all the construction of federal fortifications on Ship Island just off Biloxi in the Gulf. Pettus queried Davis, asking if caution might not be the best plan given these fears and developments, but Davis, committed at last, said no—"The moral power of steady progress must not be impaired."[66] Regardless of any moral power, steady progress was maintained. Meeting on 7 January, the Mississippi Secession Convention withdrew the state from the Union two days later.[67]

Only the most determined Unionists could resist the winds of cooperation that now whipped across the Lower South. In Florida Governor Perry received word from Pettus of Mississippi's secession, and William S. Barry, president of the Mississippi Secession Convention, sent word to his Florida counterpart, John McGehee.[68] Before this, the Florida Convention's activities had been desultory, as Edmund Ruffin discovered while visiting Tallahassee a week after Carolina's withdrawal. There to urge Floridians to the proper course, he worried over Florida's factiousness. The proceedings did not go smoothly, and the audience misbehaved. Ruffin contemptuously noted that the convention's first official act had been to observe Buchanan's day of prayer and fasting. Ruffin refused to attend these ceremonies, but he did address the convention on 7 January before departing for Montgomery.[69] Florida delegates, warming to their task, gradually overcame fears aroused by geographical and economic dependence on Georgia and Alabama. Senators Yulee and Mallory in Washington were no help. Stephen Mallory would not desert his conservatism before some overt act of the national government, while Yulee told the Florida legislature that he would gladly join the state in secession.[70] Finally, the convention agreed with McGehee's advice that Florida had to escape the Black Republican menace because "as we stand our doom is decreed."[71] The day after receiving word of Mississippi's withdrawal, Florida seceded.

In Alabama a strong cooperationist-Unionist coalition emerged after Lincoln's election. Situated mostly in the northern part of the state, this coalition was a minority but imperturbable in its resistance to any untoward, impetuous action. Radicals took care not to flaunt their newly found, but tenuous, role as the majority. Yancey, however, nearly ruined everything again. Regarded with suspicion by even his own fire-eating colleagues, he had run unopposed in Montgomery County, but the organizers of the Breckinridge campaign, who after the election had committed to disunion, wisely paired him with former Whig Thomas H. Watts, noted for a calm loyalty to Southern rights. In the convention itself, all went well for the fire-eaters thanks mainly to the management of Governor Andrew B. Moore, whose messages and guidance imparted to the proceedings an air of inevitability. But Yancey grew impatient with delay, and by 8 January, the second day of the convention, he committed yet another of his legendary stupidities. He delivered a blistering denunciation of cooperationists and Unionists that charged them with treason if they stalled Alabama's withdrawal. Watts tried to repair the damage, and Yancey provided a lame apology that unconvincingly claimed he had not been referring to anybody in the convention. In the end, the actions of Mississippi and Florida—not Yancey's golden tongue—broke the back of the minority coalition and pushed the secession ordinance to a successful vote.[72]

No place better demonstrated Unionist disarray than did Georgia. The missionary for the cause, Ruffin, after passionately arguing for Florida's secession in Tallahassee, had been enroute to Montgomery when he learned of Mississippi's, Florida's, and Alabama's withdrawal. He would have then gone to Milledgeville, where the Georgia Convention was to gather in a week, but the rumbling of imminent war drew him back to Charleston. He was confident anyway that all would proceed at the Georgia capital as the radicals wished.[73]

At first Georgia had not been a certainty for the fire-eaters. Three weeks after Lincoln's election, Ruffin traveled to Milledgeville, meeting by chance Barnwell Rhett at Waynesboro, also on his way to the Georgia capital. In Milledgeville, both of them conversed with Joe Brown, who had declared for secession, and were invited by the state Senate to take seats. Ruffin, pleased that the legislature appropriated a million dollars for arming the militia and then called a convention to meet on 16 January, realized how much dissent such moves inspired.[74]

But by the time Ruffin and Rhett arrived in Milledgeville, the central figure of that dissent had already had his say. Alexander H. Stephens addressed the Georgia legislature on 14 November to plead for discretion. The frail, little man, in his own way as much a political colossus in Georgia as the burly Robert Toombs or the careful Howell Cobb were, was appalled at the apparent insanity gripping his state. One could understand Joe Brown's stand—Stephens evidently did not intend for his estimation of the governor as "lucky" to be complimentary—and one could perhaps have predicted that Savannah's Julian Hartridge, too much imbued with Carolina carelessness, would call upon the Georgia House to have the legislature rather than a convention effect the state's withdrawal.[75] But how to explain Robert Toombs's thorough descent into radicalism, his desire for revolution without a convention, his advice to march on the customs house and treasury building? And what could one make of Thomas Cobb's confused collection of incoherences that variously defended majority rule against minority rights, then called for Georgia's secession from that premise?[76]

Obviously disturbed, Stephens, more sallow than ever, planned to bring the legislature to its senses on the night of 14 November. There was only the slightest chance he could do so, but the extended applause that greeted his entrance belied the futility of his mission just as it demonstrated the high admiration the legislature felt for him. Never weighing more than ninety-five pounds, Stephens was heavy with principle. Many of the men he now faced remembered or had been told of how, after his first election to Congress, he declared his victory fraudulent because Georgia had failed to conform with a redistricting act of 1842.[77]

There was nothing fragile about his presence on a platform. At the start of Stephens's career, went one story, Walter Colquitt first noticed the little Whig, who allegedly proved himself so well in debate, by remarking that his "hands itched to get hold of him." Colquitt soon got his wish, much to his dismay and the crowd's delight, one member of which cried,

"Your hands itch to let him go, Judge, don't they?"[78] Intelligent, scrupulous, and scrappy, Stephens was the incarnation of the boy-man, the father-son, paradoxically inspiring both reverence and empathy. Robert Toombs, who until secession had estranged them, had been Stephens's closest friend. Standing in the rear of the chamber, Toombs might have observed to himself that the tiny specimen, swallowed up by his clothes and enfolded by the cheers and applause that went on and on, was the biggest man in Georgia. There was no doubt that he would be heard, no matter what he had to say or how unpopular it was.

Their behavior nonplussed him, Stephens told the legislators. Lincoln could do nothing against the South without violating the Constitution. Then would be the time to act. He hoped that that time would never come, for secession was as tempting as the apple in Eden. "Instead of becoming gods," he envisioned, "we shall become demons, and at no distant day commence cutting one another's throats."[79] The legislature's presumption that it could speak for the popular will repelled him. The people from the "cross-roads and groceries" had to be heard. "You Legislators," he began quietly in admonition then quickly added, "I speak it respectfully—are but our servants. You are the servants of the people, and not their masters."[80]

Soon he was through, and then there was only the briefest silent pause before Toombs, who had heckled the little man throughout the address, shouted, "Three Cheers for Stephens!" He did not have to suggest it twice, and he led the "Hip-Hips" to the chorused "Hurrahs." Toombs later explained the incongruity of calling for this tribute after having so badgered Stephens during his speech by saying, "I always try to behave myself at a funeral."[81] Toombs knew that one voice, even if that of Stephens, could not turn the sweep of inevitability.

Howell Cobb, after declaring to the people of Georgia the need for immediate secession, felt it necessary to resign from Buchanan's cabinet. He hoped the president could understand and would grant a farewell unencumbered by rancor. Buchanan could not. He would not.[82]

Thus Stephens swayed no one of sufficient importance, and he became a stunning exemplar of what happened to Unionists across the South. At Milledgeville during the convention he had insisted on, he was lackadaisical. He refused to lead Unionists largely because he despised Benjamin Hill, prominent among them, so the task fell to Herschel Johnson, unpopular because of his recent campaign as vice-presidential nominee with Douglas. Stephens's only contribution was a halfhearted speech steeped in resignation. There was no question that the state would secede.[83] It did so on 19 January.

In Washington, Southern senators from withdrawn states prepared to quit the legislature. Here the inevitable result of secession became terribly real. Congressional deliberations had taken on the character of a bear garden for several weeks, what with fire-eaters—Louis Wigfall prominent among them—mocking John Crittenden's compromise efforts and persistently goading waverers to the line of immediate dissolution. On 21 January as many as a thousand spectators filled the Senate gallery to watch David Yulee, Stephen Mallory, Clement C. Clay, Benjamin Fitzpatrick, and Jefferson Davis withdraw. It was the first time in a week that Yulee and Mallory had even shown themselves in the chamber, having waited only for word of their state's ordinance to depart. Now they took rank with other Gulf Staters still in Washington to participate in the grimmest spectacle the national legislature would ever witness. When Clay announced his retirement, his wife said, "It seemed as if the blood within me congealed." She heard the droning murmur of the galleries rise and fall as women "grew hysterical and waved their handkerchiefs." Men wept. "I . . . feel that I but express their [my constituents'] desire," said Davis, "when I say I hope, and they hope, for peaceable relations with you, though we must part."[84]

The droning hum and clattering hubbub spread out into the city itself as carriages, messengers, and baggage wagons crisscrossed paths to wharves and railroad stations. Those who could not comprehend previously what all the controversy meant received a painful lesson that afternoon in Washington. A handful of days later, delegates in Montgomery, Alabama, proclaimed the provisional government of the Confederate States of America. Epochs came and passed now in hours.

Calm, commercial, tariff-loving Louisiana, home of administration moderate John Slidell and the cleverly cautious Judah P. Benjamin, became fevered and tempestuous in an almost reflexive response to its Gulf State neighbors. After Lincoln's victory, Slidell and Benjamin called for immediate secession, and newspapers charged those who wavered with treason. Presbyterian minister Benjamin Morgan Palmer devoted his Thanksgiving Day sermon to blessing secession as a divine instrument. Commissioners from independent South Carolina and Alabama hovered over the delegates to the Louisiana Convention while a regular army of six hundred rushed to garrison forts and arsenals. The militia overflowed with volunteers. New Orleans reported that nearly ten thousand were armed and drilling.[85] The *New Orleans Picayune* tried in vain to maintain its traditional "cooperationist" calm, but it lost enough subscribers to force it to militancy as well. The Louisiana Convention adopted an ordinance of secession on 26 January.[86]

Fire-eaters everywhere knew, as Edmund Ruffin knew, that as for Texas "the difficulty there will [be] in that old scoundrel & traitor to the South, Houston, being governor."[87] To be sure, that was true, but Houston found his a relatively lonely voice, although at first a strong one because only he acted as though he knew what he was doing. However, under the stinging assault of John Marshall's (Austin) *Texas State Gazette,* which referred to Houston's Unionist lieutenants as the old governor's "flunkies," even Sam Houston faltered as the chorus of disunion grew in the Lone Star State.[88] In Washington, Senator Wigfall cooperated with James L. Pugh of Alabama to prepare the "Southern Manifesto," a declaration stating that the time for talk had passed and that the time for disunion and a Southern Confederacy had come. Six other Southern senators and twenty-three Southern representatives signed the document, and it was distributed throughout the South. Such support went far in quashing moderates' optimism in Washington.[89] Likewise, fire-eaters prevailed in a Texas legislature intent upon calling a convention. The state's mood promised that the convention would take Texas out of the Union, but Houston's resistance was not to be trifled with. Although reemerging or recently converted radicals like State Comptroller Clement R. Johns or Attorney General George M. Flournoy riddled the state government, Texas would be the last of the Deep South states to quit the American Republic, doing so on 23 February.[90]

As if to prove that Texas was different in every way, Louis Wigfall and fellow Texas Senator John Hemphill remained in the Senate after their state's secession on the flimsy ground that they had not received official notice of the ordinance. Wigfall became so openly obnoxious—declaring himself a foreigner loyal to another country—that he practically invited Republican attempts to expel him. While gleefully taunting Northerners, he amused himself by secretly arming a "Breckinridge and Lane Club" in the District of Columbia, by spying on the government's plans for the forts in Charleston Harbor (and keeping Governor Pickens posted), and by recruiting a Confederate regiment to send to Charleston from Maryland. He met openly with Confederate commissioners and helped Texas Ranger Captain Ben McCulloch purchase one thousand rifles and revolvers for his state.[91] He would eventually leave Washington for the more exciting Charleston. There, at the height of the bombardment he would insinuate himself into a Sumter cannon port—where he would almost literally be not only a fire-eater but a cannonball-eater as well—to receive Robert Anderson's surrender terms. It was the last piece of real influence he would enjoy, and it, like so much of his career, was unauthorized.

Robert Barnwell Rhett and many other radicals had ceased to think about Virginia as either helping or hurting the secession cause in their respective states. Too many times Old Dominion moderation had undermined determined action, and the state's legislature had too often dampened resolution elsewhere with caution in Richmond. Disaffected Virginia fire-eaters, however, could not help caring about their native state, although Ruffin foreswore it, voluntarily exiling himself in February from any place that consented to Lincoln's government. Virginians, he said, disgusted him, and he suspected that even the instigators of the Peace Convention only wanted to prevent immediate secession so the state could again submit to the North.[92] Ruffin, in Charleston as the Sumter crisis entered its final hours, could not have been as sure as Roger Pryor, who was also in the city, that firing on Sumter would bring Virginia along with the rest of the South. "We will put her in," Pryor assured crowds two days before the batteries opened up on the fort, "if you but strike a blow."[93]

Actually, it would be just that easy, although nothing in Virginia's previous behavior promised it. When Lincoln won, slaveholders were naturally up in arms, but nonslaveholders, overseers, and poor whites reportedly grumbled that they would sit out any conflict.[94] Meanwhile, the Breckinridge organization hardly broke stride in changing its cry from "Breckinridge for President" to "Virginia out of the Union." Two Richmond newspapers, the *Enquirer* and the *Examiner,* once pitted in bitter opposition, became fast friends in the secessionist cause. Roger Pryor, James Seddon, M. R. H. Garnett, and John Randolph Tucker raised their voices for action. Tucker's kinsman, Robert Randolph, was soon shouting, "The Cry of Union at this late day is the cry of War. Secession is the only road to Peace."[95] But moderates and conservatives, gathered in a fragile coalition, would have none of it, not even to forestall Gulf-State impetuosity with Virginia's famous restraint. The great conservative hope was that some compromise would emerge from Washington. While Pryor and Mason scorned this, Mason even participating in Wigfall-like attempts to obstruct conciliation, Senator Hunter obstinately clung to moderation, and with good reason. Many Virginians openly worried that a Confederate policy of free trade would hurt the state's manufactures, and the Mississippi River promised to become the major artery for Southern commerce. Would not Virginia find more economic security with the North?[96]

Virginia's course would determine that of the Upper South.[97] In those tense weeks after the election, while Carolina prepared for its withdrawal, some Southerners tried to goad the Old Dominion to action. Robert Grinnan, a Louisianan applying Garibaldi's maxim, proposed advising Virginia "women not to allow the embrace of a husband or maid of a lover unless he took [an] active part for his freedom."[98] When the legislature did finally act on 14 January—though surely for more sophisticated reasons—it was not taken as particularly promising that the House of Delegates insisted that the convention submit any call for secession to a vote by the people. "This is all wrong," cried Grinnan. "It gives delay and will prevent decided action."[99]

In any event, the election of delegates on 4 February disappointed radicals. A severe blow fell on the Ruffins when moderate Timothy Rives defeated Edmund, Jr., in Prince George County. Willoughby Newton lost as well. The elder Ruffin took a long view, hoping for rapid events to turn men from moderation. His optimism was not without foundation, since John Minor Botts, William Cabell Rives, and John Gilmer—all confirmed Unionists—lost their races as well. Immediate secession had fallen but so had out-and-out Unionism. Virginia, even as the Deep South fell one state after another out of the Union, still steered a middle course. Conservatives, planning to stall, hoped it would be middle enough to save the nation.[100]

Moderates put the convention at a dead stop within ten days of its first meeting. Lewis Harvie and Henry A. Wise led secessionists—about thirty in number and mostly from the Tidewater and Piedmont—in nothing more than a contest of endurance with the conservative coalition.[101] By the second week in April, however, events following Lincoln's inauguration, especially in Charleston, raised popular enthusiasm for the radical stand. Denunciations of the stalemated convention and cautious

Governor Letcher led to talk of a "People's Spontaneous Convention" to convene on 16 April if the regular convention neglected its duty. Soon the talk went further, rumoring "arrests and executions." The people spreading such information carried firearms and were serious.[102]

An ill Henry A. Wise spent most of his time on a sofa at Richmond's Exchange Hotel struggling with numbing coughing fits, but he managed to rouse himself to instigate and follow through on the idea of a spontaneous convention. The extralegal body did meet on 16 April, four days after the batteries had opened on Sumter, but its plans were unclear and potentially ugly. Ensconced at Metropolitan Hall and guarded by a doorkeeper brandishing a sword, the convention elected David Chalmers as its president. Willoughby Newton, denied a place in the regular convention, was elected as one of the vice presidents. Some members from the legal convention attended the spontaneous gathering, moving back and forth between the meetings. Nervous Unionists secured adjournment at least for the day.[103]

The next day Henry Wise appeared before the regular convention. Ostentatiously displaying a pistol, he delivered an address of spitting condemnation during which he paused to announce that even as he spoke Virginia troops were seizing Harpers Ferry and that he had authorized it because of Letcher's torpor. It did not matter by then. Across town, the People's Spontaneous Convention received word that the legitimate gathering had done its duty. The vote was close on the successful ordinance—eighty-eight to fifty-five—but Virginia's conservative coalition had disintegrated a week before, and it was amazing that it took so long to get the state out of the Union.[104]

Ruffin surely must have agreed. On 9 April the old man became an honorary member of the Marion Artillery Corps stationed on Morris Island.[105] Three days later, he stood with his new comrades in the predawn darkness to stare out across the gray waters at a dark shape, the target for his and a host of other guns. Ruffin pulled the lanyard and sent off one of the shells that, in a sense, blasted his native state out of the Union. Thinking of it that way would have pleased him.

Henry L. Benning, Georgia

Although a bona fide fire-eater during most of the sectional crisis, Benning stayed in the Democratic Convention in Charleston and was the vice president of the Baltimore Convention that nominated Douglas. After Lincoln's victory, however, he called for secession. *(Courtesy of University of Georgia Libraries)*

Preston Brooks, South Carolina

He was as moderate as he was popular, and he enjoyed a reputation for courtesy only matched by the admiration of ladies for his good looks. But Brooks's beating of Charles Sumner on 22 May 1856 became one of the ugly punctuation marks of the sectional crisis. Brooks died of tuberculosis less than a year after the event. *(Courtesy of South Caroliniana Library, University of South Carolina)*

Albert Gallatin Brown, Mississippi

The feud Brown waged against Jefferson Davis in Mississippi exacerbated Stephen A. Douglas's problems within the National Democracy at the end of the 1850s. Ironically, this master politician would, in old age, counsel his two sons never to enter politics. They took the advice. *(Courtesy of Mississippi Department of Archives and History)*

John C. Calhoun, South Carolina

Seen here near the end of his life, Calhoun played out but could not complete the dangerous sectional drama of 1850. When he died in late March 1850, his last words reportedly were, "The South, the poor South." The radicals would invoke his memory in their cause, but none could assume his place nor claim his stature. *(Courtesy of Library of Congress)*

Walter T. Colquitt, Georgia

He delivered the most stunning and vehement address at the ill-fated Nashville Convention, then returned to Georgia to spend his energies for the secessionist cause. The Georgia Convention's Unionism direly disappointed him, however, and his participation in the sectional crises thereafter was slight and ineffectual. He died in 1855. *(Courtesy of University of Georgia Libraries)*

Jefferson Davis, Mississippi

Events and the activities of Albert Gallatin Brown pushed Davis toward radicalism more than any agreement with fire-eater objectives. In Charleston, he opposed Douglas but not the Democracy, and many (including Benjamin Butler) thought Davis would be the perfect compromise nominee for president. In less than a year, he would become president, but not of the United States. *(Courtesy of South Caroliniana Library, University of South Carolina)*

James Henry Hammond, South Carolina

He pictured himself as the next Calhoun, and he delivered the most famous speech of his career on 4 March 1858, eight years to the day after Calhoun's swan song. The "Cotton is King" speech proclaimed that "no power on earth dares make war on it," but Hammond was wrong about both the supremacy of cotton and his assumption of Calhoun's place. *(Courtesy of South Caroliniana Library, University of South Carolina)*

Lawrence M. Keitt, South Carolina

When Preston Brooks beat Charles Sumner, "Kit" Keitt ran interference against those who tried to intervene. He himself was involved in a fist-fight on the floor of the House during the stormy debates on the Lecompton Constitution. Keitt would die from wounds received during the Battle of Cold Harbor. *(Courtesy of South Caroliniana Library, University of South Carolina)*

William Porcher Miles, South Carolina
Erudite and charming, this mathematics professor turned politician in 1855 when conservatives backed him for mayor of Charleston. Although a fire-eating Southern nationalist in Congress, he proved a reluctant secessionist in 1860 because he did not want to seem merely Rhett's cipher. *(Courtesy of South Caroliniana Library, University of South Carolina)*

James L. Orr, South Carolina

His reorganization of South Carolina politics following the radicals'
defeat in 1851 boded well for a renewed nationalism in the Palmetto
State, but Orr resembled Hammond in always espousing the political
line of least resistance. Ultimately the South Carolina Democracy
proved too fragile to withstand the growing sectional choler of the late
1850s. By 1860, Rhett was resurgent and Orr became, at the eleventh
hour, a secessionist. *(Courtesy of South Caroliniana Library, University
of South Carolina)*

Institute Hall, Charleston, South Carolina

The site of many important meetings during the antebellum period,
Institute Hall bore the distinction of being where the Democratic party
destroyed itself in April 1860 and South Carolina broke the nation nine
months later. *(Courtesy of South Caroliniana Library, University of
South Carolina)*

John J. Pettus, Mississippi
In spite of the fiery rhetoric of his gubernatorial campaign, Pettus made sure that he had consensus from the Mississippi congressional delegation before calling a secession convention after Lincoln's election. Ultimately, Pettus could not be cautious when Jefferson Davis and A. G. Brown had finally agreed about something. *(Courtesy of Mississippi Department of Archives and History)*

John A. Quitman, Mississippi
His governorship of Mississippi was racked by controversy and turmoil, and he fell into political disfavor in the radical debacle of 1851. But in four years, the legis-lature placed him in the Senate, where he railed against the neu-trality laws he had flouted in regard to Cuba. His death in 1858 gave Jefferson Davis his Senate seat, much to the chagrin of Albert Gallatin Brown. *(Courtesy of Mississippi Department of Archives and History)*

**Robert Barnwell Rhett, Sr.,
South Carolina**

The Rhetts led the most troublesome faction in South Carolina
politics. When Rhett Jr. became
editor of the *Mercury* in 1857, the
paper became a clarion for Southern secession, with decidedly
mixed results. Rhett Sr.'s reputation for inflexible consistency
usually made him an ineffectual
leader and a failed politician.
*(Courtesy of South Caroliniana
Library, University of South
Carolina)*

**Robert Barnwell Rhett, Jr.,
South Carolina**

Edmund Ruffin, Virginia

He feared advancing age and the diminution of his mental acuity, but Ruffin remained the most resolutely committed ide-alogue of the period. He filled newspapers and pamphlets with calls for Southern seces-sion and proved nearly inde-fatigable during the secession winter of 1860–61. He would kill himself in the wake of Southern defeat. *(Courtesy of South Caroliniana Library, University of South Carolina)*

Whitemarsh Seabrook, South Carolina

As governor of South Caro-lina during the 1850 crisis, Seabrook hoped that Quitman's Mississippi would take the secessionist lead and save Carolina from isolation. Yet as the South's anger cooled, so did Sea-brook's hopes, and he finally helped to calm his state with caution as politic with the moderates as it was unpopu-lar with fire-eaters. *(Cour-tesy of South Caroliniana Library, University of South Carolina)*

William Gilmore Simms, South Carolina

As an influential literary figure, Simms hoped to explain his misunderstood South to Northerners, but his one serious attempt to do so in 1856 failed under the weight of the Brooks-Sumner incident. His lecture tour of the North devolved into disaster when audiences first jeered then stayed away. Simms fumed under the injustice. *(Courtesy of South Caroliniana Library, University of South Carolina)*

William Lowndes Yancey, Alabama

This premier fire-eater managed at one time or another to be all things to almost all people. A peerless orator and prescient observer, Yancey's political fortunes crested during the Charleston Convention when his Alabama Platform broke the Democracy. His behavior in the Alabama secession convention earned him little credit, though, and the state withdrew from the Union in spite of rather than because of his efforts. *(Courtesy of South Caroliniana Library, University of South Carolina)*

Louis T. Wigfall, Texas

Extravagantly radical and fearless before the gravest dangers, he could be a dangerous foe, as many in both the North and South discovered. As the secession crisis got underway, one of his calmer observations before the Senate was to "mend it [the Union] if you can; cement it with blood." *(Courtesy of South Caroliniana Library, University of South Carolina)*

David L. Yulee, Florida

Yulee suffered from the disaster of 1851, failing in his reelection bid for the Senate. He became involved in railroad construction in Florida during the 1850s and by 1860 was one of the most successful railroad promoters in the South, especially in his home state. Some critics would ascribe his reluctant secessionism in 1860—a reverse of his fiery attitude ten years before—to his financial success. *(Courtesy of the Florida State Archives)*

Yulee ("Traitor")

A Unionist contemporary's sentiment about Yulee's stand on secession is graphically represented in this previously unpublished photograph. *(Richard J. Ferry Collection, Courtesy of the Florida State Archives)*

CHAPTER TEN

"We Will Stand by You to the Death"

Rapidity and a high degree of organization characterized the maneuvers of the radicals during the secession crisis. Yet while haste worked toward their advantage, radicals knew that such haste created a negative perception that threatened their success. The fire-eater victory occurred in Alabama in spite of rather than because of William Lowndes Yancey. Elsewhere, the most prominent fire-eaters, those whose agitations spanned a decade or longer, helped their cause the most in those last hours when they were silent. Albert Gallatin Brown had less to do with Mississippi's course than did Jefferson Davis. Louis Wigfall raged in the Senate while in Austin more methodical operatives like John Reagan successfully marshalled secessionists against Houston men. David Yulee's heated assurances to the Florida legislature proved less effective than John McGehee's earnest addresses to the convention in Tallahassee, and Stephen Mallory, disunionist only after the fact, possessed more influence upon his return to the state. Likewise, Henry Benning and Walter Colquitt were never as effective as Robert Toombs or Howell Cobb, both of whom grimly agreed to the withdrawal of Georgia, and Cobb, only after compromise efforts had failed in Washington. And, like Yancey in Alabama, the Rhetts in Charleston contributed little more than divisiveness at the moment of their cause's most propitious opportunity.

The secessionist majorities rapidly constructed amidst the heated fears and animosities left over from the 1860 election were tenuous at best.

Stephens predicted that disunion would unleash jealousies and rivalries far more terrific than the ills it sought to correct. In fact, it did not take long before Georgians looked askance at South Carolina. Some suspected that without the war, half-mad Palmetto separatists probably would have racked the Confederacy with its own secession crisis.[1] Many viewed Carolina as imperious and arrogant, and those unaware that Montgomery had ordered Sumter reduced blamed impetuous Charlestonians for ruining any chance of accommodation with the federal government.[2]

The fire-eaters miscalculated badly about the border states. Yancey thought a wavering Kentucky would join the Southern defense after the first blow fell, but of course that was not to be. From Frankfort, Mildred Sayre wrote to her father Edmund Ruffin that in her husband's school, bluegrass boys referred to Mississippians as foreigners.[3] Ruffin himself entertained high hopes for Missouri, especially when an insurrectionary raid from Kansas led by "Jayhawker" James Montgomery pushed into the state shortly after the November election. At bottom, secessionist strength in Missouri did not exist. The convention of ninety-nine men proved that with forty-seven conditional Unionists and fifty-two unconditional Unionists. Very late in the day, in October 1861, the meteoric mayor of St. Joseph, Meriwether Jefferson Thompson, exhorted fellow Missourians to the cause of the South in order to effect reconciliation, but by then the issue was even deader in Missouri.[4]

In Arkansas heated responses cooled after initial outbursts over Lincoln's election. South Carolina's secession occasioned nothing more than a little stir. Albert Pike, in Washington on business while the congressional compromise efforts crumbled away, returned to his state to advocate secession. He wanted Arkansas to join the Confederacy before Lincoln's inauguration to better the chances for reconstructing the Union.[5] The vision, however, was that of an eccentric, but nonetheless moderate, Southerner. Arkansas left the Union on 6 May in response to the call for volunteers to repress the insurrection after Sumter.

North Carolina found itself truly caught in the middle. Governor John Ellis might have qualified as the unhappiest and most bewildered official in the South during the secession crisis. "If coercion be attempted by the General Government," he informed a South Carolinian in December, "we will stand by you to the death, whether in or out of the Union."[6] Such wording—"in or out of the Union"—gave the pronouncement the character of a reluctant promise rather than an oath of allegiance. South

Carolina's secession summoned little sympathy in North Carolina except from radicals. Ellis pondered in a quandary, explaining to Joe Brown that United States forts in Tarheel country were of little importance to the Southern cause. He urged a defensive coordination at most but began arming the state after the telegraph brought news of Georgia's secession.[7] At the same time the North Carolina legislature sat late into the night thrashing over questions about whether or not to have a convention and what kind it should be. Finally, it declared that the federal government had the right to coerce a seceding state.[8]

Soon the failed compromise efforts and Lincoln's inaugural address paralyzed the Unionist faction, in reality the majority in North Carolina. "We, the Secessionists," recorded young, newly radical David Schenck, "are laboring manfully to join [the seceded states], but the tories of 76 are not out of North Carolina yet."[9] After Sumter, Schenck was exultant. He predicted on 6 May, the day the state seceded, "If Abe Lincoln ever rules North Carolina again, it will be as a barren desert of desolation."[10]

There was little time to analyze what had happened before the killing in earnest began. More than anything, most Southerners came to the position that secession was necessary while bitterly regretting what circumstances had forced them to do.[11] In a sense, secession was an idea whose time had come for the testing. A half century of debate and theoretical argument made its own contribution to the eruption of the great crisis in 1860 and 1861, as shown by the tortured reasoning of secession conventions groping for a justification of their course. The fire-eater insistence that secession was a legal recourse legitimated by "sovereign" conventions was more than a tidy trick to manipulate heightened passion and fear. John Reagan in Texas feared that vigilante coercion from secret groups like the Knights of the Golden Circle that raucously intimidated Unionists would ruin everything. In Georgia or Alabama or South Carolina or Texas, the secessionists of 1860 were mostly lawyers, not planters, and certainly they were not madmen.[12]

Moreover, in the appearance of their success, the fire-eaters were lucky. The secession movement would *appear* at once to have been both conspiratorial and popular, but it was neither, and in 1860 it did not have to be. The events preceding the secession of the Gulf States—reaching back to Brown's raid, certainly, but in the memory of many Southerners even reaching back to David Wilmot's notorious Proviso—had in their cumulative effect made for a populace anxious for action. Meanwhile year after year, the same radical messages assailed the South with an unerring consistency. Rendered with supreme self-assurance, intolerant of dispute, arrogant in certitude, such messages found merit in consistency. Then events made the messages, so long unpopular but rigidly maintained, seem prophetic. In not one single instance did the fire-eaters shape those events. They ranted against Wilmot while calmer men pushed the offending amendment aside. They fumed at those "Bleeding Wounds" of 1850 while compromise made their dark predictions seem absurd. Moderate men fashioned the ill-fated Kansas-Nebraska Act. An old Jacksonian of the first order drafted the tangled Dred Scott decision. At Charleston in April 1860, Douglas, as much as anyone, forged the nails for his coffin, and Yancey ultimately refused to drive those nails home. Southerners feared Republicans because of warnings from men calmer than fire-eaters. Then the Republicans came to power, and something had to be done. The fire-eaters, a minority always, had the plan while the majority of moderate Southerners floundered in bewilderment. It all happened so quickly.[13]

There was no conspiracy of the Gulf-State slavocracy formulated by the fire-eaters. The true fire-eater, like Rhett, always advocated separate state action; conspiracies require cooperation, and the cooperationists were the archrivals of the radical secessionists, abided and accommodated on occasion, but never embraced. Events forced cooperation on the South, not a dark fire-eater plan; indeed, the fire-eaters had shown and would prove themselves to be about the most uncooperative, doctrinaire men in the South. At Montgomery, Rhett served as the chairman of the Committee on Foreign Affairs (whose advice was largely ignored) and as the chairman of the committee to draft the Confederate Constitution (in principle, indistinguishable from the federal Constitution); and he was the chairman of the committee to present Jefferson Davis to the Provisional Congress, this last duty really indicating the decline of his popularity and influence.[14]

President Davis, joined by Vice President Alexander H. Stephens, presided over a cabinet containing at most, and only briefly, one discernible radical—Leroy P. Walker of Alabama. Davis packed Yancey off to the Court of St. James in a diplomatically foolish move counterpoised by the felicitous event of removing him from the country. Memminger, not Rhett, joined the administration; Toombs, not Benning, went into the cabinet. Wigfall would resort to hurling sullen recriminations at Davis from the Confederate Senate floor. In temper they were much like those he had produced in Washington. As chief executive, Confederate President Davis evoked the same predictable and unrelenting enmity of Albert Gallatin Brown as had Mississippi National Democrat Davis.

A storm king during a storm may achieve the status of a prophet, but all storms eventually subside. Secession was a revolutionary act because it was born of apprehensions over tyranny as it melded into the crucible of war. At the Louisiana Convention, secessionists insisted on the constitutional legality of withdrawal. However, Unionists and cooperationists seeking delay so often used the threat of war with the North that nobody could deny at the end that a vote for separation was a revolutionary act.[15] In the precipitous speed of crisis, a nervous John Ellis plaintively cried that "revolutions do not admit of long pauses."[16] Yet as revolution was truly an American ritual, moderate Southerners in Montgomery made sure the ritual was calm and its posture conservative.

The fire-eater was a renegade, not a conspirator, not a cooperator. The knowledge among political professionals that men like Rhett and Yancey could disrupt normal political intercourse in peacetime barred them from real avenues of power in war.

Meanwhile, the rest of the South canted the liturgy of sectional nationalism, understanding little more than the fact that on distant fields percussion muskets already crackled in anger. Sarah Lois Wadley in Mississippi sat before her diary as her mother called to her for companionship on a stroll. Sarah, in her teens, filled her journal with the normal and obvious preoccupations universal to adolescent girls: boys, mainly, and sad fits of self-analysis and criticism. Sarah was short, thick, freckled, had a big nose, and was without the languorous eyes of the true belle. She cursed her towhead of hair that refused to hold the ringlets fashionable to her time.[17] But here and there phrases like "spurn the yoke of the cowardly tyrant of the United States" appear, seeming strangely out of place, out of time. Near the end of June she noted that "affairs in Virginia remain the same, both parties are concentrating their forces but there has been no fight beyond a few slight Skirmishes"—which meant, of course, that men were already killing one another, doing what Governor Ellis had promised, standing by each other to the death.[18]

The husbands, fathers, brothers, and sons surely believed, as did

Sarah, that this was a "noble enterprise," but that was apart from the torrent of words that had been spewed forth by the Yanceys, Ruffins, Rhetts, Bennings, Wigfalls and all the rest. War, like secession, might have been nothing more than an idea whose time had come for the testing. Probably stout Sarah and those soldiers understood the why of it then no better than we do now.

Notes

CHAPTER ONE
"A Disposition to Dissolve the Union"

1. Roy P. Basler, ed., *Abraham Lincoln: His Speeches and Writings* (Cleveland: World Publishing Company, 1946), 588.

2. John G. Nicolay and John Hay, *Complete Works of Abraham Lincoln*, 12 vols. (New York: The Century Company, 1905), XI, 46.

3. Eric Foner, *Politics and Ideology in the Age of the Civil War* (New York: Oxford University Press, 1980), 19.

4. James L. Roark, *Masters Without Slaves: Southern Planters in the Civil War and Reconstruction* (New York: W. W. Norton & Co., 1977), 4–5.

5. Robert Barnwell Rhett, for example, tried but with little success. See one such attempt in manuscript in the Robert Barnwell Rhett Papers, South Carolina Historical Society, Charleston, S.C.

6. Glover Moore, *The Missouri Controversy, 1819–1821* (Lexington: University of Kentucky Press, 1953), 218.

7. Garnett to John Randolph, 20 February 1820, quoted in Moore, *Missouri Controversy*, 218.

8. Tait to John W. Walker, 20 May 1820, quoted in Moore, *Missouri Controversy*, 25.

9. The Adams-Onís Treaty that sought to divide the Spanish and American possessions on the continent came under harsh scrutiny because of the Missouri Compromise Line. Northerners were angry about Florida going to the South, while Southerners complained about the renunciation of Texas. The question already was one of balance and would only become more acute in the coming years. See Moore, *Missouri Controversy*, 160–61.

10. Tucker's essay appeared as an appendix to his edition of *Blackstone's Commentaries.*

11. August O. Spain, *The Political Theory of John C. Calhoun,* 51–54.

12. Robert M. Dawidoff, *The Education of John Randolph* (New York: W. W. Norton and Company, 1979), 259–60.

13. Dumas Malone, *Jefferson and His Time: Jefferson the President, First Term, 1801–1805* (Boston: Little, Brown and Company, 1970), 468–69, 471–72.

14. Dawidoff, *Randolph,* 168.

15. There was some dispute over Randolph's sanity even during his own lifetime, although Calhoun would say after Randolph's death that he had been as sane as the next fellow. See Dawidoff, *Randolph,* 260.

16. Ibid., 60.

17. Ibid., 44–45, 60–61.

18. Turnbull's pamphlets were titled *The Crisis: Or Essays on the Usurpations of the Federal Government,* by Brutus. See U. B. Phillips, *The Course of the South to Secession,* edited by E. Merton Coulter (New York: D. Appleton-Century Company, 1939), 130; *Charleston Mercury,* 1827; Murray N. Rothbard, *The Panic of 1819: Reactions and Policies* (New York: Columbia University Press, 1962), 187; Samuel Rezneck, "The Depression of 1819–1822, A Social History," *American Historical Review* 39 (October 1933): 41–42.

19. William W. Freehling, *Prelude to Civil War: The Nullification Crisis in South Carolina, 1816–1836* (New York: Harper and Row, 1966), 158–59.

20. Jesse T. Carpenter, *The South as a Conscious Minority, 1789–1861* (New York: New York University Press, 1930), 26–29.

21. Peter Harvey, *Reminiscences and Anecdotes of Daniel Webster* (Boston: Little, Brown and Company, 1921), 152; also see William R. Taylor, *Cavalier and Yankee: The Old South and American National Character* (Cambridge: Harvard University Press, 1979), 110–11.

22. Lindsay Swift, ed., *The Great Debate Between Robert Y. Hayne of South Carolina and Daniel Webster of Massachusetts* (Boston: Houghton Mifflin Company, 1898), 216–17.

23. William A. Schaper, "Sectionalism and Representation in South Carolina," *Annual Report of the American Historical Association for the Year 1900,* Vol. 1 (Washington: Government Printing Office, 1901): 250–52, 443–44.

24. James Hamilton, Jr., to John Taylor, *et al.,* 14 September 1830 in *Charleston Mercury,* 29 September 1830.

25. William W. Freehling, ed., *The Nullification Era: A Documentary Record* (New York: Harper Torchbooks, University Library, Harper & Row, 1967), 98. Also see Thomas F. Jones to John F. Patterson, 24 November 1832, quoted in Richard E. Ellis, *The Union at Risk: Jacksonian Democracy, States' Rights, and the Nullification Crisis* (New York: Oxford University Press, 1987), 73.

26. Freehling, *Nullification Era,* 189–90; also see David Franklin Houston, *A Critical Study of Nullification in South Carolina* (New York: Longmans, Green, and Co., 1908), 136.

27. Freehling, *Nullification Era,* 189; also see Laura A. White, *Robert Barnwell Rhett: Father of Secession* (New York: The Century Co., 1931), 136.

28. Journal entry of 30 March 1833, quoted in Lillian Adele Kibler, *Benjamin F. Perry, South Carolina Unionist* (Durham: Duke University Press, 1946), 156.

29. "Cooper's Value of the Union Speech, 2 July 1827," in Freehling, *Nullification Era*, 25.

30. Houston, *Critical Study of Nullification*, 138–40.

31. Major L. Wilson, "'Liberty and Union': An Analysis of Three Concepts Involved in the Nullification Controversy," *Journal of Southern History* 33 (1967): 138–40.

32. Littleton Waller Tazewell, *A Review of the Proclamation of President Jackson of the 10th of December, 1832 in a Series of Numbers Originally Published in the "Norfolk and Portsmouth Herald" Under the Signature of "A Virginian"* (Norfolk: J. D. Ghiselin, 1888), 110, 112.

33. Phillips, *Course of the South to Secession*, 130.

34. Evidence suggests that Turner's interpretation of a solar eclipse in February 1831 as portentous had more to do with his actions than familiarity with Garrison's writings. See David M. Potter and Don Fehrenbacher, *The Impending Crisis, 1848–1861* (New York: Harper & Row, 1976), 454.

35. Moore, *Missouri Controversy*, 343–45.

36. Disunion sentiment was growing in Georgia out of frustration over the Texas annexation question. See Samuel Dickson to J. M. Berrien, 3 February 1845, John MacPherson Berrien Papers, Southern Historical Collection, University of North Carolina, Chapel Hill, N.C. William Lowndes Yancey argued for the annexation of Texas, openly stating that he did so because the South was losing ground in the national legislature, that this was a result of the Missouri Compromise removing any chance for the South to maintain equality, and that the world was against slavery in the South and Texas was necessary for its protection. See Henry Wilson, *History of the Rise and Fall of the Slave Power in America* 9th ed., 3 vols. (Boston: Houghton, Mifflin and Company, 1872–77), I, 611–12.

37. The phrase is Major L. Wilson's in "Three Concepts of the Nullification Controversy," 354.

38. *Charleston Mercury,* 20 March 1846.

39. Chaplain W. Morrison, *Democratic Politics and Sectionalism: The Wilmot Proviso Controversy* (Chapel Hill: University of North Carolina Press, 1967), 5, 9, 16–17.

40. *Richmond Times,* quoted in the *Charleston Mercury,* 13 January 1846.

41. In spite of Yancey's efforts Westerners were mainly unconvinced. See Morrison, *Democratic Politics,* 12–13.

42. *Charleston Mercury,* 15 January, 3 February 1846.

43. Wilmot did not take up the fight for the Proviso in the first session of the 30th Congress. Coincidentally, Preston King, along with a number of other Van Burenites from New York, had retired. See Morrison, *Democratic Politics,* 181n.

44. Allan Nevins, *Ordeal of the Union: Fruits of Manifest Destiny, 1847–1852* (New York: Charles Scribner's Sons, 1947), 9.

45. Morrison, *Democratic Politics,* 19, 32–33. The Wilmot Proviso as well as the appropriation bill was introduced as the Congress was about to adjourn.

46. Ibid., 36–37. A decade later John Tyler claimed that he "would not have

negotiated a Treaty of Peace" without settling the slave question in that treaty. He felt that "the omission to do which was a great blunder." See Tyler to Thomas Jefferson Green, 28 February 1856, Thomas Jefferson Green Papers, Southern Historical Collection, University of North Carolina, Chapel Hill, N.C.

47. Morrison, *Democratic Politics,* 49.

48. Ibid. Calhoun took the precaution of employing agents at this convention who were instrumental in guiding it toward the adoption of the Virginia Resolutions, passed the previous March, which sought to prohibit congressional intrusion respecting slavery.

49. Taylor had qualities that recommended him to a number of Southerners. As South Carolinian James Henry Hammond told Edmund Ruffin, Taylor was "a Southern man—a slaveholder & I hope a Free Trader—honest & able." While he was not a politician, neither did he have "the makings of a military despot." Hammond was for Taylor "as far as I know now." Hammond to Ruffin, 1 June 1847, Edmund Ruffin Papers, Southern Historical Collection, University of North Carolina, Chapel Hill, N.C.

50. Morrison, *Democratic Politics,* 111–13.

51. Ibid., 114–17. The philosophy of Yancey's Alabama Platform turned up in other parts of the nation, including, strangely enough, Springfield, Massachusetts, where the Whig state convention in September 1847 had seen an attempt to place an amendment on the report of the resolutions committee that Whigs support no one for president who was known to oppose the extension of slavery. It was defeated, of course, though it must have shocked Charles Sumner and Daniel Webster to hear it even suggested. See Wilson, *Rise and Fall of the Slave Power,* II, 123.

52. Yulee to Mrs. D. L. Yulee, 9 May 1848, in David L. Yulee Papers, P. K. Yonge Library of Florida History, University of Florida, Gainesville, Fla.

53. Circular letter in Berrien Papers. The circular was signed by, among others, Georgians Walter Colquitt and George Washington Towns and South Carolinian Franklin H. Elmore.

54. Wilson, *Rise and Fall of the Slave Power,* II, 129–30.

55. Ibid., 133; also see Morrison, *Democratic Politics,* 140–42.

56. Morrison, *Democratic Politics,* 157–61.

57. Douglas to Cass, 13 June 1848, in Robert W. Johannsen, ed., *The Letters of Stephen A. Douglas* (Urbana: University of Illinois Press, 1961), 346.

58. Morrison, *Democratic Politics,* 162.

59. D. H. Lewis to William Lowndes Yancey, 29 June 1848, Dixon Hall Lewis Papers, Auburn University Archives, Ralph Brown Draughon Library, Auburn University, Auburn, Ala.

60. Biographical sketch in Lewis Papers.

61. Morrison, *Democratic Politics,* 110.

62. Lewis to Yancey, 29 June 1848, in Lewis Papers. "If anything will defeat you in South Carolina," Taylor was advised, "it will be Genl Cass's pledge to veto the *Wilmot Proviso.*" See Thomas Jefferson Green to Zachary Taylor, 12 October 1848, Green Papers.

63. Edmund Ruffin, Jr., to Edmund Ruffin, 16 October 1847 [*sic*], Ruffin Papers.

64. See for example Avery O. Craven, *Civil War in the Making, 1815–1860* (Baton Rouge: Louisiana State University Press, 1959), 74.

65. Gerald M. Capers, *John C. Calhoun, Opportunist: A Reappraisal* (Gainesville: University of Florida Press, 1960), 233–34.

66. Calhoun to the Executive Committee organizing for a Southern Rights Association, Charleston, 28 September 1847, in *Charleston Mercury,* 3 May 1847.

67. Capers, *Calhoun,* 244.

68. Calhoun to Executive Committee, 28 September 1847, *Charleston Mercury,* 5 May 1847.

69. Calhoun to Henry S. Foote, 3 August 1849, in *Charleston Mercury,* 4 June 1851.

CHAPTER TWO
"Leadership of This Generation"

1. Frederick William Seward, *Reminiscences of a War-Time Statesman and Diplomat, 1830–1915* (New York: G. P. Putnam's Sons, 1916), 71.

2. Hammond to Catherine Hammond, 17 April 1836, J. H. Hammond Papers, Southern Historical Collection, University of North Carolina, Chapel Hill, N.C.

3. Henry Washington Hilliard, *Politics and Pen Pictures at Home and Abroad* (New York: G. P. Putnam's Sons, 1892), 3–4, 199. The move for Southern unity was early in the making, and this congressional caucus seemed a grand opportunity for realizing it. "It would be an excellent thing," a correspondent wrote to Calhoun early in 1848, ". . . thus some course should be determined that the whole South could unite upon. . . . I think that it might be done by yourself and the representatives of the Southern states in Washington." Henry Gourdin to Calhoun, 19 January 1848, in J. Franklin Jameson, ed., *Correspondence of John C. Calhoun,* American Historical Association *Annual Report,* 1899, pt. 2. For a detailed account of the maneuvering attendant to the issue of the Southern Address see Charles Wiltse, *John C. Calhoun: Sectionalist, 1840–1850* (Indianapolis: Bobbs-Merrill Company, Inc., 1951), 337–88.

4. Hilliard, *Politics and Pen Pictures,* 199–200.

5. Roy F. Nichols, *The Stakes of Power, 1845–1877,* American Century Series, David Donald, ed. (New York: Hill and Wang, 1961), 37–38. Also see J. B. Kendall to John M. Berrien, 4 January 1849, Berrien Papers.

6. Henry Quitman to Eliza Quitman, 4 March 1850, Quitman Family Papers, Southern Historical Collection, University of North Carolina, Chapel Hill, N.C.

7. To some Southerners this practice seemed a deadly error in its implications. See John Chrisfield to Henry Page, 20 January 1861, Henry Page Papers, Southern Historical Collection, University of North Carolina, Chapel Hill, N.C.

8. Yulee to Mrs. D. L. Yulee, 10 December 1847, Yulee Papers.

9. Yulee to Mrs. D. L. Yulee, 12 December 1847, Yulee Papers. The charge that Douglas owned slaves would reappear as part of the North's vilification of him after the passage of the Kansas-Nebraska Act. See Gerald M. Capers, *Stephen A. Douglas: Defender of the Union* (Boston: Little, Brown and Company, 1959), 119.

10. David Gavin Diary, entry of 4 July 1856, Southern Historical Collection, University of North Carolina, Chapel Hill, N.C.

11. White, *Rhett,* 99–100; also see *Charleston Mercury,* 22 December 1848, 15–31 January, February 1849.

12. White, *Rhett,* 182.

13. A draft of Rhett's speech can be found in the Robert Barnwell Rhett Papers, Southern Historical Collection, University of North Carolina, Chapel Hill, N.C.

14. White, *Rhett,* 70–74, 100–101.

15. Rhett to Calhoun, 19 July 1849, quoted in White, *Rhett,* 105.

16. Cleo Hearon, *Mississippi and the Compromise of 1850* (Mississippi Historical Society Publications 14 [1913]: 7–299; reprint edition, New York: AMS Press, 1972), 40–44.

17. William J. Cooper, *The South and the Politics of Slavery, 1828–1856* (Baton Rouge: Louisiana State University Press, 1978), 57–58; James Roger Sharp, *The Jacksonians versus the Banks: Politics in the States after the Panic of 1837* (New York: Columbia University Press, 1970), 111–12.

18. Sharp, *Politics in the States,* 275–77.

19. Kenneth S. Greenberg, "The Second American Revolution: South Carolina Politics, Society, and Secession, 1776-1860," Ph.D. diss., University of Wisconsin, 1976.

20. Arthur C. Cole, "The South and the Right of Secession in the Early Fifties," *Mississippi Valley Historical Review* 1 (December 1914): 377.

21. Never again would men not totally swept away in radicalism wish for South Carolina to act alone. "We must unite the South," wrote Hammond. "Every head, heart, every hand must be devoted to that purpose. The impatient must be restrained; the timid and the wavering must be encouraged; the laggard must be whipped in and the deserter shot." Hammond to Beverley Tucker, 11 March 1836, in Freehling, *Nullification Era, 205.* Butler, from Edgefield, and Barnwell, from Beaufort, nevertheless reflected the conservatism endemic to Charleston.

22. N. W. Stephenson, "Southern Nationalism in South Carolina in 1851," *American Historical Review* 36 (1931): 316–17. South Carolina was also beset during this time by factional haggling over the issue of the state bank. See John A. Calhoun to John C. Calhoun, 14 December 1849, in Chauncey S. Boucher and Robert R. Brooks, eds., *Correspondence Addressed to John C. Calhoun, 1837–1849,* American Historical Association *Annual Report,* 1929, 532–33.

23. Hammond to Edmund Ruffin, 7 May 1850, Ruffin Papers.

24. Holman Hamilton, *Prologue to Conflict: The Crisis and Compromise of 1850* (Lexington: University of Kentucky Press, 1964), Chapter 1.

25. James Byrne Ranck, *Albert Gallatin Brown: Radical Southern Nationalist* (New York: D. Appleton-Century Company, Inc., 1937), 61–63; Ray Holder, "The Brown-Winans Canvass for Congress, 1849," *Journal of Mississippi History* 40 (November 1978): 353–73.

26. *Mississippi Free Trader,* 19 January 1850, cited in Ranck, *Brown,* 64. Also see *Congressional Globe,* 31st Congress, 1st session, 257–61.

27. Calhoun to David L. Yulee, 19 October 1849, Yulee Papers.

28. A. Hutchinson to Calhoun, 5 October 1849, in *Correspondence of Calhoun.*

29. Calhoun to Collin S. Tarpley, 9 July 1849, quoted in Hearon, *Mississippi and the Compromise of 1850,* 62.

30. J. F. H. Claiborne, ed., *Life and Correspondence of John A. Quitman,* 2 vols. (New York: Harper & Brothers, 1860), II, 25.

31. Hearon, *Mississippi and the Compromise of 1850,* 61–68.

32. Cooper, *Politics of Slavery,* 292.

33. Thomas J. Green to Editor, *Southern Press,* 29 September 1850, Green Papers. Also see Edmund Ruffin's blistering castigation of Houston in William Kauffman Scarborough, ed., *The Diary of Edmund Ruffin: Volume 1, Toward Independence, October, 1856–April, 1861* (Baton Rouge: Louisiana State University Press, 1972), 33–34.

34. Houston's dislike of Calhoun perhaps stemmed from the South Carolinian's role in the Nullification crisis, but there were rumors that the real source of enmity stretched back to when Houston, serving as subagent for the Cherokee Indians, had been reprimanded by Calhoun, then secretary of war in James Monroe's cabinet. See Thomas J. Green to Editor, *Southern Press,* 29 September 1850, Green Papers.

35. Anna Irene Sandbo, "Beginning of the Secession Movement in Texas," *Southwestern Historical Quarterly* 18 (July 1972): 46–48.

36. Ibid., 44–45.

37. Randolph B. Campbell, "Texas and the Nashville Convention," *Southwestern Historical Quarterly* 76 (July 1972): 2–4.

38. The Virginia Resolutions are reprinted in the *Charleston Mercury,* 16 February 1850.

39. Campbell, "Texas and the Nashville Convention," 3–4.

40. Ibid., 6–8.

41. Charles C. Mills to Governor Peter H. Bell, 18 January 1850, quoted in Campbell, "Texas and the Nashville Convention," 14.

42. *Charleston Mercury,* 31 January 1850.

43. *Concordia Intelligencer,* 5 January 1850.

44. John Gardner Cooper, "Winning the Lower South to the Compromise of 1850," Ph.D. diss., Louisiana State University and Agricultural and Mechanical College, 1974, 2 vols., II, 33. See also Avery O. Craven, *The Growth of Southern Nationalism, 1848–1861* (Baton Rouge: Louisiana State University Press, 1953), 86; also James K. Greer, "Louisiana Politics, 1845-61," *Louisiana Historical Quarterly* 12 (October 1929): 573–74; also M. J. White, "Louisiana and the

Secession Movement of the Early Fifties," *Proceedings of the Mississippi Valley Historical Association for the Year 1914–1915,* vol. 8 (Cedar Rapids, Iowa: Torch Press, 1916); 277–88.

45. Craven, *Southern Nationalism,* 87–88.

46. Quoted in Craven, *Southern Nationalism,* 83.

47. Venable to Calhoun, 7 August 1849, in *Correspondence to Calhoun,* 521–22.

48. Nor was there among their colleagues. Bedford Brown took an active part in attempts to relieve tensions and provide for compromise. See Brown to William Brown, 4 March 1850, Brown Papers.

49. Craven, *Southern Nationalism,* 84–85.

50. W. H. Haywood, Jr., to F. P. Blair, 7 May 1850, quoted in Joseph Carlyle Sitterson, *The Secession Movement in North Carolina,* James Sprunt Studies in History and Political Science, vol. 23, no. 2 (Chapel Hill: University of North Carolina Press, 1939), 62.

51. John H. McHenry to R. M. T. Hunter, 21 February 1850, in Charles H. Ambler, ed., *Correspondence of R. M. T. Hunter, 1826–1876,* American Historical Association Annual Report, 1916, pt. 2.

52. William E. Parrish, *David Rice Atchison of Missouri: Border Politician,* University of Missouri Studies, vol. 34, no. 1 (Columbia: University of Missouri Press, 1961), 101. Benton had reversed his anti-Northern sentiments of 1819. See Moore, *Missouri Controversy,* 260.

53. *Boston Daily Advertiser,* 23 February 1850, quoted in Herbert D. Foster, "Webster's Seventh of March Speech and the Secession Movement of 1850," *American Historical Review* 27 (1921–1922): 252.

54. Joseph H. Parks, "John Bell and the Compromise of 1850," *Journal of Southern History* 9 (August 1943): 328.

55. St. George Sioussat, "Tennessee, the Compromise of 1850, and the Nashville Convention," *Mississippi Valley Historical Review* 2 (December 1915): 323–24. Also see Parks, "Bell and the Compromise," 345–46. Also Craven, *Southern Nationalism,* 87.

56. Yulee had suffered at the hands of his opponents because of his family. Branded an unnaturalized alien in 1845, he was harassed by the stratagems of a group of Florida Whigs to remove him from the Senate. See [W. J. Wait] to J. M. Berrien, 28 April 1845, Berrien Papers. Yulee claimed that his father was naturalized under the treaty of cession from Spain, but there was a question as to whether his father had been in Florida at the time of the treaty. See David [Durham] to Berrien, 24 November 1845, Berrien Papers. As signatures (some of them alleged to have been forged) were collected on petitions in Florida demanding Yulee's removal from the Senate, responsible Whigs in Washington attempted to stop the initiative out of fear that it would make the party indistinguishable from the Native Americans. See Durham to Berrien, 29 December 1845; J. D. Westcott, Jr., to Berrien, 22 January 1846; [James Keough] to Durham, 18 March 1846, Berrien Papers. Also see Box 27 of the Yulee Papers for an extensive body of documents connected to this controversy.

57. Yulee to Calhoun, 10 July 1849, Yulee Papers.

58. Dorothy Dodd, "The Secession Movement in Florida, 1850–1861," *Florida Historical Quarterly* 12 (July 1933): 3–7.

59. D. L. Yulee, Jackson Morton, and E. C. Cabell to Governor Thomas Brown, 6 February 1850, Yulee Papers.

60. Brown to Yulee, Morton, and Cabell, 22 February 1850, Yulee Papers.

61. John Meador, "Florida and the Compromise of 1850," *Florida Historical Quarterly* 29 (1960–61): 17–18; also see Craven, *Southern Nationalism,* 88.

62. Quoted in Ulrich B. Phillips, *The Life of Robert Toombs* (New York: Macmillan Company, 1913), 77.

63. Craven, *Southern Nationalism,* 85. Also see Richard H. Shryock, *Georgia and the Union in 1850* (Durham, N.C.: Duke University Press, 1926), 217–18, 220.

64. William Garrett, *Reminiscences of Public Men in Alabama for Thirty Years* (Atlanta: Plantation Publishing Company's Press, 1872), 544–45.

65. John Witherspoon DuBose, *The Life and Times of William Lowndes Yancey: A History of Political Parties in the United States from 1834 to 1864; Especially as to the Origin of the Confederate States* (Birmingham: Roberts & Son, 1892), 203. Also see Joseph Hodgson, *The Cradle of the Confederacy; or, The Times of Troup, Quitman, and Yancey: A Sketch of Southwestern Political History from the Formation of the Federal Government to A. D. 1861* (Mobile: Mobile Register Publishing Office, 1876), 271–72.

66. DuBose, *Life and Times of Yancey,* 188.

67. Ibid., 188–89.

68. Hilliard, *Politics and Pen Pictures,* 200; also see DuBose, *Life and Times of Yancey,* 241.

69. Lewy Dorman, *Party Politics in Alabama from 1850 through 1860* (Wetumpka, Ala.: Wetumpka Publishing Company, 1935), 43–44; also see Craven, *Southern Nationalism,* 86.

70. Foster, "Webster's Seventh of March Speech," 257–59.

71. Cooper, *Politics of Slavery,* 293.

72. Ibid., 294.

73. *Charleston Mercury,* 24 January 1850.

74. Wiltse, *Calhoun: Sectionalist,* 386–87; Jameson, *Correspondence of Calhoun,* 783; Hilliard, *Politics and Pen Pictures,* 220.

75. Hilliard, *Politics and Pen Pictures,* 222. Also see Foster, "Webster's Seventh of March Speech," 257–59.

76. Hilliard, *Politics and Pen Pictures,* 225–26. Calhoun dictated a set of resolutions a few days prior to his death in which he set forth the main points of his 4 March speech. His last appearance in the Senate was on 13 March, when a heated exchange between him and Mississippi Senator Henry S. Foote, who had broken with Southern Democrats on the issue of a Southern movement, nearly caused the sick man to collapse on the Senate floor. Jefferson Davis and Andrew Pickens Butler intervened and escorted Calhoun from the Senate. He never returned. He died on 31 March at 7 A.M. See David M. Potter and Don

Fehrenbacher, *Impending Crisis,* 101n; also Wiltse, *Calhoun: Sectionalist,* 471–72, 475.

77. Quoted in Foster, "Webster's Seventh of March Speech," 255.

78. Calhoun to James H. Hammond, 14 February 1849, in *Correspondence of Calhoun.*

79. Wiltse, *Calhoun: Sectionalist,* 483.

80. Hammond to Calhoun, 6 March 1850, quoted in Hamilton, *Prologue to Conflict,* 74. On the posthumous appearance of Calhoun's last work, Hammond would say that "since Aristotle, there has been nothing like it." Hammond to Ruffin, 30 September 1851, Ruffin Papers.

81. Webster to Franklin Haven, 5 September 1850, quoted in Claude Moore Fuess, *Daniel Webster,* 2 vols. (Boston: Little, Brown, and Company, 1930), II, 221.

82. Bedford Brown to William Brown, 4 March 1850, Brown Papers. Brown never forgave Calhounites in the North Carolina legislature for opposing his bid for the United States Senate. See Cooper, *Politics of Slavery,* 116.

83. Calhoun to Hammond, 7 March 1849, in *Correspondence of Calhoun.*

84. Henry L. Benning to Howell Cobb, 1 July 1849, in Ulrich B. Phillips, ed., *The Correspondence of Robert Toombs, Alexander H. Stephens, and Howell Cobb,* American Historical Association *Annual Report,* 1911, pt. 2.

85. Julian Ruffin to Edmund Ruffin, 5 April 1850, Ruffin Papers.

86. Tucker to James H. Hammond, 4 December 1849, quoted in Robert J. Brugger, *Beverley Tucker: Heart over Head in the Old South* (Baltimore: Johns Hopkins University Press, 1978), 178.

CHAPTER THREE
"A Partial Affair"

1. Bedford Brown to William Brown, 4 March 1850, Brown Papers.

2. Henry S. Foote to John C. Calhoun, 25 September 1849, in *Correspondence of Calhoun.* Also see Craven, *Coming of the Civil War,* 258.

3. An illegal duel had caused Foote's departure from Alabama in 1826, but the pugnacious side of his character was far from cooled. Four more duels, two with Sargent S. Prentiss, had punctuated an admittedly bellicose public career. See Clayton Rand, *Men of Spine in Mississippi* (Gulfport: The Dixie Press, 1940), 161.

4. Holman Hamilton, *Zachary Taylor: Soldier in the White House* (Indianapolis: Bobbs-Merrill Company, Inc., 1951), 326–27. Also see Parrish, *Atchison,* 99–100.

5. Columbus *Enquirer,* 19 February 1850.

6. Ibid., 9 April, 21 May 1850.

7. *Daily National Intelligencer,* 30 April 1850.

8. Shryock, *Georgia and the Union, 257–58;* also see the *Charleston Mercury,* 19 February 1850.

9. *Concordia Intelligencer,* 6 April 1850.

10. *Richmond Whig,* 17 May 1850.

11. Henry T. Shanks, *The Secession Movement in Virginia, 1847–1861* (Richmond: Garrett and Massie, 1934), 29–30.

12. Ibid., 30; Craven, *Southern Nationalism,* 84.

13. *Richmond Whig,* 17 May 1850.

14. Julian Ruffin to Edmund Ruffin, 5 April 1850, Ruffin Papers.

15. Edmund Ruffin, Jr., to Edmund Ruffin, 3 April 1850, Ruffin Papers.

16. Tucker to James H. Hammond, 26 March 1850, quoted in Shanks, *Secession Movement in Virginia,* 31–32.

17. Ibid., 33–34. See also Brugger, *Tucker,* 181. Wise gave up his place to Tucker because he did not want to go, but he claimed that the Virginia Constitutional Convention required his presence in the state. Tucker did not care for Wise, so he must have considered it fortunate that he would take his place at Nashville. See Craig M. Simpson, *A Good Southerner: The Life of Henry A. Wise of Virginia* (Chapel Hill: University of North Carolina Press, 1985.), 75–76.

18. Moore, *Missouri Controversy,* 241–42, 259–60.

19. Tucker to William Gilmore Simms, February 1851, quoted in Shanks, *Secession Movement in Virginia,* 69.

20. Brugger, *Tucker,* xiii.

21. Ibid., iv, 170–71.

22. Ibid., 66, 74.

23. Ibid., iv.

24. William P. Trent, *William Gilmore Simms* (Boston: Houghton, Mifflin and Company, 1892), 82, 111, 324–25.

25. Ibid., 10–11.

26. Brugger, *Tucker,* 175–76.

27. Hamilton, *Prologue to Conflict,* 60.

28. The phrase is Robert Winthrop's, quoted in Foster, "Webster's Seventh of March Speech," 255.

29. Tucker to Hammond, 8 February 1850, cited in Brugger, *Tucker,* 179.

30. Tucker to Lucy Tucker, n.d., cited in Brugger, *Tucker,* 181-82; Tucker's acerbic commentary on Cincinnati appeared in the *Charleston Mercury,* 25 July 1850.

31. Tucker to Lucy Tucker, n.d., cited in Brugger, *Tucker,* 182.

32. Carol Bleser, ed., *The Hammonds of Redcliffe* (New York: Oxford University Press, 1981), 4–5.

33. Ibid., 6. Hammond's health always was a source of his complaints. He described it on one occasion as "monstrous." See Hammond to Catherine Hammond, 27 November 1841, Hammond Papers.

34. Bleser, *Hammonds of Redcliffe,* 9. Why Hammond fondled his nieces over a two-year period has elicited a number of explanations. Hammond made

excuses at the time, proving that it is nothing new to describe improper behavior as merely an error in judgment. For a modern defense of Hammond that employs psychological and sociological ruminations, see Drew Gilpin Faust, *A Sacred Circle: The Dilemma of the Intellectual in the Old South, 1841–1860* (Baltimore: Johns Hopkins University Press, 1977), 41.

35. Bleser, *Hammonds of Redcliffe,* 10.

36. Hammond to Ruffin, 20 November 1845, Ruffin Papers.

37. Bleser, *Hammonds of Redcliffe,* 10. While Hampton's efforts to damage Hammond were successful in 1846, they were purchased at high cost for his daughters, none of whom ever married. See Drew Gilpin Faust, *James Henry Hammond and the Old South: A Design for Mastery* (Baton Rouge: Louisiana State University Press, 1982), 299.

38. Hammond to Ruffin, 12 January 1850, Ruffin Papers.

39. Ibid.

40. Hammond to Ruffin, 8 February 1850, Ruffin Papers.

41. Hammond to Ruffin, 7 May 1850, Ruffin Papers.

42. Ibid.

43. J. H. Ingraham, ed., *The Sunny South, or The Southerner at Home: Embracing Five Years' Experience of a Northern Governess in the Land of Sugar and Cotton* (Philadelphia: G. G. Evans, 1860), 72–74.

44. F. Garvin Davenport, *Cultural Life in Nashville on the Eve of the Civil War* (Chapel Hill: University of North Carolina Press, 1941), 199–200.

45. Ibid., 202–3.

46. Sioussat, "Tennessee and the Compromise of 1850," 323–34; also see Parks, "John Bell and the Compromise of 1850," 345–46; Craven, *Southern Nationalism,* 87; Ingraham, *Sunny South,* 136.

47. Sioussat, "Tennessee and the Compromise of 1850," 330.

48. Ingraham, *Sunny South,* 136.

49. Ibid., 136–37.

50. C. B. Strong to John M. Berrien, 19 May 1850, Berrien Papers.

51. Sioussat, "Tennessee and the Compromise of 1850," 229–30.

52. B. C. Yancey to Committee of Electoral Delegates, 20 April 1850, Microfilm, B. C. Yancey Papers, Ralph Brown Draughon Library, Auburn University, Auburn, Ala.

53. Craven, *Southern Nationalism,* 93–96.

54. Thelma Jennings, *The Nashville Convention: Southern Movement for Unity, 1848–1851* (Memphis: Memphis State University Press, 1980), 126–29. William F. Gordon of Albermarle County would attend both sessions of the Nashville Convention—the only Virginian to do so. Willoughby Newton was, in 1850, a Unionist and a Compromiser, although later in the decade anger would overwhelm his moderation to make him an ardent secessionist. W. O. Goode and R. H. Claybrooke were Compromisers. See Shanks, *Secession Movement in Virginia,* 121–22.

55. *Congressional Globe,* 31st Congress, 1st session, 13 August 1850, pt. 2,

1536; also see Campbell, "Texas and the Nashville Convention," 1–14; Jennings, *Nashville Convention,* 121–22.

56. Dorman, *Politics in Alabama,* 44–45.

57. Jennings, *Nashville Convention,* 120, 122–25, 130.

58. Ingraham, *Sunny South,* 138–40. Pillow's conduct in Mexico during the war had been, according to Winfield Scott, unseemly. Combined with the political maneuvering that had caused James K. Polk to install Pillow on Scott's staff, this was all the worse. Beyond this, Pillow had been involved in the last piece of business before the House of Representatives that John Quincy Adams had heard. It was a resolution, sponsored by a Whig, thanking Scott, that was intruded upon by a rider, sponsored by a Democrat, to include Pillow. Undoubtedly it was pure coincidence, but during the vote on this question Adams had been stricken. Thus, a stretch of the imagination could say that among Pillow's many sins was the murder of John Quincy Adams, if only because of the legislative temerity of his champions. See Hilliard, *Politics and Pen Pictures,* 183–84.

59. Jennings, *Nashville Convention,* 114.

60. Foster, "Webster's Seventh of March Speech," 225. Foote would vote against the admission of California, but he supported the Compromise in sum. See John McCardell, *The Idea of a Southern Nation: Southern Nationalism and Southern Nationalists, 1830–1860* (New York: W. W. Norton and Company, 1979), 303.

61. Robert W. Dubay, *John Jones Pettus, Mississippi Fire-Eater: His Life and Times, 1813–1867* (Jackson: University Press of Mississippi, 1975), 13–14. A report prepared by Pettus for the Mississippi legislature in February showed how far his thinking had advanced on the subjects of secession and, indirectly, civil war. In studying the Southern Railroad Company, Pettus concluded that expanded rail service would not only profit the state commercially but would also prove advantageous militarily "should protection and defense be needed."

62. Jennings, *Nashville Convention,* 116–19; also see Beth G. Crabtree and James W. Patton, *"Journal of a Secesh Lady": The Diary of Catherine Devereaux Edmonston, 1860–1866* (Raleigh: North Carolina Division of Archives and History, 1979), 744.

63. Cheves was described by Cave Johnson as "very old and said to be intemperate and of course useless except [for] his name." Johnson to James Buchanan, 6 June 1850, quoted in Sioussat, "Tennessee and the Compromise of 1850," 333n. See also Jennings, *Nashville Convention,* 107–11.

64. White, *Rhett,* 105.

65. Ingraham, *Sunny South,* 132–34. Hammond had used articles by Ruffin to try to persuade Georgia to the cause since Georgian envy and suspicion of South Carolina tended to undermine advice from Carolinians. See Hammond to Ruffin, 8 February, 7 May 1850, Ruffin Papers.

66. Ingraham, *Sunny South,* 134.

67. Ibid., 140.

68. Ibid., 135.

69. Jennings, *Nashville Convention,* 137–45.

70. William O. Goode to R. M. T. Hunter, 20 April 1850, in *Correspondence of Hunter.*

71. Hiram Warner to Howell Cobb, 17 March 1850, in *Correspondence of Toombs,* Stephens, and Cobb.

72. *Charleston Mercury,* 4 March 1850.

73. Buchanan to Davis, 16 March 1850, John Bassett Moore, *The Works of James Buchanan, Comprising his Speeches, State Papers, and Private Correspondence,* 12 vols. (New York: Antiquarian Press, 1960), VIII, 372.

74. Shryock, *Georgia and the Union,* 270–71.

75. Jennings, *Nashville Convention,* 145.

76. White, *Rhett,* 106–7; also see Jennings, *Nashville Convention,* 147–49; *Charleston Mercury,* 20 June 1850.

77. Hammond to Calhoun, 5 March 1850, in *Correspondence of Calhoun.*

78. M. W. Cluskey, ed., *The Political Textbook or Encyclopedia Containing Everything Necessary for the Reference of the Politicians and Statesmen of the United States,* 12th ed. (Philadelphia: Jas. B. Smith & Co., 1860), 595–96. The most important of these additional resolutions was the last, which called for the reassembly of the convention in November in order to evaluate the progress of the compromise action. See Jennings, *Nashville Convention,* 146–47.

79. Reuben Davis, *Recollections of Mississippi and Mississippians,* reprint (Jackson: University and College Press of Mississippi, 1972), 325–26. Also see Jennings, *Nashville Convention,* 149–50.

80. Ingraham, *Sunny South,* 137–38.

81. Jennings, *Nashville Convention,* 154.

82. Brugger, *Tucker,* 184–87; Shanks, *Secession Movement in Virginia,* 34–35; Ingraham, *Sunny South,* 184.

83. Brugger, *Tucker,* 187.

84. Johnson to Buchanan, 6 June 1850, quoted in Sioussat, "Tennessee and the Compromise of 1850," 133n.

85. White, *Rhett,* 108.

86. Potter and Fehrenbacher, *Impending Crisis,* 105.

CHAPTER FOUR
"That We Were All Such Traitors!"

1. Craven, *Southern Nationalism,* 97–98.

2. *Charleston Mercury,* 20 July 1850.

3. Ibid., 16 August 1850.

4. White, *Rhett,* 109–11; *Columbus Enquirer,* 9 July 1850; *Charleston Mercury,* 20 July 1850.

5. Sioussat, "Tennessee and the Nashville Convention," 338–40; *Charleston Mercury,* 20 July 1850.

6. J. A. Campbell to Calhoun, 20 December 1847, in *Correspondence of Calhoun.*

7. *Dictionary of American Biography,* 1931 ed., s.v. "George Goldwaithe," by Albert B. Moore; DuBose, *Life and Times of Yancey,* 247–48.

8. DuBose, *Life and Times of Yancey,* 248; Hilliard, *Politics and Pen Pictures,* 255; G. F. Mellen, "Henry W. Hilliard and William Lowndes Yancey," *Sewanee Review* 17 (January 1909): 47.

9. DuBose, *Life and Times of Yancey,* 248–49.

10. Simms to Tucker, 11 July 1850, *Letters of Simms.*

11. Kenneth F. Neighbors, "The Taylor-Neighbors Struggle over the Upper Rio Grande Region of Texas in 1850," *Southwestern Historical Quarterly* 61 (April 1958): 458.

12. Phillips, *Correspondence of Toombs, Stephens, and Cobb,* 193; Loomis Morton Ganaway, *New Mexico and the Sectional Controversy, 1846–1861* (Albuquerque: University of New Mexico Press, 1944; reprint edition, Philadelphia: Porcupine Press, 1976), 14–34.

13. *Matagorda Tribune,* quoted in *Charleston Mercury,* 16 July 1850; Peter H. Bell to Zachary Taylor, 14 June 1850, *Charleston Mercury,* 10 August 1850; Holman Hamilton, *Zachary Taylor: Soldier in the White House* (Indianapolis: Bobbs-Merrill Company, Inc., 1951), 387.

14. Duvall to R. M. T. Hunter, 13 August 1850, *Correspondence of Hunter.*

15. Hamilton, *Taylor,* 388–91.

16. Phillips, *Correspondence of Toombs, Stephens, and Cobb,* 217–18.

17. Robert J. Rayback, *Millard Fillmore: Biography of a President* (East Aurora, N.Y.: Henry Stewart, Inc., 1972), 247, 250.

18. Neighbors, "The Taylor-Neighbors Struggle," 458.

19. John N. Moffit to Rusk, 28 August 1850, quoted in Hamilton, *Prologue to Conflict,* 151–52. "The storm Kings," mused the *Columbus Enquirer,* "despairing of success in their efforts to drag the people into revolution and disunion if California is admitted as a state, have turned their attention to the protection of the rights of Texas hoping to find some point . . . where they can place their lever and overturn the constitution." See 3 September 1850.

20. Quitman to J. Pinckney Henderson, 18 August 1850, *Quitman Correspondence.*

21. Reuben Davis, *Recollections,* 308; Rosalie Q[uitman] Duncan, "Life of General John A. Quitman," *Publications of the Mississippi Historical Society* 4 (1901): 421; Hamilton, *Prologue to Conflict,* 152; Quitman to Henderson, *Quitman Correspondence,* II, 42; also see Quitman to F. C. Jones, *Charleston Mercury,* 4 September 1850. Jones was the editor of the *Vicksburg Sentinel.*

22. Neighbors, "The Taylor-Neighbors Struggle," 461, 461n.

23. A copy of the "Agreement between Turney, Barnwell, Soulé, and others to Defeat the California Compromise, 2 August 1850" was provided to Rhett two

years later. See Turney to Rhett, 1 May 1852, Rhett Papers, Chapel Hill; also see Georgia *Telegraph,* 27 August 1850; *Concordia Intelligencer,* 14 September 1850; Nevins, *Ordeal of the Union: Fruits of Manifest Destiny,* 343.

24. Louisa A. Quitman to John A. Quitman, 23 September 1850, Quitman Family Papers, Southern Historical Collection, University of North Carolina, Chapel Hill, N.C.

25. Hammond to Simms, 27 June 1850; also see Hammond to H. W. Conner, 17 June 1850, quoted in Hamer, *Secession Movement in South Carolina,* 65–66; Hamer, *Secession Movement in South Carolina,* 73–74.

26. Barnwell to Quitman, 19 September 1850, quoted in Hamer, *Secession Movement in South Carolina,* 71.

27. Seabrook to Quitman, 20 September 1850; Seabrook to Quitman, 23 October 1850, in *Correspondence of Quitman.*

28. James W. Garner, "The First Struggle Over Secession in Mississippi," *Publications of the Mississippi Historical Society* 4 (1901): 95–98.

29. Towns to Seabrook, 25 September 1850, in Shryock, *Georgia and the Union,* 65; Seabrook to Towns, 8 October 1850, cited in Hamer, *Secession Movement in South Carolina,* 69.

30. "Memorandum for Proclamation, September 1850," Quitman Family Papers. There are two drafts of this memorandum, the second not fully listing Southern grievances. Also see Felix Huston to Quitman, 19 September 1850, quoted in Hearon, *Mississippi and the Compromise of 1850,* 156; also see Quitman to Louisa T. Quitman, 1 October 1850, Quitman Family Papers.

31. Hearon, *Mississippi and the Compromise of 1850,* 167–70; also see Ranck, *Brown,* 76–80.

32. Brugger, *Tucker,* 189; Garner, "Secession in Mississippi," 98; also see *Mississippian,* 16, 25 October 1850.

33. Garner, "Secession in Mississippi," 99, 99n; *Correspondence of Quitman,* II, 45–46. Quitman's attention was turned away abruptly from these matters in February 1851 upon his arrest for alleged connections with a Cuban filibuster arranged by the notorious Lopez. See *Correspondence of Quitman,* II, 74–75.

34. *Montgomery Advertiser and State Gazette,* 8 October 1850; *Charleston Mercury,* 23 October 1850; Dorman, *Politics in Alabama,* 46–48; *Huntsville Democrat,* 17 October 1850; Jennings, *Nashville Convention,* 180–81.

35. Howard C. Perkins, "A Neglected Phase of the Movement for Southern Unity, 1847–1852," *Journal of Southern History* 12 (May 1946): 187; White, *Rhett,* 112; Parrish, *Atchison,* 160.

36. Calhoun to A. P. Calhoun, 22 October 1850, in *Correspondence of Calhoun; Charleston Mercury,* 13 July 1850; James Gadsden to Thomas J. Green, 19 May 1853, Green Papers. Because of the cholera epidemic and the easier accessibility of Milledgeville, the Georgia capital had been suggested as an alternate meeting place, but such notions had been disregarded. See *Milledgeville Federal Union,* quoted in *Charleston Mercury,* 22 May 1850.

37. Jennings, *Nashville Convention,* 189–97.

38. Hamer, *Secession Movement in South Carolina,* 71.

39. *Charleston Mercury,* 22 November 1850; Jennings, *Nashville Convention,* 195.

40. Sioussat, "Tennessee and the Nashville Convention," 344–47; Brown would ultimately adopt the South Carolina position, thus causing a bitter rivalry with Nicholson and splitting the Democracy in Tennessee in the process.

41. Jennings, *Nashville Convention,* 192–97; see also Cluskey, *Political Textbook,* 596–98 for the radical preamble and resolutions, and 598–99 for Tennessee's moderate resolutions; also the *Charleston Mercury,* 23 November 1850.

42. Jennings, *Nashville Convention,* 197.

43. Cole, "The South and the Right of Secession," 383–84.

44. Rutherford to Howell Cobb, 16 April 1850, *Correspondence of Toombs, Stephens, and Cobb;* "Governor Collier to the Citizens of Alabama," *Mobile Advertiser,* 3, 4 November 1850.

45. *Natchez Free Trader,* 25 September 1850.

46. *Dallas Gazette,* 4 June 1850; Cole, "The South and the Right of Secession," 384.

47. Edmund Ruffin, Jr., to Edmund Ruffin, 24 October 1850, Ruffin Papers.

48. Edmund Ruffin, Jr., to Edmund Ruffin, 2, 21 November 1850, also see 13 June, 13 July 1850, Ruffin Papers; Craven, *Ruffin,* 113–16.

49. Brugger, *Tucker,* 188.

50. *Charleston Mercury,* 16 July 1850.

51. *Letters of Simms,* III, 59; Tucker to Simms, 5 December 1850, cited in Trent, *Simms,* 180.

52. Perry, *Biographical Sketches,* 115.

53. *Charleston Mercury,* 30 November, 19, 20 December 1850.

54. Hamilton to the people of South Carolina, *Charleston Mercury,* 28 November 1850; N. W. Stephenson, "Southern Nationalism in South Carolina in 1851," *American Historical Review* 36 (1931): 321–23; Hamer, *Secession Movement in South Carolina,* 76–78.

55. Shryock, *Georgia and the Union,* 274–75, 278; also see Phillip Cook, et al., to J. M. Berrien, 23 October 1850, Berrien Papers.

56. *Charleston Mercury,* 16 August 1850, 23 August 1850. "Speech of the Honorable R. B. Rhett delivered at the Mass Meeting at Macon, Georgia, on 27 August 1850," Rhett Papers, Chapel Hill; also see *Georgia Telegraph,* 20 August 1850.

57. *Charleston Mercury,* 28, 30 August 1850; *Georgia Telegraph,* 27 August 1850. The *Southern Press* had predicted that if the California Bill passed, Georgia would take "decisive and effective measures." See 12 August 1850.

58. *Southern Banner,* 29 August 1850.

59. White, *Rhett,* 111; also see Shryock, *Georgia and the Union,* 284–85.

60. *Savannah Daily Morning News,* 24 August 1850.

61. Shryock, *Georgia and the Union,* 286–87.

62. Ibid., 304–5.

63. *Charleston Mercury,* 15 August 1850.

64. *Columbus Enquirer,* 16 July 1850.

65. John B. Lamar to Howell Cobb, 3 July 1850, in *Correspondence of Toombs, Stephens, and Cobb.*

66. William Woods to Howell Cobb, 15 September 1850, *Correspondence of Toombs, Stephens, and Cobb.*

67. Elwood Fisher to R. M. T. Hunter, 29 October 1850, in *Correspondence of Hunter.*

68. Henry L. Benning to Howell Cobb, 1 July 1849, in *Correspondence of Toombs, Stephens, and Cobb.*

69. Shryock, *Georgia and the Union,* 289–91, 306, 308; Jennings, *Nashville Convention,* 183. James M. Berrien and James Jackson of Georgia advocated this course as did Virginian John B. Floyd and Arkansas Governor John Seldon Roane.

70. Simms to Tucker, 11 September 1850, *Letters of Simms.*

71. The other exception was Democratic Representative H. A. Haralson. See Shryock, *Georgia and the Union,* 308n, 311.

72. Towns to Berrien, 17 April 1851, Berrien Papers.

73. R. M. Smith, et al., to Berrien, 28 October 1850, Berrien Papers; also see *Georgia Telegraph,* 3 September 1850; Shryock, *Georgia and the Union,* 296–97, 319. The Unionists captured about 46,000 votes to the Southern Rights total of 24,000.

74. John H. Lumpkin to Howell Cobb, 6 October 1850, in *Correspondence of Toombs, Stephens, and Cobb;* also see *Charleston Mercury,* 26 November 1850 for election tabulations.

75. Shryock, *Georgia and the Union,* 327–28.

76. Ibid., 327–29, 314, 332–33.

77. Parrish, *Atchison,* 599–600. Peter Knupfer has argued that by the 1850s the act of compromise had become more important than the substance it contained. Participants deluded themselves that any compromise should automatically be venerated, and that its term would constitute a final settlement of differences. See Peter B. Knupfer, *The Union As It Is: Constitutional Unionism and Sectional Compromise, 1787–1861* (Chapel Hill: University of North Carolina Press, 1991). Such an attitude characterized the convention that adopted the Georgia Platform at the end of 1850.

78. Shryock, *Georgia and the Union,* 335–36, 340.

79. Towns to Berrien, 17 April 1851, Berrien Papers.

80. Roy F. Nichols, *The Democratic Machine, 1850–1854* (New York: Longmans, Green & Co., 1923), 26. Florida was an exception for although fitting, in some cases, into the Democratic decline, it was for reasons more to do with state railroad construction than with the sectional controversy. David Yulee was defeated by the Compromise Democrat Stephen R. Mallory, but primarily because Yulee wanted a Fernandina to Cedar Key Route while Whigs wanted a Jacksonville to Pensacola route; South Florida Democrats in the legislature did not want a railroad at all. The Whigs and South Florida Democrats hence combined for Mallory. Whig Edward C. Cabell ran against the Democratic nominee John Beard during the summer of 1850, and Beard lost by so strongly resisting the

Compromise and advocating disunion as an alternative. Yet the high returns for Beard, about 47 percent from the sparse southern and eastern parts of Florida, matched well against Cabell's support from the wealthier cotton and tobacco counties. While Beard's support was not entirely of disunionist bent, it did indicate a high presence of discontent that would lead within a year to the formation of small, yet vocal Southern Rights Associations in Gadsden, Leon, Jefferson, and Madison Counties. To further muddy Florida trends, in 1850 Democrats recaptured the state legislature, which they had lost to the Whigs in 1848. See Dodd, "Secession Movement in Florida," 10–12; Meador, "Florida and the Compromise of 1850," 21; and Herbert J. Doherty, Jr., *Richard Keith Call: Southern Unionist* (Gainesville: University of Florida Press, 1961), 142–43.

81. [Lottie P.] to Sarah Yancey, 14 December 1850, B. C. Yancey Papers.

82. Parrish, *Atchison,* 160–61.

83. Lillian Kibler, *Benjamin F. Perry: South Carolina Unionist,* 253; Hamer, *Secession Movement in South Carolina,* 76–82; Percy S. Flippin, *Herschel V. Johnson of Georgia: States Rights Unionist* (Richmond: Dietz Publishing Co., 1931), 30.

84. Cooper, *Politics of Slavery,* 296–97, 308–9.

85. Quoted in the *Charleston Mercury,* 28 November 1850. Craven, *Coming of the Civil War,* 269–70.

86. Duncan, "Life of Quitman," 243.

87. Shryock, *Georgia and the Union,* 334n. The inscription remains the same to this day.

88. Hamer, *Secession Movement in South Carolina,* 82–83.

89. Frederick Law Olmstead, *A Journey in the Seaboard Slave States with Remarks on Their Economy* (New York: Dix and Edwards, 1856), 404.

90. *Charleston Mercury,* 20, 21 December 1850.

CHAPTER FIVE
"Ungrateful, Cowardly, Stupid State"

1. *Concordia Intelligencer,* 15 June 1850; also see A. F. Rightor to Andrew McCollam, 25 July 1851, McCollam Papers.

2. White, *Rhett,* 121.

3. Mrs. Roger A. Pryor, *Reminiscences of Peace and War* (New York: The Macmillan Company, 1905), 9; Louise Wigfall Wright, *A Southern Girl in '61: The War-Time Memoirs of a Confederate Senator's Daughter* (New York: Doubleday, Page & Company, 1905), 21.

4. Elizabeth Rhett to Rhett, 7 January 1851, Rhett Papers, Charleston.

5. Drayton Nance to Rhett, 28 January 1851, Rhett Papers, Charleston.

6. Elizabeth Rhett to Rhett, 11 January 1851, Rhett Papers, Charleston.

7. Pryor, *Reminiscences,* 8–9, 14.

8. "Speech of R. B. Rhett, 15, 16 December on the Resolution submitted by

Henry S. Foote on the Compromise of 1850," *Charleston Mercury,* 29 December 1851.

9. Craven, *Southern Nationalism,* 146, 149. Rhett could have never matched the combustible language of Charles Sumner of Massachusetts who, in reviling the Southerner exercising his privilege under the Fugitive Slave Law, vowed that "the cities, towns and villages [of Massachusetts] shall refuse to receive the monster; they shall vomit him forth, never again to disturb the repose of our community." See *Charleston Mercury,* 24 May 1851. Not all Northerners, however, were against the law. See Stanley Campbell, *The Slave Catchers: Enforcement of the Fugitive Slave Law, 1850–1860* (Chapel Hill: University of North Carolina Press, 1968), 70, 120.

10. *Mississippi Free Trader,* 5 March 1851; John G. Barnwell, Jr., "Love of Order: The Origins and Resolution of South Carolina's First Secession Crisis," Ph.D. diss., University of North Carolina, Chapel Hill, 1979, 365–66.

11. Entry of 21 February 1856, David Gavin Diary, Southern Historical Collection, University of North Carolina, Chapel Hill, N.C.

12. Two South Carolina slaves, Cato and Team, in the course of their flight, turned upon pursuing dogs. Cato wounded two badly and then botched the lunge for his own throat. Entry of 2 March 1856, Gavin Diary.

13. John Hope Franklin, *The Militant South, 1800–1861* (Cambridge: Belknap Press of Harvard University Press, 1956), 90–91; Alfred Nathaniel Hunt, "The Influence of Haiti on the Antebellum South, 1791–1865," Ph.D. diss., University of Texas at Austin, 1975, 135–37. Stories of slave plots resembled Northern stories about Irish servants plotting to murder employers. See Michael F. Holt, *The Political Crisis of the 1850s* (New York: Wiley, 1978), 240.

14. John Lofton, *Insurrection in South Carolina: The Turbulent World of Denmark Vesey* (Yellow Springs, Ohio: Antioch Press, 1964), 146–47.

15. Robert A. Starobin, ed., *Denmark Vesey: The Slave Conspiracy of 1822* (Englewood Cliffs, N.J.: Prentice-Hall, Inc., 1970), 89; also see *Charleston City Gazette,* 14, 21 August 1822. Richard Wade in "The Vesey Plot: A Reconsideration," *Journal of Southern History* 30 (May 1964): 148–61, challenged the notion that there was a conspiracy, claiming that it existed only in the imaginations of hysterical Charlestonians. Sterling Stuckey, "Remembering Denmark Vesey," *Negro Digest* 15 (February 1966): 28–41, and William Freehling, *Prelude to Civil War,* 53–61, maintain that the plot was real and serious.

16. Franklin, *Militant South,* 78–79; also see Joseph Clarke Robert, *The Road from Monticello: A Study of the Virginia Slavery Debate of 1832,* Historical Papers of the Trinity College Historical Society, Series 24 (Durham, N.C.: Duke University Press, 1941); and Alison Goodyear Freehling, *Drift Toward Dissolution: The Virginia Slavery Debate, 1831–1832* (Baton Rouge: Louisiana State University Press, 1982), 262–63; and Larry Tise, *Proslavery: A History of the Defense of Slavery in America, 1701–1840* (Athens: University of Georgia Press, 1987), 288–89.

17. Francis Butler Simkins and Charles Pierce Roland, *A History of the South,* 4th ed. (New York: Alfred A. Knopf, 1972), 153.

18. *Charleston Mercury,* 21 February 1851.

19. Ibid., 22 February 1851.

20. Ibid., 28 February, 4 March 1851.

21. Ibid., 22 February 1851.

22. Quitman to Eliza Quitman, 24 May 1848, Quitman Family Papers.

23. Eliza Quitman to Quitman, 6 June, 10 June 1850, 4 March 1851, Quitman Family Papers.

24. Ray Broussard, "Governor John A. Quitman and the Lopez Expedition of 1850-1851," *Journal of Southern History* 28 (May 1966): 107–8; also see Robert E. May, *The Southern Dream of a Caribbean Empire, 1854–1861* (Baton Rouge: Louisiana State University Press, 1973), 25–29.

25. Ibid., 109–10; Claiborne, *Quitman Correspondence,* II, 53–54.

26. William L. Barney, *The Road to Secession: A New Perspective on the Old South* (New York: Praeger Publishers, 1972), 88.

27. It was later alleged that Quitman had also supplied Lopez with arms from the Mississippi arsenal. See Broussard, "Quitman and Lopez," 112.

28. Ibid., 111.

29. See *National Intelligencer* beginning 8 June 1850.

30. The second expedition got underway on 2 August aboard the *Pampero.* The force landed in Cuba ten days later and quickly fell captive to Spanish authorities who executed Lopez and fifty Americans. Quitman's eldest son was mistakenly thought to have been among the doomed. See Robert Laws to Andrew McCollam, 21 August 1851, McCollam Letters; Claiborne, *Quitman Correspondence,* II, 83, 90–91; Eliza Quitman to Quitman, 4 July 1850, Quitman Family Papers.

31. Quitman to Eliza Quitman, 21 September 1851, Quitman Family Papers.

32. *Mississippian,* 7 February 1851; Quitman to Jacob Thompson, 15 August 1850; Quitman to Robert Barnwell Rhett, 24 January 1851, *Quitman Correspondence.* Not the least of the ramifications of Quitman's resignation was the functional discomfiture for the betrothed of Mississippi. The vacancy of the governor's chair meant that no marriage licenses could be issued until probate clerks could make bonds of office to a sitting governor. See *Mississippi Free Trader,* 19 November 1851.

33. *Mississippi Free Trader,* 19 February, 12 March 1851; *Mississippian,* 14 February 1851.

34. Rosalie Quitman Duncan, "Life of General John A. Quitman," *Publications of the Mississippi Historical Society* 4 (1901): 114; also see "President of the United States to John A. Quitman," Quitman Family Papers.

35. *Mississippi Free Trader*, 12 March 1851.

36. Note of John A. Quitman, 10 March 1851; Quitman to Eliza Quitman, 22 February 1851, Quitman Family Papers.

37. Quitman to Preston, 29 March 1851, *Quitman Correspondence.*

38. Entry of 19 May 1851, David Schenck Books, Southern Historical Collection, University of North Carolina, Chapel Hill, North Carolina.

39. *Charleston Mercury,* 8 January, 27 January 1851.

40. Ibid., 20 January 1851.

41. Ibid., 11 February 1851.

42. Drayton Nance to Rhett, 28 January 1851, Rhett Papers, Charleston.

43. *Charleston Mercury,* 7 February 1851. The importance attached to the convention was not a new concept. Calhoun had propounded the theory before the Nullification crisis that a sovereign convention did not merely represent the people, but rather it *was* the people. The sovereign convention, claiming for itself eminent domain, was accountable to no one. See Laura A. White, "The Fate of Calhoun's Sovereign Convention in South Carolina," *American Historical Review* 34 (July 1929): 762; *Charleston Mercury,* 10 December 1850.

44. *Charleston Mercury,* 7, 8 February 1851.

45. Ibid., 7 January, 14 February 1851.

46. Dorman, *Politics in Alabama,* 53; Marshal J. Rachleff, "Racial Fear and Political Factionalism: A Study of the Secession Movement in Alabama, 1819– 1861," Ph.D. diss., University of Massachusetts, 1974, 176. Radicals suffering under the appellation "fire-eater" called their moderate adversaries "dirt-eaters." See *Mississippian,* 11 April 1851.

47. *Alabama Journal,* 8 February 1851.

48. *Montgomery Advertiser and State Gazette,* 19 February 1851.

49. Rachleff, "Racial Fear," 177; Ralph Brown Draughon, Jr., "William Lowndes Yancey: From Unionist to Secessionist, 1814–1852," Ph.D. diss., University of North Carolina, Chapel Hill, 1968, 224–25; J. Mills Thornton, *Politics and Power in a Slave Society: Alabama, 1800–1860* (New York and Oxford: Oxford University Press, 1978), 190.

50. Draughon, "Yancey," 241–43; *Mobile Daily Register,* 27 March 1851.

51. Julian Ruffin to Edmund Ruffin, 8 November 1850, Ruffin Papers.

52. Shanks, *Secession Movement in Virginia,* 38–39; *Mississippian,* 11 April 1851.

53. Edmund Ruffin, Jr., to Ruffin, [spring of 1851], Ruffin Papers.

54. Simms to Tucker, 7 April 1851, *Letters of Simms.* Young Ruffin's attitude did not improve. In autumn he wrote to his father that "as we submit & back out, they [Northerners] show their determination to throw off the Compromise." See Ruffin, Jr., to Ruffin, 14 October 1851, Ruffin Papers.

55. *Charleston Mercury,* 12 April 1851; Barnwell, "South Carolina's First Secession Crisis," 367.

56. Simms to Tucker, 2 March 1851, *Letters of Simms.*

57. "Speech of Robert Barnwell Rhett to Southern Rights Association at Hibernian Hall, 7 April 1851," *Charleston Mercury,* 15 April 1851. The *Greenville Mountaineer* queried, "Who is going to invade us? Will there be a standing army in North Carolina or Georgia to invade our territory?" Quoted in *Charleston Mercury,* 15 April 1851.

58. *Charleston Mercury,* 7, 9 May 1851; see 17 May for A. P. Butler's speech; 27 May for Robert Barnwell's; and 30 May for J. L. Orr's. Cheves did not attend, but sent his advice in a letter that was read to the convention. The *New York Tribune,* Horace Greeley's paper, called the Southern Rights convention in South Carolina silly and talky with only having the good effect of bringing to an end "the whole wearisome stupidity of disunion." Such remarks showed, according

to the *Mercury,* "neither good taste, good breeding, or good manners." See 21 May 1851.

59. Means to Quitman, 12 May 1851; Gregg to Quitman, 9 May, 15 May 1851, *Quitman Correspondence;* also see Barnwell, "South Carolina's First Secession Crisis," 374–75; Hamer, *Secession Movement in South Carolina,* 90, 98–99. "If we can carry you in Mississippi and McDonald in Georgia," Rhett wrote to Quitman that summer, "the game is up, and the South will be redeemed without a blow. God grant you success." Rhett to Quitman, 22 July 1851, quoted in McCardell, *Idea of a Southern Nation,* 246.

60. Quitman had early suspected that he would be nominated by the convention in Jackson. See Quitman to Eliza Quitman, 17 May 1851, Quitman Family Papers; also see *Mississippi Free Trader,* 14 April, 14 May 1851; *Mississippian,* 16 May 1851; Claiborne, *Quitman Correspondence,* II, 136; R. Davis, *Recollections,* 315–17.

61. Foote to Howell Cobb, 9 July 1851, *Correspondence of Toombs, Stephens, and Cobb.*

62. See statement of John Guion, 8 August 1851, Quitman Family Papers; Barnwell, "South Carolina's First Secession Crisis," 416.

63. R. Quitman to Eliza Quitman, 13 August 1851, Quitman Family Papers; Davis, *Recollections,* 317–20; Claiborne, *Quitman Correspondence,* II, 136; *Mississippi Free Trader,* 8 October 1851. The Mississippi Convention met on 10 November in Jackson and promptly adopted an emulation of the Georgia Platform. The convention also chided the legislature for calling a convention without a general referendum to obtain the sense of the people. The legislature was bluntly instructed to never do so again.

64. John H. Lumpkin to Cobb, 16 February 1851; Cobb to Abraham H. Chappell and others, 7 February 1851, *Correspondence of Toombs, Stephens, and Cobb.*

65. Barnwell, "South Carolina's First Secession Crisis," 412–13.

66. Rachleff, "Racial Fear," 180–81; *Montgomery Advertiser and State Gazette,* 25 May 1851.

67. Rachleff, "Racial Fear," 182–84; Draughon, "Yancey," 227–28, 245. Neither Yancey nor Hilliard was seeking election in 1851, but they were campaigning for candidates contesting the Second Congressional District seat vacated by Hilliard. The Union party, in close association with the Whigs, pitted planter James Abercrombie, a Tuskegee Whig, against John Cochrane, a lawyer identified with the radical Eufaula Regency. Although Cochrane moderated his politics in line with the Southern Rights Convention in June, Abercrombie won by 1,600 votes. See "A Paper Addressed to the People of the Second Congressional District of Alabama, Declining Reelection to Congress, 3 December 1850," in Henry W. Hilliard, *Speeches and Addresses* (New York: Harper & Brothers, Publishers, 1855), 325–32; Draughon, "Yancey," 248, 250; Hilliard, *Politics and Pen Pictures,* 252–54.

68. Rachleff, "Radical Fear," 188.

69. Stephens to Cobb, 23 June 1851; John B. Lamar to Cobb, 3 July 1851,

Correspondence of Toombs, Stephens, and Cobb; Barnwell, "South Carolina's First Secession Crisis," 412–13, 420–21; *Mississippian,* 19 September 1851; Rhett also said that the charge of his and Quitman's collaboration was untrue. See Rhett to the editor of the *Charleston Standard,* 5 September 1851.

70. Nathaniel W. Stephenson, "Southern Nationalism in South Carolina in 1851," *American Historical Review* 36 (January 1931): 333.

71. *Charleston Mercury,* 2, 10, 12, 13, 14, 24 July 1851; R. B. Rhett, Jr., to Ruffin, 5 April 1860, Ruffin Papers. The original Southern Rights Association, failing to meet, had its members absorbed by either the auxiliary or an association formed by the cooperationists. See *Charleston Mercury,* 6 October 1851.

72. Barnwell, "South Carolina's First Secession Crisis," 402–3.

73. Ibid., 406; Means to Rhett, 30 July 1851, Rhett Papers, Chapel Hill; *Charleston Mercury,* 21 August 1851.

74. White, *Rhett,* 123.

75. *Charleston Mercury,* 16 October 1851; Elizabeth Rhett to Rhett, 17 October 1851, Rhett Papers, Charleston. The northern lights, a celestial phenomenon very unusual for South Carolina, appeared in the Charleston sky several times during September 1851. Maxcy Gregg said the event "added to the panic among the ignorant classes." See McCardell, *Idea of a Southern Nation,* 305.

76. Hammond to Ruffin, 7 February 1851, Ruffin Papers.

77. Hammond to Ruffin, 20 July 1851, Ruffin Papers; Drew Gilpin Faust, *James Henry Hammond and the Old South: A Design for Mastery* (Baton Rouge: Louisiana State University Press, 1982), 297, 300–301.

78. Elizabeth Rhett to Rhett, 7 November 1850, Rhett Papers, Charleston.

79. Hammond to Ruffin, 7 February 1851, Ruffin Papers.

80. Simms to Hammond, 30 January 1851, *Letters of Simms.*

81. "An Oration of the Life, Character, and Services of John Caldwell Calhoun, Delivered on the 21st November, 1850, in Charleston, S.C., at the Request of the City Council," in James H. Hammond, *Selections from the Letters and Speeches of the Hon. James H. Hammond of South Carolina* (New York: John F. Trow & Co., 1866; reprint, Spartanburg, S.C.: Reprint Company, 1978), 231–300.

82. Hammond to Simms, 23 December 1850; Simms to Hammond, 30 January 1851; Simms to Tucker, 7 April 1851, *Letters of Simms.*

83. Hammond to Ruffin, 7 February 1851, Ruffin Papers.

84. *Charleston Mercury,* 2 May 1851.

85. White, *Rhett,* 114-15.

86. Hammond to Ruffin, 21 November 1851, Ruffin Papers; Betty L. Mitchell, *Edmund Ruffin: A Biography* (Bloomington: Indiana University Press, 1981), 75–76.

87. Hammond to Ruffin, 21 November 1851, Ruffin Papers; White, *Rhett,* 124–25.

88. White, *Rhett,* 125, 132; Hamer, *Secession Movement in South Carolina,* 140–41; Schultz, *Secession in South Carolina,* 37–41.

89. William Ford De Saussure was appointed in Rhett's place. He was later elected to complete the term ending on 3 March 1853. Cooperationist Josiah

James Evans, judge of the Western Circuit Court from 1829 to 1852, would occupy the seat until his death on 6 May 1858. See *Letters of Simms,* III, 221n.

CHAPTER SIX
"The Sympathy of Angels"

1. *Charleston Mercury,* 31 December 1851.

2. Note of John M. Berrien, 24 January 1851, Berrien Papers. Robert Toombs ran in Berrien's place and won. See Phillips, *Georgia and State Rights,* 166. Berrien continued to be solicited by exuberant radicals looking for a champion. "We believe that you," he was told, "faithful of the faithless, have not yet suffered yourself to be *slimed over* by the great Boa Constrictor of the North." See T. P. Jones to Berrien, 9 June 1851, Berrien Papers.

3. Laura A. White, "The National Democrats in South Carolina, 1852–1860," *South Atlantic Quarterly* 28 (October 1929): 371.

4. Ulrich Bonnell Phillips, "The Course of the South to Secession. VI. The Fire Eaters," *Georgia Historical Quarterly* 22 (March 1938): 47; Hardy Perritt, "The Fire Eaters," in *Oratory in the Old South, 1828–1860,* ed. Waldo W. Braden with the assistance of Jeffrey Auer and Bert E. Bradley (Baton Rouge: Louisiana State University Press, 1970), 243; Rhett wrote an unsigned article, "Tract on Government," for Simms's *Southern Quarterly Review* April 1854 issue. See *Letters of Simms,* III, 289n. Also see *Charleston Courier,* 1 March 1854; *Charleston Evening News,* 8 March 1854.

5. Hammond to Ruffin, 24 October, 19 December 1853, 1 May 1854, Ruffin Papers; Faust, *Hammond and the Old South,* 335.

6. Turney to Rhett, 1 May 1852, Rhett Papers, Charleston.

7. Craven, *Ruffin,* 5; Mitchell, *Ruffin,* 76–77, 81–82, 84–85.

8. *Mississippian,* 19 September 1851. Quitman revived, in the winter and spring of 1854, a plan to seize Cuba. He obtained the support of Gallatin Brown in the Senate, but not of Davis in the cabinet. John Slidell attempted to gain the suspension of American neutrality laws but only succeeded in prompting Pierce, with Davis's approval, to issue on 31 May 1854 a reaffirmation of neutrality. Brown unsuccessfully tried to gain a suspension of this latest proclamation in February 1855. See Ranck, *Brown,* 98, 130–31, 134.

9. John E. Gonzalez, "Henry Stuart Foote: A Forgotten Unionist of the Fifties," *Southern Quarterly* 1 (October 1963): 129–39; Dubay, *Pettus,* 16–17. Foote joined the Native American party in California but deserted it in 1856 after Buchanan's election. He returned to Mississippi in 1859, became an ardent secessionist in March 1861, and accepted a seat in the Confederate House of Representatives.

10. Ranck, *Brown,* 88.

11. *Mississippi Free Trader,* 26 February 1851.

12. Ranck, *Brown,* 89–90, 100.

13. Rachleff, "Racial Fear," 189; Dorman, *Politics in Alabama,* 78–80; S. D. Moore to J. M. Berrien, 23 August 1852; Berrien to Moore, 9 September 1852, Berrien Papers; George W. Jones to Howell Cobb, 25 January 1852; Cobb to John B. Lamar, 18 September 1852, *Correspondence of Toombs, Stephens, and Cobb;* Cooper, *Politics of Slavery,* 334.

14. Stephens to Cobb, 5 December 1851; also see John E. Ward and Henry R. Jackson to Cobb, 28 February 1852, *Correspondence of Toombs, Stephens, and Cobb.*

15. White, "National Democrats," 374.

16. Ibid., 374; Frank L. Owsley, *Plain Folk of the Old South* (Baton Rouge: Louisiana State University Press, 1949), 141–42; Clay-Clopton, *A Belle of the Fifties,* 23. Whether Alabama Whig or Democrat, the worst thing a politician could be perceived as was an aristocrat. See Thornton, *Politics and Power,* 17, 53.

17. Arney R. Childs, *Rice Planter and Sportsman: The Recollections of J. Motte Alston, 1821–1909* (Columbia: University of South Carolina Press, 1953), 21.

18. King, *Wigfall,* 75; see G. W. Means to Robert Barnwell Rhett, 18 January 1852, Rhett Papers, Charleston, for evidence of South Carolina natives carrying secession to Florida. The radical Eufaula Regency in Alabama also reflected transplanted South Carolina influence. See *Ruffin Diary,* entry of 3 January 1861. Also see White, "National Democrats," 373n.

19. Schultz, *Sectionalism in South Carolina,* 22–23; Roger P. Leemhuis, *James L. Orr and the Sectional Conflict* (Washington: University Press of America, 1979), 3–4.

20. Leemhuis, *Orr and Sectional Conflict,* 10–11, 30–31.

21. White, "National Democrats," 374–75.

22. Schultz, *Sectionalism in South Carolina,* 73; Leemhuis, *Orr and Sectional Conflict,* 30–31; Brooks had been a cooperationist candidate for the Southern Congress from the Fifth District in 1851. He withdrew from the election. See *Charleston Mercury,* 8 October 1851. Also see Brooks to John Perkins, 27 August 1855, John Perkins Papers, Southern Historical Collection, University of North Carolina, Chapel Hill, North Carolina.

23. Charges about Southern moderates' desire for federal emoluments were common coin of radical anger. William Sharkey's appointment by Fillmore to a consular post in Havana drew scornful derision since it appeared as though Sharkey's desertion of the Southern movement had been bought and paid for. See *Charleston Mercury,* 29 March, 23 October 1851. Yet the tables could be turned. William Gilmore Simms's desire for a diplomatic post in Naples from the Pierce administration impressed B. F. Perry as laughably hypocritical. See Simms to Perry, 15 March 1853, *Letters of Simms.* Simms did not receive the appointment. Also see Schultz, *Sectionalism in South Carolina,* 16–18; Quitman to Keitt, 23 July 1857, Quitman Papers. Keitt would be drawn closer to Buchanan by more than party loyalty, for he was wooing Buchanan's niece, Harriet Lane. See *Letters of Simms,* III, 442n.

24. Ranck, *Brown,* 102–3, 124–25.

25. Craven, *Southern Nationalism,* 295.

26. Shanks, *Secession Movement in Virginia,* 43–47; see Seddon to R. M. T. Hunter, 7 February 1852, *Correspondence of Hunter.* Ruffin said that Wise was "as reliable as is a weathercock to indicate when the wind has changed, & the direction in which it blows." See *Ruffin Diary,* entry of 11 November.

27. Edmund Ruffin, Jr., to Ruffin, 13 July 1850, Ruffin Papers.

28. Tucker to Simms, 17 March 1851, quoted in Trent, *Simms,* 186.

29. Leemhuis, *Orr and Sectional Conflict,* 35–36. In Milledgeville, Georgia, in 1860, Thomas Butler King's daughter would disparage the "*crowds* of *people*" whose main attributes were "more of *quantity* than of *quality*," resulting in situations where "introductions are given without the asking. So the clerk of the office—the hotel keeper—the lawyer and the Statesman have almost an equal chance!" See Georgia King to R. Cuyler King, 13 November 1860, Thomas Butler King Papers, Southern Historical Collection, University of North Carolina, Chapel Hill, N.C. Women naturally exerted a powerful, if indirect influence on the attitudes of the antebellum South. Far from being the sheepish helpmate, the Southern woman had definite opinions on politics and society and did not hesitate to express them. See Mildred Ruffin Sayre to Ruffin, 21 November 1860, Ruffin Papers; entry of 8 November 1860, Schenck Books; [Sallie B. Putman], *Richmond During the War: Four Years of Personal Observations by a Richmond Lady* (New York: G. W. Carleton & Co., Publishers, 1867), 17, 22; John B. Jones, *A Rebel War Clerk's Diary of the Confederate States Capitol,* 2 vols. (Philadelphia: J. B. Lippincott & Co., 1866), I, 19, for a sample of such opinions.

30. Gayle to Rhett, 23 December 1851, Rhett Papers, Charleston.

31. Quoted in Barney, *Road to Secession,* 85.

32. White, *Rhett,* 123; Barney, *Road to Secession,* 91–92.

33. David R. Goldfield, *Urban Growth in the Age of Sectionalism: Virginia, 1847–1861* (Baton Rouge: Louisiana State University Press, 1977), 166. Traditionalists in the North also found fundamental change difficult. See Faust, *A Sacred Circle,* 89.

34. Robert G. Gunderson, "The Southern Whigs," in *Oratory in the Old South, 1828–1860,* 134. Also see Holt, *Political Crisis of the 1850s,* 118–19.

35. Schultz, *Sectionalism in South Carolina,* 68, 78.

36. Phillips, *Georgia and State Rights,* 178; Stephens to Thomas W. Thomas, 9 May 1855, *Milledgeville* (Georgia) *Federal Union,* 22 May 1855; also see Toombs to T. Lomax, 6 June 1855, *Correspondence of Toombs, Stephens, and Cobb.*

37. Dorman, *Politics in Alabama,* 117, 119; Donald W. Zacharias, "The Know-Nothing Party and the Oratory of Nativism," in *Oratory in the Old South, 1828–1860,* 232; Dale A. Somers, "James P. Newcomb: The Making of a Radical," *Southwestern Historical Quarterly* 72 (April 1969): 453.

38. Zacharias, "Oratory of Nativism," 220.

39. Dorman, *Politics in Alabama,* 102, 119.

40. Harvie to R. M. T. Hunter, 5 March 1855 *Correspondence of Hunter.*

41. Entry of 9 November 1855, Gavin Diary.

42. Schultz, *Sectionalism in South Carolina,* 79–83; Leemhuis, *Orr and Sectional Conflict,* 48–49; White, "National Democrats," 372.

43. William Y. Thompson, *Robert Toombs of Georgia* (Baton Rouge: Louisiana State University Press, 1966), 117–18.

44. King, *Wigfall,* 19, 23, 32–33, 35–36, 46–47, 51–52; *Ruffin Diary,* entry of 19 June 1860.

45. King, *Wigfall,* 55–56.

46. Clay-Clopton, *A Belle of the Fifties,* 98–99.

47. King, *Wigfall,* 58–59; Walter L. Buenger, *Secession and the Union in Texas* (Austin: University of Texas Press, 1984), 28.

48. King, *Wigfall,* 61–63; Buenger, *Secession in Texas,* 28.

49. Buenger, *Secession in Texas,* 32, 34.

50. White, "National Democrats," 378–79.

51. Channing, *Crisis of Fear,* 153–55; *Ruffin Diary,* entry of 13 May 1857.

52. Richard K. Crallé to Rhett, 13 October 1854, Rhett Papers, Charleston. "The hostility of Rhett to you," A. P. Butler was informed, "flashes out in the *Mercury* on every occasion." See Isaac E. Holmes to Butler, 17 March 1856, in *Correspondence of Hunter;* also see "Introduction to the Attempt," in *Ruffin Diary,* 16.

53. *Ruffin Diary,* entry of 1 May 1858.

54. Ibid., entry of 8 May 1858; R. D. Arnold to John W. Forney, 26 November 1856, *Letters of Richard D. Arnold, M.D., 1808–1876: Mayor of Savannah, Georgia; First Secretary of the American Medical Association,* Papers of Trinity College Historical Society, Double Series, 18–19 (Durham, N.C.: Duke University Press, 1929; reprint, New York: AMS Press, Inc., 1979). The commercial convention activities of the radicals would come to grief when they split over the issue of the African slave trade to be discussed in the next chapter.

55. Owen Peterson, "Speaking in the Southern Commercial Conventions," in *Oratory of the Old South, 1828–1860,* 198–99.

56. *Mississippian,* quoted in *Charleston Mercury,* 6 July 1850; see also Shanks, *Secession Movement in Virginia,* 82; Peterson, "Southern Commercial Conventions," 204–5.

57. John G. Van Deusen, *The Ante-Bellum Southern Commercial Conventions,* Historical Papers published by the Trinity College Historical Society, Series 16 (Durham: Duke University Press, 1926), 101; Walter L. Brown, "Rowing Against the Stream: The Course of Albert Pike from National Whig to Secessionist," *Arkansas Historical Quarterly* 39 (Autumn 1980): 232–33; Mark Keller and Thomas A. Belser, Jr., eds., "Albert Pike's Contribution to the *Spirit of the Times,* Including His 'Letter from the Far, Far West,'" *Arkansas Historical Quarterly* 37 (Winter 1978): 331–32; Peterson, "Southern Commercial Conventions," 208–9.

58. Peterson, "Southern Commercial Conventions," 217.

59. Thomas P. Kettell, *Southern Wealth and Northern Profits, As Exhibited in Statistical Facts and Official Figures* (New York: George W. & John A. Wood, 1860), estimated that the South spent over $53 million per season in the North;

but Hinton R. Helper, *The Impending Crisis of the South: How to Meet It* (New York: A. B. Burdick, 1859), calculated that by 1857 Southerners were spending as much as $123 million a year. See John Hope Franklin, *A Southern Odyssey: Travelers in the Antebellum North* (Baton Rouge: Louisiana State University Press, 1976), 40–43.

60. Franklin, *Southern Odyssey,* 110, 208, 255–56; Platt K. Dickinson to Mrs. John G. Dabney, 27 July 1859, 29 August 1860, Dickinson Letters; Shanks, *Secession Movement in Virginia,* 77–79; *Richmond Enquirer,* 14 June 1854.

61. *Letters of Simms,* III, 161n; DeBow to Andrew McCollam, 28 April 1852, McCollam Papers; DeBow to John Perkins, 14 June 1855, John Perkins Papers.

62. Goldfield, *Urban Growth,* xvi-xviii, xxiii-xxv; *Richmond Enquirer,* 23 August 1855; Craven, *Southern Nationalism,* 248, 264–65, 267–68.

63. Mitchell, *Ruffin,* 99; "Memorandum handed to a member of the Texas legislature, Mr. Powell. February 8, 1858," Thomas Butler King Papers; also see H. L. P. King to R. B. King, Jr., 31 January 1858; Lorenzo Sherwood to Honorable L. T. Wigfall, 8 February 1858, King Papers; T. J. Green to Executive Committee, Southern Pacific Railroad Company, 14 October 1856, Green Papers. Jefferson Davis was accused in 1859 of using his position as Pierce's secretary of war to further a Southern route. Davis strenuously objected to the charge. See W. P. Trent, ed., *Southern Writers: Selections in Prose and Verse* (New York: Macmillan Company, 1910), 205.

64. *Ruffin Diary,* entry of 14 January 1857. Professor of mathematics D. H. Hill wrote a textbook, *Elements of Algebra,* for use in his North Carolina College classes. One of eleven word problems read: "A Yankee mixes a certain number of wooden nutmegs, which cost him ¼ cent apiece, with a quantity of real nutmegs, worth 4 cents apiece, and sells the whole assortment for $44; and gains $3.75 by the fraud. How many wooden nutmegs were there?" See Phillips, "The Fire Eaters," 69. See McCardell, *Idea of a Southern Nation,* 92–106, for a good overview of why Southern distinctiveness and economic self-sufficiency were incompatible.

65. Stephens to J. Henley Smith, 5 January 1860, *Correspondence of Toombs, Stephens, and Cobb.*

66. Shanks, *Secession Movement in Virginia,* 71–72. Republican congressman James McKean of New York stated what many Southerners, although from a different perspective, already suspected: that manufacturing would "create demands which ignorant, indolent slave labor cannot meet, and which intelligent, free labor can alone supply." See Barney, *Road to Secession,* 48; also see Goldfield, *Urban Growth,* 250–51, 259–60; Huston, "Panic of 1857," 933–35.

67. Drew Gilpin Faust, "The Rhetoric and Ritual of Agriculture in Antebellum South Carolina," *Journal of Southern History* 45 (November 1979): 546; Robert J. Brugger, "The Mind of the Old South: New Views," *Virginia Quarterly Review* 56 (Spring 1980): 288. Also see Faust, *A Sacred Circle,* 2, 12.

68. Faust, "Rhetoric and Ritual," 551, 557–59, 566; David Donald, "The Proslavery Argument Reconsidered," *Journal of Southern History* 37 (February 1971): 16. Bertram Wyatt-Brown has argued that slavery established the South-

ern hierarchy and solidified concepts of honor. See *Yankee Saints and Southern Sinners,* 9.

69. Shanks, *Secession Movement in Virginia,* 72.

CHAPTER SEVEN
"Glory Enough for One Day"

1. Benning to Cobb, 2 September 1852, *Correspondence of Toombs, Stephens, and Cobb;* Simms to Orr, 30 August 1856, *Letters of Simms.*

2. Craven, *Southern Nationalism,* 369. Spratt's *Charleston Standard* was described by Carolina Know-Nothing David Gavin as a "dirty and foreign principled sheet." Gavin Diary, entry of 1 August 1856; also see Peterson, "Southern Commercial Conventions," 210–12 for a view of the lead-up to the gathering at Montgomery.

3. Mitchell, *Ruffin,* 123–24.

4. Ibid., 125–26; also see *Ruffin Diary,* entry of 11 May 1858; also see D. H. Hamilton to William Porcher Miles, 20 April 1860, Miles Papers, for an example of Southern sensitivity about the impression that the issue created in the South.

5. *Ruffin Diary,* entry of 13 May 1858. Even as the convention in Montgomery was thrashing about with these problems, some Southerners were testing the waters on removing the prohibition by a fait accompli. In Charleston Harbor a ship, the *Echo,* appeared loaded with Negroes. Papers had been denied to the firm in Charleston intending to import the Negroes into slavery. Federal officers seized the illegal cargo and detained the Negroes at Fort Sumter. Rhett wanted something done about the matter, and as the controversy continued throughout the summer, so did Buchanan. The president proposed a commission, tactfully including Rhett, that would make arrangements to return the Africans to their native land. Buchanan asked Rhett to use his influence to make the removal peaceful and without incident. See Buchanan to Rhett, 3 September 1858, Rhett Papers, Charleston.

6. White, *Rhett,* 148–49, 152.

7. Earl Fornell, "Agitation in Texas for Reopening the Slave Trade," *Southwestern Historical Quarterly* 60 (October 1956): 251, 256.

8. Mitchell, *Ruffin,* 138–39; Schultz, *Sectionalism in South Carolina,* 183; Shanks, *Sectionalism,* 131; John Cunningham to Bedford Brown, 20 December 1860, Brown Papers.

9. Dorman, *Politics in Alabama,* 128–29.

10. Ibid., 135.

11. Cooper, *Politics of Slavery,* 358–59.

12. Mitchell, *Ruffin,* 93.

13. Crabtree and Patton, *Journal of a Secesh Lady,* entry of 4 July 1860, 4.

14. A. Dudley Mann to John Perkins, 28 July 1856, Perkins Papers.

15. Atchison to Hunter, 4 March 1855, *Correspondence of Hunter.*

16. Dorman, *Politics in Alabama,* 130; Craven, *Southern Nationalism,* 218–19.

17. Richard K. Crallé to Hunter, 24 October 1857, *Correspondence of Hunter.*

18. John S. Barbour to Hunter, 1 August 1857; A. D. Banks to Hunter, 24 July 1857, *Correspondence of Hunter.*

19. Quoted in Capers, *Douglas,* 137.

20. *Congressional Globe,* 34th Congress, 1st Sess., Appendix, 530, 543.

21. Louise Wigfall Wright, *A Southern Girl in '61: The War-Time Memoirs of a Confederate Senator's Daughter* (New York: Doubleday, Page & Company, 1905), 31; also see Robert Neil Mathis, "Preston Smith Brooks: The Man and His Image," *South Carolina Historical Magazine* (October 1978): 304.

22. Schultz, *Sectionalism in South Carolina,* 116–17. Brooks's action was not unprecedented. In South Carolina, James Henry Hammond had chastised an editor, C. F. Daniels, for an offensive editorial during the Nullification crisis by bludgeoning him on the streets of Camden. Daniels had shown himself not to be a gentleman and was thus unfit for challenge. See Faust, *Hammond and the Old South,* 55–56. Also in 1832, Sam Houston had beaten Ohio Congressman William Stanbery senseless with a walking stick on the streets of Washington for an insulting remark the congressman made about Houston's fondness for Cherokee women. See A. W. Terrel, "Recollections of General Sam Houston," *Southwestern Historical Quarterly* 16 (October 1912): 125.

23. Quoted in Schultz, *Sectionalism in South Carolina,* 118.

24. Gavin Diary, entry of 23 July 1856; Green to H. S. Foote, 29 July 1856; Green to [editor] *Daily News,* 24 October 1856, Green Papers. Not all Southerners were in agreement with the necessity of Brooks's response. See Simeon Colton Diary, entry of 4 June 1856, Southern Historical Collection, University of North Carolina, Chapel Hill, North Carolina.

25. Gavin Diary, entry of 23 July 1856. William Gilmore Simms in the autumn of 1856 attempted a lecture tour in the North where he planned to speak on South Carolina's role in the American Revolution. He had appeared only three times, when heckling about the Brooks incident forced him to defend South Carolina with such vehemence that nobody would purchase tickets to future lectures. "The game of the Black Republicans," he muttered, "was to identify me with Brooks." He returned to South Carolina, where he retreated increasingly into a morbid irritability. See Franklin, *Southern Odyssey,* 237–43; also see Simms to James Chesnut, Jr., 16 December 1856, *Letters of Simms;* Trent, *Simms,* 224–25.

26. Phillips, "The Fire-Eaters," 62.

27. Quitman to Keitt, 23 July 1857, Quitman Family Papers; T. J. Green to Buchanan, November 1856, Green Papers.

28. Toombs to W. W. Burwell, 11 July 1857, *Correspondence of Toombs, Stephens, and Cobb.*

29. Potter, *The Impending Crisis,* 301.

30. Cobb to Stephens, 5 October 1857; Thomas W. Thomas to Stephens, 15 June 1857, *Correspondence of Toombs, Stephens, and Cobb.*

31. Cobb to Stephens, 5 October 1857, *Correspondence of Toombs, Stephens, and Cobb.*

32. Dorman, *Politics in Alabama,* 138–39.

33. DeBow to Miles, 4 September 1857, Miles Papers.

34. Keitt to Miles, 15 June 1857, Miles Papers.

35. Quitman to Keitt, 23 July 1857, Quitman Family Papers.

36. Allan J. Green to Hammond, 7 March 1858, quoted in Schultz, *Sectionalism in South Carolina,* 154n.

37. Brown to Stephens, 9 February, 26 March, 7 May 1858, *Correspondence of Toombs, Stephens, and Cobb.*

38. Craven, *Southern Nationalism,* 288–89; Dorman, *Politics in Alabama,* 143–44; also see *Ruffin Diary,* entry of 23 April 1858.

39. Yancey to Slaughter, 15 June 1858, quoted in Garrett, *Reminiscences,* 685.

40. *Ruffin Diary,* entry of 27 July 1860.

41. Ibid., 14 May 1858.

42. Mitchell, *Ruffin,* 102–3, 131.

43. Ibid., 96–97.

44. Shanks, *Secession Movement in Virginia,* 62–63. *The South* ceased publication shortly after the summer of 1858.

45. Mitchell, *Ruffin,* 129–31.

46. *Charleston Mercury,* 7 November 1856; *Charleston Courier,* 14, 19 November 1856.

47. White, *Rhett,* 137–38; also see *Letters of Simms,* III, 176n, 446n. McGrath's withdrawal left only John Cunningham, dogged by a Native American past, and William Porcher Miles, mayor of Charleston, in the field. Miles had previously been an assistant professor of mathematics at the College of Charleston since 1843 and was agreeable to the nationalists because he had never been notably against them. He would become a fire-eater.

48. Hammond to editor, *Charleston Mercury,* 2 October 1857. Hammond to Simms, 13 August 1857; Bleser, *Hammonds of Redcliffe,* 28–33. Also see White, "National Democrats," 380–81; *Letters of Simms,* III, 506n.

49. Gregg to Rhett, 14 September 1858, Rhett Papers, Charleston.

50. Shanks, *Secession Movement in Virginia,* 70.

51. George Petrie, "William F. Samford, Statesman and Man of Letters," *Transactions of the Alabama Historical Society, 1899–1903,* edited by Thomas McAdory Owen (Montgomery: Alabama Historical Society, 1904), 475.

52. Ibid., 477.

53. Perrit, "The Fire-Eaters," 53.

54. Walker sat next to Ruffin at Yancey's dinner party in May and told him that Indians in Nicaragua were perfectly suited to slavery if Americans successfully conquered the area. See *Ruffin Diary,* 14 May 1858, 189; also see Dorman, *Politics in Alabama,* 152.

55. Robert R. Russel, "The Issues in the Congressional Struggle over the Kansas-Nebraska Bill, 1854," *Journal of Southern History* 39 (May 1963): 199, 205n.

56. Capers, *Douglas,* 152. James L. Orr said virtually the same thing about local law and slavery being hopelessly intertwined. See Robert W. Johannsen, *Stephen A. Douglas* (New York: Oxford University Press, 1973), 570.

57. Ranck, *Brown,* 160; also see Quitman to Douglas, 4 May 1853, Quitman Family Papers. James Rawley argues that Douglas's opposition to the Lecompton Constitution rather than his statement at Freeport turned Southerners against him. See *Race and Politics,* 231.

58. Damon Wells, *Stephen Douglas: The Last Years, 1857–1861* (Austin: University of Texas Press, 1971), 162, states that Yancey and Rhett and other radicals' anger at Douglas grew over the decade "into an almost pathological hatred greater than they had for any other Yankee, including Lincoln and Sumner." They would defeat Douglas, Wells contends, "even if that meant the demise of the Democratic Party and the destruction of the Union." Wells has it precisely backwards.

59. Ranck, *Brown,* 138–39.

60. N. A. Richardson to Quitman, 16 February 1857; John D. McConnel to Quitman, 13 June 1856, Quitman Family Papers.

61. Ranck, *Brown,* 160–61, 163–64.

62. Brown's expression of continued admiration for Douglas is quoted in Ranck, *Brown,* 176; also see Capers, *Douglas,* 187. After the passage of the Kansas-Nebraska Act, Brown wrote to Douglas, "If your *friends* failed to make you President in 1852, your enemies will succeed in making you the first man in the republic in 1856." Brown to Douglas, 8 September 1854, quoted in Johannsen, *Douglas,* 454.

63. Dubay, *Pettus,* 24–25, 28–32.

64. White, *Rhett,* 154.

65. *Charleston Mercury,* 25 April 1859.

66. Rhett's speech appeared in the *Charleston Mercury,* 7 July 1859.

67. *Charleston Mercury,* 14 July 1859.

68. Orr served as the Speaker of the House of Representatives from 1857 to 1859.

CHAPTER EIGHT
"One of the Most Aristocratic Cities of the Union"

1. *Charleston Mercury,* 13 October 1859.

2. Ibid., 7 December 1859.

3. Ibid., 6 December 1859.

4. White, *Rhett,* 158–59.

5. Schultz, *Sectionalism in South Carolina,* 191; also see White, "National Democrats," 382.

6. Wooster Sherman to Hunter, 10 December 1859, *Correspondence of Hunter;* Cobb to the People of Georgia, 6 December 1860, *Correspondence of Toombs, Stephens, and Cobb;* Stephen B. Oates, *To Purge This Land with Blood: A Biography of John Brown* (New York: Harper & Row, 1970), 353–56; Platt K. Dickinson to Mrs. John C. Dabney, 12 November 1859, Dickinson Letters.

7. White, "National Democrats," 383.

8. Biography of Christopher G. Memminger in Memminger Papers.

9. When Banks had been elected Speaker, David Gavin had written, "Woe! be to the South, for she will not heed the voice of warning." Gavin Diary, entry of 6 February 1856.

10. Victor B. Howard, "John Brown's Raid at Harper's Ferry and the Sectional Crisis in North Carolina," *North Carolina Historical Review* 19 (Autumn 1978): 334–36; Channing, *Crisis of Fear,* 105–6, 111–12; Gist to Miles, 20 December 1859, Miles Papers.

11. Miles to Memminger, 10 January 1860, Memminger Papers.

12. Miles to Memminger, 18 January 1860, Memminger Papers.

13. Thomas to Memminger, 7 January 1860, Memminger Papers.

14. Ruffin to Ruffin, Jr., 14 January 1860, Ruffin Papers.

15. Harvie to Beverley R. Wellford, Jr., 22 October 1859, White-Wellford-Taliaferro-Marshal Papers, Southern Historical Collection, University of North Carolina, Chapel Hill, N.C.

16. Harvie to Hunter, 18 October 1859, *Correspondence of Hunter.*

17. Rhett opposed vigilance committees in the raw, unorganized form they took, especially after an incident in Kingstree. A mob threatened two Northern schoolteachers, already at odds for personal reasons with some members of the community, and consequently they fled. Rhett deplored "dealing with men as if they were guilty without proof." He thought that vigilance was necessary, but he did strive to have the formation of committees controlled and maintained under authoritative auspices. The passion against abolitionism, however, continued with a frenzy akin to witchhunting. See Channing, *Crisis of Fear,* 31–34; also see *Charleston Mercury,* 5 December 1859. As one young girl in Mississippi noted later, "The Abolitionists have sowed the seeds of disunion and insurrection among us." See Sarah Lois Wadley Diary, Southern Historical Collection, University of North Carolina, Chapel Hill, N.C.

18. Shanks, *Secession Movement in Virginia,* 94–96. Hunter was being advised to counter Wise's position, which had gathered extremists and alarmists around it, by recommending "distinct measures of independent state action" as "essential to our success in Charleston." See William Old, Jr., to Hunter, 1 January 1860, *Correspondence of Hunter;* also see Simpson, *A Good Southerner,* 213.

19. Civilians were barred from the execution, but Ruffin became an honorary member of the Society of Cadets of the Virginia Military Institute so he could be present for Brown's hanging on 2 December. See W. G. Paxton to Ruffin, 30 January 1860, Ruffin Papers. Ruffin obtained one of Brown's pikes that day and pasted to the handle the message, "Sample of the favors designed for us by our Northern Brethren." He arranged with the master armorer, Alfred M. Barbour, to have a number of the pikes sent to him. After considerable delays, Ruffin received the pikes and stored them in Washington in the rooms of Alabama Senator Clement C. Clay, Jr., much to the discomfort of Mrs. Clay. She complained that "for four months my parlour was made an arsenal for the storing of a dozen lengthy spears." She thought they were "for some decorative purpose." See Ruffin to Ruffin, Jr., and Julian, 3 December 1859; Barbour to Ruffin, 15 March 1860, Ruffin Papers; also see Clay-Clopton, *A Belle of the Fifties,* 145–46.

20. *Ruffin Diary,* entry of 31 December 1859.

21. Miles to Memminger, 10 January 1860, Memminger Papers.

22. Memminger to Letcher, 6 February 1860; Memminger to Gist, 13 February 1860, Memminger Papers.

23. Dorman, *Politics in Alabama,* 154.

24. Ibid., 155; also see Austin L. Venable, "The Conflict Between the Douglas and Yancey Forces in the Charleston Convention," *Journal of Southern History* 8 (May 1942): 233.

25. "If Southern States remain in convention," Hunter heard by the telegraph, "Douglas nomination impossible. If they go out his is certain." See Thomas S. Bocock to Hunter, 25 April 1860, telegram, *Correspondence of Hunter.*

26. Quoted in Capers, *Douglas,* 173.

27. Potter and Fehrenbacher, *The Impending Crisis,* 408.

28. Robert Toombs believed afterward that the Douglas people agreed to vote on the platform first to drive radicals from the convention. See Toombs to Stephens, 12 May 1860, *Correspondence of Toombs, Stephens, and Cobb;* also see Wells, *Douglas' Last Years,* 219.

29. Charles Linsley to Hunter, 26 March 1860, *Correspondence of Hunter.* Linsley was from Rutland, Vermont.

30. Seddon to Hunter, 26 December 1859, *Correspondence of Hunter.* "I would as soon have a baboon for my leader," Seddon said of the unrefined, tobacco-chewing Wise. See Simpson, *A Good Southerner,* 159.

31. Rhett, Jr., told Ruffin that Wise had ruined himself with the cotton states because of the position he had taken on the Kansas question of 1857. See Rhett, Jr., to Ruffin, 5 April 1860, Ruffin Papers.

32. Shanks, *Secession Movement in Virginia,* 105.

33. Wells, *Douglas' Last Years,* 205; Pugh was an anti-Republican Democrat of the first order who had never been an adherent of the querulous Northern faction of the Democracy. He and his beautiful wife, Therese, ate regularly in Washington with the Clays and Fitzpatricks of Alabama, Larry Orr and James Chesnut of South Carolina, and L. Q. C. ("Moody") Lamar of Mississippi. See Clay-Clopton, *A Belle of the Fifties,* 43–44.

34. Later and for good reason there would be rumors that Douglas had not wanted Stuart at Charleston for fear that he might threaten the harmony of the convention. Douglas, however, had expressly requested him to attend on the Michigan delegation. See Douglas to Stuart, 15 January 1860, Johannsen, *Douglas Letters.*

35. Ranck, *Brown,* 183–85; Craven, *Southern Nationalism,* 295. Davis also had his eyes on the possibility of a deadlocked convention, for he was popular with Northern Democrats. James G. Blaine thought that Davis might have been nominated in 1864 had not secession intervened. See James G. Blaine, *Twenty Years of Congress from Lincoln to Garfield with A Review of the Events which Led to the Political Revolution of 1860,* 2 vols. (Norwich, Conn.: Henry Bill, 1884), I, 245–46; also see King, *Wigfall,* 82–85.

36. Toombs to Stephens, 10 February 1860, *Correspondence of Toombs, Stephens, and Cobb.*

37. Walter Buenger maintains that Wigfall owed his Senate election not to the reaction after John Brown's raid but rather to Wigfall's appealing to party loyalty; the fiery Texan had moderated his views while also collecting political debts by campaigning for John Reagan and Hardin Runnells, neither of whom Wigfall liked. See Buenger, *Secession in Texas,* 72; also see Billy D. Ledbetter, "The Election of Louis T. Wigfall to the United States Senate, 1859: A Reevaluation," *Southwestern Historical Quarterly* 77 (October 1973): 241–42. Houston would finally lose control of Texas because of his inability to match his predecessor's success in acquiring federal help to protect the Texas frontier from Indian attacks. See Craven, *Southern Nationalism,* 376.

38. Sitterson, *Secession Movement in North Carolina,* 162; Green to Yancey, 22 April 1860, Green Papers.

39. Schultz, *Sectionalism in South Carolina,* 210–11; White, "National Democrats," 383–84; Barnwell Rhett, Jr., called the delegation "a packed jury trimming to keep in with Douglas." See Rhett, Jr., to Miles, 17 April 1860, Miles Papers.

40. Craven, *Southern Nationalism,* 327; Wells, *Douglas' Last Years,* 211.

41. Hammond to Miles, 16 July 1860, Miles papers; also see Clement Eaton, *Jefferson Davis* (New York: The Free Press, 1977), 115–16, 117. Hunter was consoled as the convention tottered on the brink of disruption with the observation that he was "young enough to make a good fight four years hence." See Charles Mason to Hunter, 30 April 1860, *Correspondence of Hunter.*

42. Platt K. Dickinson to Mrs. J. L. Dabney, 11 May 1857, Dickinson Letters.

43. Craven, *Southern Nationalism,* 327–28; Gavin Diary, entry of 24 April 1860; Paul H. Langdon to Thomas J. Green, 18 March 1860, Green Papers.

44. Craven, *Southern Nationalism,* 327–28; *Charleston Mercury,* 24 April 1860; Green to Wharton Jackson Green, 24 April 1860, Green Papers.

45. D. H. Hamilton to Miles, 26 April 1860, Miles Papers.

46. Craven, *Southern Nationalism,* 328.

47. Ibid., 329–30.

48. Nichols, *Disruption of American Democracy,* 304.

49. As noted earlier, Stuart was at Charleston at Douglas's behest, and his performance in Institute Hall at this crucial moment must be scrutinized in that light. As Nichols, *Disruption of American Democracy,* 304, has pointed out, Stuart's action was prohibitively risky if the Douglas people were apprised, as they surely were by now, of the depth of Southern resentment. But also Douglas managers had shown a remarkable degree of control over areas of the convention they could control. Stuart's speech was unduly provocative, but that it was made very probably surprised no one in the Douglas camp. Robert Johannsen softens Douglas's complicity in prompting Stuart's performance. He also states that the size of the Southern withdrawal stunned Douglas's managers.

50. Channing, *Crisis of Fear,* 107–8; Wells, *Douglas' Last Years,* 237.

51. Venable, "Douglas and Yancey Conflict," 239; Anthony W. Dillard, "William Lowndes Yancey, The Sincere and Unfaltering Advocate of Southern Rights," *Southern Historical Society Papers,* vol. 21 (Richmond: Southern His-

torical Society, 1893), 156; J. E. D. Yonge, "The Conservative Party in Alabama, 1848–1860," *Transactions of the Alabama Historical Society,* 1899–1903, vol. 4 (Montgomery: Alabama Historical Society, 1904), 509.

52. Craven, *Southern Nationalism,* 331; Schultz, *Sectionalism in South Carolina,* 215–16; Shanks, *Secession Movement in Virginia,* 106; Rhett, Jr., to Miles, 12 May 1860, Miles Papers.

53. Rhett, Jr., to Miles, 10 May 1860, Miles Papers. Also see Thomas Butler King to J. Floyd King, 1 May 1860, King Papers, for thoughts concerning the possible reconciliation of the divided party.

54. King to Robert Collins and Others, 11 May 1860, King Papers. King had written and then crossed ". . . until we shall have failed, if fail we must, at Baltimore."

55. Florence King to J. Floyd King, 25 May 1860, King Papers.

56. Cobb to Robert Collins and Others, 9 May 1860; Toombs to Collins and Others, 10 May 1860; Toombs to Stephens, 16 May 1860, *Correspondence of Toombs, Stephens, and Cobb.*

57. Georgia King to J. Floyd King, 11 May 1860, King Papers.

58. Georgia King to J. Floyd King, 14 May 1860, King Papers; Phillips, *Georgia and State Rights,* 190. The original Georgia delegation would be the cause of the breakup of the Baltimore Convention.

59. Dubay, *Pettus,* 58, 60; Ranck, *Brown,* 188–89.

60. Dorman, *Politics in Alabama,* 157–58. Clement C. Clay, L. P. Walker, and Reuben Chapman were exceptions to the Unionism prevalent in the northern part of the state.

61. Crabtree and Patton, *Journal of a Secesh Lady,* entries of 16, 20 July 1860; Mitchell, *Ruffin,* 156–57.

62. "By the way," wrote Trescott to Miles, "don't send any more of my letters to Barnwell Rhett for reasons I will explain when I see you." See 8 May 1860, Miles Papers.

63. White, "National Democrats," 385.

64. Ibid., 386–87; White, *Rhett,* 165–66, 169; Channing, *Crisis of Fear,* 224; Charles Edward Cauthen, "South Carolina's Decision to Lead the Secession Movement," *North Carolina Historical Review* 18 (October 1941): 362.

65. Letcher to Hunter, June 1860, *Correspondence of Hunter.*

66. Bachman to Ruffin, 23 May 1860, Ruffin Papers.

67. *Ruffin Diary,* entries of 2, 10, 15 June 1860.

68. Ibid., entry of 13 June 1860.

69. Ibid., entries of 11, 12, 22 June 1860; Channing, *Crisis of Fear,* 225.

70. Kibler, "Unionist Sentiment in South Carolina," 352; Cauthen, *South Carolina Goes to War,* 50; *Charleston Mercury,* 10 August 1860.

71. Hammond to Miles, 16 July 1860, Miles Papers. Hammond straddled the issue of disunion as long as he could because he was being warned of intrigue against his Senate place arising from either Rhett's quarter or that of Governor Gist. See Isaac W. Hayne to Hammond, 15 September 1860; Keitt to Hammond, 23 October 1860, cited in Cauthen, *South Carolina Goes to War,* 49.

72. Hammond to Miles, 16 July 1860; also see Trescott to Miles, 27 July 1860, Miles Papers.

73. *Charleston Mercury,* quoted in Faust, *Hammond and the Old South,* 347.

74. Faust, *Hammond and the Old South,* 99, 345.

75. Channing, *Crisis of Fear,* 226.

CHAPTER NINE
"Instruments in the Hands of God"

1. G. Bailey to Miles, 13 October 1856, Miles Papers; John M. Perkins to Dr. Delaney and Others, 28 September 1856, Perkins Papers; also see Schultz, *Sectionalism in South Carolina,* 125–26; Cauthen, *South Carolina Goes to War,* 25–27.

2. Green to Foote, 29 June 1856, Green Papers.

3. J. D. Ashman to Miles, 30 July 1860, Miles Papers.

4. *Charleston Mercury,* 8 October 1851; Chesnut told Ruffin in August 1860 that if enough cotton states went out, European concern for textile manufacturing would make the diplomatic difference in the success of secession. See *Ruffin Diary,* entry of 12 August 1860.

5. Orr stated that he was for South Carolina's withdrawal only if Alabama, Mississippi, and Georgia cooperated, prompting Benjamin F. Perry to scoff that predicating Palmetto secession on Georgia was rather like waiting for the moon to withdraw from the earth. See Cauthen, "South Carolina's Decision to Lead the Secession Movement," *North Carolina Historical Review* 18 (October 1941): 362.

6. William B. McCash, *Thomas R. R. Cobb (1823–1862): The Making of a Southern Nationalist* (Macon, Georgia: Mercer University Press, 1983), 184–85, 193.

7. Schenck Books, entry of 1 October 1860.

8. Gavin Diary, entry of 1 October 1860; also see Dubay, *Pettus,* 64–65.

9. Slidell to E. G. W. Barker, 25 August 1860, quoted in Peyton McCary, Clark Miller, and Dale Baum, "Class and Party in the Secession Crisis: Voting Behavior in the Deep South, 1856–1861," *Journal of Interdisciplinary History* 8 (Winter 1978): 440n.

10. James Golden, "The Southern Unionists, 1850–1860," in *Oratory in the Old South,* 1828–1860, 280; Shanks, *Secession Movement in Virginia,* 112.

11. Branch to John U. Kirkland, 13 August 1860, William H. Branch Family Papers, Southern Historical Collection, University of North Carolina, Chapel Hill, N.C.

12. Ranck, *Brown,* 193–95, 197.

13. *Atlantic Monthly* 6 (October 1860): 501.

14. Wells, *Douglas' Last Years,* 254–55.

15. Channing, *Crisis of Fear,* 261–63; William Tennent, Jr., to Ruffin, 29 October 1860, Ruffin Papers.

16. *Ruffin Diary,* entries of 5, 11 September 1860.

17. Buenger, *Secession in Texas,* 55–56, 75–76. Bickley is quoted in Ollinger Crenshaw, "The Knights of the Golden Circle: The Career of George Bickley," *American Historical Review* 47 (October 1941): 37; also see Channing, *Crisis of Fear,* 269–71. William White, "The Texas Slave Insurrection in 1860," *Southwestern Historical Quarterly* 52 (January 1949): 259–86, believes that the "Texas Troubles" were the result of abolitionist plots, but that they were badly organized and executed because of paltry numbers.

18. Fite, *Campaign of 1860,* 180.

19. Alto L. Garner and Nathan Scott, "William Lowndes Yancey: Statesman of Secession," *Alabama Review* 15 (July 1962): 200–201; Craven, *Southern Nationalism,* 341–42; Fite, *Campaign of 1860,* 323; Franklin, *Southern Odyssey,* 250–52; Ruffin to Yancey, 29 October 1860, *Ruffin Diary,* Appendix E.

20. Frank Steele to Anna Steele, 8 December 1860, Frank F. Steele Letters, Southern Historical Collection, University of North Carolina, Chapel Hill, N.C.; Lizzie Buford to Anne Mercer, 17 December 1860, Mrs. T. P. Waring Collection, Southern Historical Collection, University of North Carolina, Chapel Hill, N.C.

21. Gavin Diary, entry of 1 October 1860; Hunter to James R. Micon and Others, 10 December 1860, *Correspondence of Hunter.*

22. A. R. Blakey to Beverley Wellford, 3 December 1860, White-Wellford-Taliaferro-Marshal Papers.

23. Craven, *Southern Nationalism,* 373; Gist to Pettus, 6, 8 November 1860, quoted in Dubay, *Pettus,* 66; Mitchell, *Ruffin,* 160–61; Gist to Ellis, 5 October 1860, typescript, White-Wellford-Taliaferro-Marshal Papers.

24. Craven, *Southern Nationalism,* 369; Schultz, *Sectionalism in South Carolina,* 224.

25. Rhett to Ruffin, 20 October 1860, Ruffin Papers.

26. Schultz, *Sectionalism in South Carolina,* 225–26.

27. Kibler, "Unionist Sentiment in South Carolina," 354; *Ruffin Diary,* entry of 7 November 1860.

28. Hammond to Marcellus Hammond, 12 November 1860, Bleser, *Hammonds of Redcliffe.*

29. Quoted in Faust, *Hammond and the Old South,* 360–61. "The other U. S. Senator of S. C.," Ruffin recorded, "Hammond, had also resigned." The oblique reference perhaps pointed to the Virginian's dissatisfaction with his friend over his nationalism. See *Ruffin Diary,* entry of 12 November 1860.

30. Rhett to Miles, 8 November 1860, Miles Papers.

31. Ruffin to Ruffin, Jr., and Julian, 11 November 1860, Ruffin Papers.

32. Cauthen, "South Carolina's Decision to Lead Secession," 369; Ruffin to Ruffin, Jr., and Julian, 11 November 1860, Ruffin Papers.

33. Gavin Diary, entry of 6 December 1860.

34. Kibler, "Unionist Sentiment in South Carolina," 359.

35. Jeannette and Charles Holst to Isabella Woodruff, 18 November 1860, Isabella Ann Roberts Woodruff Papers, Southern Historical Collection, University of North Carolina, Chapel Hill, N.C. The Holsts were from Chester. Woodruff was a schoolteacher in Charleston.

36. *Ruffin Diary,* entry of 9 November 1860.

37. Quoted in White, *Rhett,* 177.

38. Rhett to Miles, 4 December 1860, Miles Papers. Also see Richardson Miles to James M. Mason, 1 December 1860, Miles Papers.

39. White, *Rhett,* 183–85; *Ruffin Diary,* entry of 17 December 1860.

40. Cauthen, "South Carolina's Decision to Lead Secession," 371–72.

41. C. D. Evans to Mrs. C. D. Evans, 18 December 1860, Chesley D. Evans Letters, Southern Historical Collection, University of North Carolina, Chapel Hill, N.C. It has been posed that the smallpox scare was merely a ruse to justify the moving of the convention to a place more hospitable to the radicals. On the other hand, the move promised delay and consequently was opposed by some extremists like William Porcher Miles. See Kibler, "Unionist Sentiment in South Carolina," 363; also see Cauthen, "South Carolina Goes to War," 69n.

42. William Henry Trescott to Howell Cobb, 14 December 1860, *Correspondence of Toombs, Stephens, and Cobb;* Buchanan to Pickens, 18 December 1860, copy, Memminger Papers.

43. *Ruffin Diary,* entry of 20 December 1860. According to one Northern reporter, the people attending the secession convention were stunned rather than festive upon the signing. See *New York Tribune,* 24 December 1860.

44. White, *Rhett,* 188–90; also see *Charleston Mercury,* 21 November 1860.

45. *Ruffin Diary,* entry of 22 December 1860.

46. Pryor, *Reminiscences,* 111.

47. *Journal of a Secesh Lady,* entry of 22 December 1860. Williams, sixty-three years old, would die within a year.

48. Cauthen, *South Carolina Goes to War,* 32–33; Hammond is quoted in White, *Rhett,* 182.

49. Gavin Diary, entry of 26 January 1861.

50. Thomas Butler Gunn to Jesse Haney, 22 January 1861, Jesse Haney Papers, Southern Historical Collection, University of North Carolina, Chapel Hill, N.C.

51. Dickinson to Mrs. John Dabney, 8 January 1861, Dickinson Letters.

52. Tunnard to Maggie Sawer, 14 March 1861, William H. Tunnard Letters, Southern Historical Collection, University of North Carolina, Chapel Hill, N.C.

53. Ibid.

54. Green to Buchanan, 15 January 1861, Green Papers. The letter is a draft and might never have been sent.

55. Ibid.

56. *Ruffin Diary,* entries of 27, 29 June 1860.

57. Ibid., entry of 26 December 1860.

58. White, *Rhett,* 186–87; Miles to Cobb, 17 January 1861, *Correspondence of Toombs, Stephens, and Cobb; Ruffin Diary,* entry of 2 April 1861; Pugh to Miles, 24 January 1861, Miles Papers.

59. Mildred Ruffin Sayre to Ruffin, 4 February 1861, Ruffin Papers.

60. Ruffin, Jr., to Ruffin, 24 November 1860, Ruffin Papers.

61. Ellis to Hon. J. W. Garrot, 30 January 1861, typescript, White-Wellford-Taliaferro-Marshal Papers; Pickens to Miles, 7 February 1861, Miles Papers.

62. "Speech of Armistead Burt to the Mississippi Secession Convention," John Francis Hamtramck Claiborne Papers, Southern Historical Collection, University of North Carolina, Chapel Hill, N.C.

63. Dubay, *Pettus,* 68–69.

64. Davis to Rhett, Jr., 10 November 1960, Rhett Papers, Charleston.

65. Ranck, *Brown,* 201–2; Clement Eaton, *Jefferson Davis* (New York: The Free Press, 1977), 121, 123. Upon the formation of the House Committee of Thirty-Three in December, Reuben Davis was appointed to serve for Mississippi. When he stated his intention to serve, Jefferson Davis walked over from the Senate to ask if this were true. Upon being told that it was, Senator Davis looked levelly at his colleague and said, "then it is useless to say anything to you," and walked away. See R. Davis, *Recollections,* 396. Jefferson Davis did serve on the Senate Committee of Thirteen, however, but he and other Southern members deserted it when it proved impotent to answer Southern complaints concretely.

66. Pettus to Davis, 27 December 1860; Davis to Pettus, 4 January 1861, quoted in Dubay, *Pettus,* 78–79.

67. "Proceedings and Debates of the Mississippi State Convention of 1861," reported by J. L. Power, Claiborne Papers. The convention would remain in session until 26 January, the day that Louisiana seceded.

68. Pettus to Perry, 8 January 1861, telegram; Barry to McGehee, 9 January 1861, telegram, "Documents Relating to Secession in Florida," *Florida Historical Quarterly* 4 (April 1926): 184.

69. *Ruffin Diary,* entries of 5, 7 January 1861.

70. Ralph A. Wooster, "The Florida Secession Convention," *Florida Historical Quarterly* 36 (April 1958): 382; Craven, *Southern Nationalism,* 368.

71. "Documents Relating to Florida's Secession," 189.

72. William L. Barney, *The Secessionist Impulse: Alabama and Mississippi in 1860* (Princeton: Princeton University Press, 1974), 248, 301–2. Robert Jemison of Tuscaloosa angrily inquired if Yancey planned to hang dissenters "by families, by neighborhoods, by counties, by Congressional Districts?" See Wyatt-Brown, *Yankee Saints and Southern Sinners,* 206.

73. Mitchell, *Ruffin,* 171–72.

74. *Ruffin Diary,* entries of 20, 21, 22 November 1860.

75. Alexander H. Stephens, *Recollections of Alexander H. Stephens: His Diary When a Prisoner at Fort Warren, Boston Harbor, 1865; Giving Incidents and Reflections of his Prison Life and Some Letters and Reminiscences,* Myrta Lockett Avary, ed. (New York: Doubleday, Page, & Company, 1910), 353; William B. Bates, "The Last Stand for the Union in Georgia," *Georgia Review* 7 (Winter 1953): 455–56.

76. Georgia King to J. Floyd King, 10 November 1860, King Papers; McCash, *Thomas R. R. Cobb,* 188.

77. Lindsey S. Perkins, "The Moderate Democrats, 1830–1860," in *Oratory in the Old South, 1828–1860,* 150.

78. Myrta Lockett Avary's "Introduction" to Stephens, *Recollections,* 47.

79. Trent, ed., *Southern Writers,* 252.

80. Henry Cleveland, ed., *Alexander H. Stephens in Public and Private with*

Letters and Speeches Before, During, and Since the War (Philadelphia: National Publishing Company, 1866), 252. There would be a convention but never a popular referendum on the secession issue in Georgia. See Bates, "Last Stand for the Union in Georgia," 465–66. "We [the convention delegates] are the People," Toombs proclaimed, "owing no allegiance to any Prince, Potentate, Power, or anything under Heaven, but ourselves and our society." See Johnson, *Patriarchal Republic,* 153.

81. Stephens, *Recollections,* 57–58.

82. Cobb to People of Georgia, 6 December 1860; Cobb to Mrs. Cobb, 7, 10 December 1860; Cobb to Buchanan, 8 December 1860, *Correspondence of Toombs, Stephens, and Cobb.*

83. Bates, "Last Stand for the Union in Georgia," 462.

84. King, *Wigfall,* 101–2; Yulee and Mallory to Governor Perry, 15 January 1861, telegram,, cited in "Documents Relating to Florida's Secession," 183; Clay-Clopton, *A Belle of the Fifties,* 147–48; Trent, ed., *Southern Writers,* 207.

85. Charles P. Roland, "Louisiana and Secession," *Louisiana History* 19 (Fall 1978): 395–96; Robert H. Grinnan to Beverley Wellford, 21 January 1861, White-Wellford-Taliaferro-Marshal Papers.

86. Grinnan to Wellford, 24 January 1861, White-Wellford-Taliaferro-Marshal Papers.

87. *Ruffin Diary,* entry of 12 November 1860.

88. Anna Irene Sandbo, "First Session of the Secession Convention of Texas," *Southwestern Historical Quarterly* 18 (October 1914): 181; Larry Jay Gage, "The Texas Road to Secession and War: John Marshall and the *Texas State Gazette,*" *Southwestern Historical Quarterly* 62 (October 1958): 206.

89. King, *Wigfall,* 104.

90. George F. Durham to Cobb, 17 January 1861, *Correspondence of Toombs, Stephens, and Cobb.*

91. King, *Wigfall,* 113–14.

92. *Ruffin Diary,* entries of 4, 27 February 1861.

93. Shanks, *Secession Movement in Virginia,* 198.

94. W. H. Janson to Ruffin, 28 November 1860, Ruffin Papers.

95. Speech of Robert Randolph in Millwood, Clark County, 26 January 1861, White-Wellford-Taliaferro-Marshal Papers.

96. Shanks, *Secession Movement in Virginia,* 126–27; A. R. Blakey to Beverley Wellford, 3 December 1860, White-Wellford-Taliaferro-Marshal Papers; Junius Hillyer to Cobb, 30 January 1861, *Correspondence of Toombs, Stephens, and Cobb.* Mississippi's Fulton Anderson, Georgia's Henry L. Benning, and South Carolina's John Smith Preston sought to allay Virginia's economic fears in addresses to the Virginia Convention. Benning promised the Old Dominion that the proposed Confederacy would institute a 10 percent tariff and would not renew the African slave trade. See Shanks, *Secession Movement in Virginia,* 161.

97. J. N. Chrisfield to Henry Page, 20 January 1861, Page Papers.

98. Robert H. Grinnan to B. R. Wellford, 26 December 1860, White-Wellford-Taliaferro-Marshal Papers.

99. Grinnan to Wellford, 21 January 1861, White-Wellford-Taliaferro-Marshal Papers.

100. *Ruffin Diary,* 8 February 1861; Shanks, *Secession Movement in Virginia,* 150, 156–57; Goldfield, *Urban Growth,* 264–69.

101. James A. Seddon to John Randolph Tucker, 26 February 1861, Tucker Family Papers, Southern Historical Collection, University of North Carolina, Chapel Hill, N.C.; Shanks, *Secession Movement in Virginia,* 159; David F. Riggs, "Robert Young Conrad and the Ordeal of Secession," *Virginia Magazine of History and Biography* 86 (July 1978): 265.

102. John B. Jones, *A Rebel War Clerk's Diary at the Confederate States Capital,* 2 vols. (Philadelphia: J. B. Lippincott & Co., 1866), entries of 10, 11 April 1861; also see Simpson, *A Good Southerner.* 242.

103. Shanks, *Secession Movement in Virginia,* 202; Jones, *Rebel War Clerk's Diary,* entries of 11, 16 April 1861. Wise said that he wanted this "select" convention to organize a resistance party for the upcoming spring elections, not to overthrow the legitimate convention. See Simpson, *A Good Southerner,* 245.

104. Jones, *Rebel War Clerk's Diary,* entry of 17 April 1861; Shanks, *Secession Movement in Virginia,* 203.

105. John F. Douglas to Ruffin, 11 April 1861, Ruffin Papers.

CHAPTER TEN
"We Will Stand by You to the Death"

1. A. S. Alderman Collection, vol. 5, 6–7, Southern Historical Collection, University of North Carolina, Chapel Hill, N.C.

2. Ibid., 6; Colton Diary, entry of 20 April 1861.

3. Blanton Duncan to Miles, 11 February 1861, Miles Papers; Mildred Ruffin Sayre to Ruffin, 21 January 1861, Ruffin Papers.

4. *Ruffin Diary,* entries of 26, 28 November 1860; William Roed, "Secessionist Strength in Missouri," *Missouri Historical Review* 72 (July 1978): 421; "An Address to the Citizens of the State of Missouri by M. J. Thompson, 27 October 1861," Meriwether Jefferson Thompson Papers, Southern Historical Collection, University of North Carolina, Chapel Hill, N.C.

5. Brown, "Course of Albert Pike," 241–42.

6. Ellis to Robert N. Gourdin, 15 December 1860, typescript, White-Tellford-Taliaferro-Marshal Papers.

7. Sitterson, *Secession Movement in North Carolina,* 196; Ellis to Brown, 14, 19 January 1861, typescript, White-Wellford-Taliaferro-Marshal Papers.

8. A. L. Williamson to Thomas David Smith McDowell, 15 January 1861, Thomas David Smith McDowell Papers, Southern Historical Collection, University of North Carolina, Chapel Hill, N.C.

9. Schenck Books, entry of 18 March 1861; Sitterson, *Secession Movement in North Carolina,* 230–33; also see John Gilchrist McCormick's memorandum

in McCormick Papers, Southern Historical Collection, University of North Carolina, Chapel Hill, N.C.

10. Schenck Books, entry of 20 May 1861.

11. See, for example, Sarah Lois Wadley Diary, entry of 16 February 1861.

12. Buenger, *Secession in Texas,* 155.

13. Perritt, "The Fire Eaters," 253–54; Potter, *The Impending Crisis,* 502; Wyatt-Brown, *Yankee Saints and Southern Sinners,* 208; Thornton, *Politics and Power,* 455.

14. Perritt, "Rhett's Grahamville Speech," 106–7; Holt, *Political Crisis of the 1850s,* 221.

15. Roland, "Louisiana and Secession," 398. Also see Johnson, *Patriarchal Republic,* 29–30, 33–34.

16. Ellis to Garrot, 30 January 1861, typescript, White-Wellford-Taliaferro-Marshal Papers.

17. Wadley Diary, entry of 4 January 1861.

18. Ibid., entry of 19 June 1861.

Bibliography

PRIMARY SOURCES

Manuscript Collections

Auburn University, Auburn, Alabama
    Dixon Hall Lewis Papers
    B. C. Yancey Papers

University of Florida, Gainesville
    David L. Yulee Papers

University of North Carolina, Chapel Hill, Southern Historical
Collection
    S. S. Alderman Collection
    Edward Clifford Anderson Papers
    John MacPherson Berrien Papers
    Branch Family Papers
    John Francis Hamtramck Claiborne Papers
    Simeon Colton Diary
    Platt K. Dickinson Letters
    Chesley D. Evans Letters
    David Gavin Diary

Thomas Jefferson Green Papers
James Henry Hammond Papers
Jesse Haney Papers
Thomas Butler King Papers
Edward M. L'Engle Papers
Andrew McCollam Letters
John Gilchrist McCormick Papers
Thomas David Smith McDowell Papers
William Porcher Miles Papers
Henry Page Papers
John Perkins Papers
Quitman Family Papers
Robert Barnwell Rhett Papers
Edmund Ruffin Papers
David Schenck Books
Frank F. Steele Letters
Meriwether Jefferson Thompson Papers
Tucker Family Papers
William H. Tunnard Letters
Sarah Lois Wadley Diary
Mrs. T. P. Waring Collection
White-Wellford-Taliaferro-Marshal Papers
Isabella Ann Roberts Woodruff Papers

South Carolina Historical Society Archives, Charleston
Bacot-Huger Collection
Robert Barnwell Rhett Papers

Published Materials

Ambler, Charles H., ed. *Correspondence of R. M. T. Hunter,*
1826–1876. American Historical Association *Annual Report,*
1916, pt. 2.
Basler, Roy P., ed. *Abraham Lincoln: His Speeches and Writings.*
Cleveland: The World Publishing Company, 1946.
Blaine, James G. *Twenty Years of Congress from Lincoln to Garfield,*
With a Review of the Events Which Led to the Political Revolu-
tion of 1860. 2 vols. Norwich, Conn.: Henry Bill, 1884.

Bleser, Carol, ed. *The Hammonds of Redcliffe.* New York: Oxford University Press, 1981.

Boucher, Chauncey S., and Robert P. Brooks, eds. *Correspondence Addressed to John C. Calhoun, 1837–1849.* American Historical Association *Annual Report,* 1929.

Childs, Arney R., ed. *Rice Planter and Sportsman: The Recollections of J. Motte Alston, 1827–1909.* Columbia: University of South Carolina Press, 1953.

Claiborne, J. F. H., ed. *Life and Correspondence of John A. Quitman.* 2 vols. New York: Harper & Brothers, 1860.

Clay-Clopton, Virginia. *A Belle of the Fifties: Memoirs of Mrs. Clay of Alabama, Covering Social and Political Life in Washington and the South, 1853–66, Gathered and Edited by Ada Sterling.* New York: Doubleday, Page & Company, 1904.

Clayton, Victoria. *White and Black Under the Old Regime.* Reprint. Freeport, N.Y.: Books for Libraries Press, 1970.

Cleveland, Henry, ed. *Alexander H. Stephens in Public and Private with Letters and Speeches Before, During, and Since the War.* Philadelphia: National Publishing Company, 1866.

Cluskey, M. W., ed. *The Political Textbook or Encyclopedia Containing Everything Necessary for the Reference of the Politicians and Statesmen of the United States.* 12th ed. Philadelphia: Jas. B. Smith & Co., 1860.

Crabtree, Beth G., and James W. Patton, eds. *"Journal of a Secesh Lady:" The Diary of Catherine Anne Devereaux Edmonston, 1860–1866.* Raleigh: North Carolina Division of Archives and History, 1979.

Davis, Reuben. *Recollections of Mississippi and Mississippians.* Reprint. Jackson: University and College Press of Mississippi, 1972.

Dillard, Anthony W. "William Lowndes Yancey: The Sincere and Unfaltering Advocate of Southern Rights." *Southern Historical Society Papers,* vol. 21, 151–59. Edited by R. A. Brock. Richmond: Southern Historical Society, 1893.

DuBose, John Witherspoon. *The Life and Times of William Lowndes Yancey: A History of Political Parties in the United States from 1834 to 1864; Especially as to the Origin of the Confederate States.* Birmingham, Ala.: Roberts & Son, 1892.

Duncan, Rosalie Quitman. "Life of General John A. Quitman." *Publications of Mississippi Historical Society* 4 (1901): 415–520.

Easterby, J. H., ed. *The South Carolina Rice Plantation as Revealed in the Papers of Robert F. W. Allston.* Chicago: University of Chicago Press, 1945.

Freehling, William W., ed. *The Nullification Era: A Documentary Record.* New York: Harper Torchbook, 1967.

Garrett, William. *Reminiscences of Public Men in Alabama for Thirty Years.* Atlanta: Plantation Publishing Company's Press, 1872.

Hammond, James H. *Selections from the Letters and Speeches of the Hon. James H. Hammond of South Carolina.* New York: John F. Trow & Co., 1866.

Harvey, Peter. *Reminiscences and Anecdotes of Daniel Webster.* Boston: Little, Brown and Company, 1921.

Hilliard, Henry Washington. *Politics and Pen Pictures at Home and Abroad.* New York: G. P. Putnam's Sons, 1892.

_____. *Speeches and Addresses.* New York: Harper & Brothers, 1855.

Ingraham, J. H., ed. *The Sunny South, or the Southerner at Home: Embracing Five Years Experience of a Northern Governess in the Land of Sugar and Cotton.* Philadelphia: G. G. Evans, 1860.

Jameson, J. Franklin, ed. *Correspondence of John C. Calhoun.* American Historical Association *Annual Report,* 1899, pt.2.

Johannsen, Robert W. ed. *The Letters of Stephen A. Douglas.* Urbana: University of Illinois Press, 1961.

Jones, John B. *A Rebel War Clerk's Diary at the Confederate States Capital.* 2 vols. Philadelphia: J. P. Lippincott & Co., 1866.

Moore, John Bassett, ed. *The Works of James Buchanan, Comprising His Speeches, State Papers, and Private Correspondence.* 12 vols. Reprint. New York: Antiquarian Press Ltd., 1960.

Oliphant, Mary C. Simms, Alfred Taylor Odell, and T. C. Duncan Eaves, eds. *The Letters of William Gilmore Simms.* 5 vols. Columbia: University of South Carolina Press, 1952–56.

Olmstead, Frederick Law. *A Journey in the Seaboard Slave States, With Remarks on their Economy.* New York: Dix and Edwards, 1856.

Perry, Benjamin Franklin. *Biographical Sketches of Eminent American Statesmen with Speeches, Addresses and Letters.* Philadelphia: Feree Press, 1887.

Phillips, Ulrich B., ed. *Correspondence of Robert Toombs, Alexander H. Stephens, and Howell Cobb.* American Historical Association *Annual Report,* 1911, pt. 2.

Pryor, Mrs. Roger A. *Reminiscences of Peace and War.* New York: The Macmillan Company, 1905.

Putnam, Sallie B. *Richmond During the War: Four Years of Personal Observations by a Richmond Lady.* New York: G. W. Carleton & Company, Publishers, 1867.

Scott, Edwin J. *Random Recollections of a Long Life, 1805 to 1876.* Columbia, S.C.: Charles Calvo, Jr., 1884.

Seward, Frederick W. *Reminiscences of a War-Time Statesman and Diplomat, 1830–1915.* New York: G. P. Putnam's Sons, 1916.

Shryock, Richard H., ed. *Letters of Richard D. Arnold, M. D., 1808–1876: Mayor of Savannah, Georgia; First Secretary of the American Medical Association.* Durham, N.C.: Duke University Press, 1929.

Starobin, Robert S., ed. *Denmark Vesey: The Slave Conspiracy of 1822.* Englewood Cliffs, N.J.: Prentice-Hall, Inc., 1878.

Stephens, Alexander H. *Recollections of Alexander H. Stephens: His Diary Kept When a Prisoner at Fort Warren, Boston Harbor, 1865; Giving Incidents and Reflections of His Prison Life and Some Letters and Reminiscences.* Edited by Myrta Lockett Avary. New York: Doubleday, Page & Company, 1910.

Swift, Lindsay, ed. *The Great Debate Between Robert Young Hayne of South Carolina and Daniel Webster of Massachusetts.* Boston: Houghton Mifflin Company, 1898.

Tazewell, Littleton Waller. *A Review of the Proclamation of the 10 of December, 1832, in a Series of Numbers Originally Published in the Norfolk and Portsmouth* Herald *Under the Signature of "A Virginian."* Norfolk: J. D. Ghiselin, 1888.

Trent, W. P., ed. *Southern Writers: Selections in Prose and Verse.* New York: The Macmillan Company, 1910.

Watson, William. *Life in the Confederate Army Being the Observations and Experiences of an Alien in the South During the American Civil War.* New York: Scribner and Welford, 1888.

Wilson, Clyde N., ed. *Selections from the Letters and Speeches of the Hon. James Henry Hammond of South Carolina.* Reprint. Spartanburg, S.C.: The Reprint Company, 1978.

Wright, Louise Wigfall. *A Southern Girl in '61: The War-Time Memories of a Confederate Senator's Daughter.* New York: Doubleday, Page & Company, 1905.

Younger, Edward, ed. *Inside the Confederate Government: The Diary of Robert Garlick Hill Kean, Head of the Bureau of War.* New York: Oxford University Press, 1957.

Newspapers and Periodicals

Atlantic Monthly
Charleston Courier
Charleston Mercury
Columbus (Georgia) *Enquirer*
Concordia (Louisiana) *Intelligencer*
(Jackson) *Mississippian*
Milledgeville (Georgia*) Federal Union*
Mobile Daily Register
Montgomery Advertiser and State Gazette
Montgomery Alabama Journal
(Natchez) *Mississippi Free Trader*
National Intelligencer
Niles Weekly Register
Richmond Enquirer
Richmond Whig
United States Congress *Congressional Globe*

SECONDARY SOURCES

Books

Allmendinger, David F., Jr. *Ruffin: Family and Reform in the Old South.* New York: Oxford University Press, 1990.

Bancroft, Frederic. *Calhoun and the South Carolina Nullification Movement.* Baltimore: Johns Hopkins Press, 1928.

Banks, Ronald F. *Maine Becomes a State: The Movement to Separate Maine from Massachusetts, 1785–1820.* Middleton, Conn.: Wesleyan University Press, 1970.

Barney, William L. *The Road to Secession: A New Perspective on the Old South.* New York: Praeger Publishers, 1972.

_____. *The Secessionist Impulse: Alabama and Mississippi in 1860.* Princeton: Princeton University Press, 1974.

Binkley, William Campbell. *The Expansionist Movement in Texas,
1836–1850.* Reprint. Millwood, N.Y.: Kraus Reprint Co., 1974.

Boucher, Chauncey Samuel. *The Nullification Controversy in South
Carolina.* Chicago: University of Chicago Press, 1916.

Brugger, Robert J. *Beverley Tucker: Heart Over Head in the Old South.*
Baltimore: Johns Hopkins University Press, 1978.

Buenger, Walter L. *Secession and the Union in Texas.* Austin: University of Texas Press, 1984.

Campbell, Stanley W. *The Slave Catchers: Enforcement of the Fugitive
Slave Law, 1850–1860.* Chapel Hill: University of North Carolina
Press, 1968.

Capers, Gerald M. *John C. Calhoun, Opportunist: A Reappraisal.*
Gainesville: University of Florida Press, 1960.

_____. *Stephen A. Douglas: Defender of the Union.* Boston: Little,
Brown and Company, 1959.

Carpenter, Jesse T. *The South as a Conscious Minority, 1789–1861.*
Reprint. Gloucester, Mass.: Peter Smith, 1963.

Cauthen, Charles E. *South Carolina Goes to War, 1860–65.* Chapel
Hill: University of North Carolina Press, 1950.

Channing, Stephen A. *Crisis of Fear: Secession in South Carolina.*
New York: Simon and Schuster, 1970.

Cole, Arthur Charles. *The Whig Party in the South.* Reprint. Gloucester,
Mass.: Peter Smith, 1962.

Cooper, William J., Jr. *The South and the Politics of Slavery,
1828–1856.* Baton Rouge: Louisiana State University Press,
1978.

Craven, Avery O. *Civil War in the Making, 1815–1860.* Baton Rouge:
Louisiana State University Press, 1959.

_____. *Edmund Ruffin, Southerner: A Study in Secession.* New
York: D. Appleton and Company, 1932.

_____. *The Coming of the Civil War.* New York: Charles Scribner's
Sons, 1942.

_____. *The Growth of Southern Nationalism, 1848–1861.* Baton
Rouge: Louisiana State University Press, 1953.

Davenport, F. Garvin. *Cultural Life in Nashville on the Eve of the Civil
War.* Chapel Hill: University of North Carolina Press, 1941.

Davis, William H. *The Whig Party of Louisiana.* Lafayette, La.: University of Southwestern Louisiana, 1973.

Dawidoff, Robert. *The Education of John Randolph.* New York: W. W. Norton & Company, 1979.

Doherty, Herbert J., Jr. *Richard Keith Call: Southern Unionist.* Gainesville: University of Florida Press, 1961.

Dorman, Lewy. *Party Politics in Alabama from 1850 Through 1860.* Wetumpka, Ala.: Wetumpka Publishing Company, 1935.

Dubay, Robert W. *John Jones Pettus, Mississippi Fire Eater: His Life and Times, 1813–1867.* Jackson: University Press of Mississippi, 1975.

DuBose, John Witherspoon. "W. L. Yancey in History: The Memorable Debate on the Slave Trade at Montgomery, Alabama, in 1858." *Southern Historical Society Papers,* vol. 27. Richmond: Southern Historical Society, 1899.

Dumond, Dwight Lowell. *The Secession Movement, 1860–1861.* New York: The Macmillan Company, 1931.

Eaton, Clement. *Jefferson Davis.* New York: The Free Press, 1977.

Edmunds, John B., Jr. *Francis W. Pickens and the Politics of Destruction.* Chapel Hill: University of North Carolina Press, 1986.

Ellis, Richard E. *The Union at Risk: Jacksonian Democracy, States' Rights, and the Nullification Crisis.* New York and Oxford: Oxford University Press, 1987.

Faust, Drew Gilpin. *A Sacred Circle: The Dilemma of the Intellectual in the Old South, 1840–1860.* Baltimore: Johns Hopkins Press, 1977.

_____. *James Henry Hammond and the Old South: A Design for Mastery.* Baton Rouge: Louisiana State University Press, 1982.

Fite, Emerson D. *The Presidential Campaign of 1860.* New York: The Macmillan Company, 1911.

Flippin, Percy S. *Herschel V. Johnson of Georgia: States Rights Unionist.* Richmond: Dietz Printing Co., 1931.

Ford, Lacy F., Jr. *Origins of Southern Radicalism: The South Carolina Upcountry, 1800–1860.* New York and Oxford: Oxford University Press, 1988.

Franklin, John Hope. *A Southern Odyssey: Travelers in the Antebellum North.* Baton Rouge: Louisiana State University Press, 1976.

_____. *The Militant South, 1800–1861.* Cambridge: Belknap Press of Harvard University, 1956.

Freehling, Alison Goodyear. *Drift Toward Dissolution: The Virginia*

Slavery Debate, 1831–1832. Baton Rouge: Louisiana State University Press, 1982.

Freehling, William W. *Prelude to Civil War: The Nullification Controversy in South Carolina, 1816–1836.* New York: Harper & Row, 1966.

_____. *The Road to Disunion: Secessionists at Bay, 1776–1854.* New York: Oxford University Press, 1990.

Fuess, Claude Moore. *Daniel Webster.* 2 vols. Boston: Little, Brown and Company, 1930.

Ganaway, Loomis Morton. *New Mexico and the Sectional Controversy, 1846–1861.* Albuquerque: University of New Mexico Press, 1944.

Golden, James. "The Southern Unionists, 1850–1860." In *Oratory in the Old South, 1828–1860,* 258–90. Edited by Waldo W. Braden with the assistance of J. Jeffrey Auer and Bert E. Bradley. Baton Rouge: Louisiana State University Press, 1970.

Goldfield, David R. *Urban Growth in the Age of Sectionalism: Virginia, 1847–1861.* Baton Rouge: Louisiana State University Press, 1977.

Gunderson, Robert G. "The Southern Whigs." In *Oratory in the Old South, 1828–1860,* 104–41. Edited by Waldo W. Braden with the assistance of J. Jeffrey Auer and Bert E. Bradley. Baton Rouge: Louisiana State University Press, 1970.

Hamer, Philip May. *The Secession Movement in South Carolina, 1847–1852.* Reprint. New York: Da Capo Press, 1971.

Hamilton, Holman. *Prologue to Conflict: The Crisis and Compromise of 1850.* Lexington: University of Kentucky Press, 1964.

_____. *Zachary Taylor: Soldier in the White House.* Indianapolis: Bobbs-Merrill Company, Inc., 1951.

Hearon, Cleo. *Mississippi and the Compromise of 1850.* Reprint. New York: AMS Press, 1972.

Hodder, Frank Heywood. "Side Lights on the Missouri Compromises." American Historical Association *Annual Report,* 1909.

Hodgson, Joseph. *The Cradle of the Confederacy: or, the Times of Troup, Quitman and Yancey: A Sketch of Southwestern Political History from the Formation of the Federal Government to A.D. 1861.* Mobile: *Mobile Register* Publishing Office, 1876.

Hoffman, William S. *Andrew Jackson and North Carolina Politics.*

James Sprunt Studies in History and Political Science, vol 40. Reprint. Gloucester, Mass.: Peter Smith, 1971.

Holt, Michael F. *The Political Crisis of the 1850s.* New York: Wiley, 1978.

Houston, David Franklin. *A Critical Study of Nullification in South Carolina.* New York: Longmans, Green, and Co., 1908.

Jack, Theodore Henley. *Sectionalism and Party Politics in Alabama, 1819–1842.* Reprint. Spartanburg, S.C.: The Reprint Company, 1975.

Jennings, Thelma. *The Nashville Convention: Southern Movement for Unity, 1848–1851.* Memphis: Memphis State University Press, 1980.

Jervey, Theodore D. *Robert Y. Hayne and His Times.* New York: The Macmillan Company, 1909.

Johannsen, Robert W. *Stephen A. Douglas.* New York: Oxford University Press, 1973.

Johnson, Michael P. *Toward a Patriarchal Republic: The Secession of Georgia.* Baton Rouge: Louisiana State University Press, 1977.

Kibler, Lillian Adele. *Benjamin F. Perry: South Carolina Unionist.* Durham, N.C.: Duke University Press, 1970.

King, Alvy L. *Louis T. Wigfall: Southern Fire Eater.* Baton Rouge: Louisiana State University Press, 1970.

Knupfer, Peter B. *The Union As It Is: Constitutional Unionism and Sectional Compromise, 1787–1861.* Chapel Hill: University of North Carolina Press, 1991.

Leemhuis, Roger P. *James L. Orr and the Sectional Conflict.* Washington, D.C.: University Press of America, 1979.

Lofton, John. *Insurrection in South Carolina: The Turbulent World of Denmark Vesey.* Yellow Springs, Ohio: Antioch Press, 1964.

Mathew, William M. *Edmund Ruffin and the Crisis of Slavery in the Old South: The Failure of Agricultural Reform.* Athens: University of Georgia Press, 1988.

May, Robert E. *John A. Quitman: Old South Crusader.* Baton Rouge: Lousiana State University Press, 1985.

————. *The Southern Dream of a Caribbean Empire, 1854–1861.* Baton Rouge: Louisiana State University Press, 1973.

McCardell, John. *The Idea of a Southern Nation: Southern Nationalists* and *Southern Nationalism, 1830–1860*. New York: W. W. Norton & Company, Inc., 1979.

McCash, William B. *Thomas R. R. Cobb (1832–1862): The Making of a Southern Nationalist.* Macon, Ga.: Mercer University Press, 1983.

Mitchell, Betty L. *Edmund Ruffin: A Biography.* Bloomington: Indiana University Press, 1981.

Moore, Glover. *The Missouri Controversy, 1819–1821.* Lexington: University of Kentucky Press, 1953.

Morrison, Chaplain W. *Democratic Politics and Sectionalism: The Wilmot Proviso Controversy.* Chapel Hill: University of North Carolina Press, 1967.

Munford, Beverley B. *Virginia's Attitude Toward Slavery and Secession.* New York: Longmans, Green, and Co., 1909.

Murray, Paul. *The Whig Party in Georgia, 1825–1853.* James Sprunt Studies in History and Political Science, vol 29. Chapel Hill: University of North Carolina Press, 1948.

Nevins, Allan. *Ordeal of the Union: Volume 1: Fruits of Manifest Destiny.* New York: Charles Scribner's Sons, 1947.

Nichols, Roy F. *The Democratic Machine, 1850–1854.* New York: Longmans, Green & Co., 1923.

_____. *The Disruption of American Democracy.* New York: The Macmillan Company, 1948.

_____. *The Stakes of Power, 1845–1877.* New York: Hill and Wang, 1961.

Oates, Stephen B. *To Purge this Land With Blood: A Biography of John Brown.* New York: Harper & Row, 1970.

Owsley, Frank L. *Plain Folk of the Old South.* Baton Rouge: Louisiana State University Press, 1949.

Parrish, William E. *David Rice Atchison of Missouri: Border Politician.* Columbia: University of Missouri Press, 1961.

Perkins, Lindsey S. "The Moderate Democrats, 1830–1860." In *Oratory in the Old South, 1828–1860,* 142–68. Edited by Waldo W. Braden with the assistance of J. Jeffrey Auer and Bert E. Bradley. Baton Rouge: Louisiana State University Press, 1970.

Perritt, H. Hardy. "Robert Barnwell Rhett's Speech, July 4, 1859." In *Antislavery and Disunion, 1858–1861: Studies in the Rhetoric of*

Compromise and Conflict, 145–52. Edited by J. Jeffrey Auer.
New York: Simon and Schuster, 1963.

Perritt, H. Hardy. "The Fire Eaters." In *Oratory in the Old South,
1828–1860*, 234–57. Edited by Waldo W. Braden with the assistance of J. Jeffrey Auer and Bert E. Bradley. Baton Rouge:
Louisiana State University Press, 1970.

Peterson, Owen. "Speaking in the Southern Commercial Conventions,
1837–1859." In *Oratory of the Old South, 1828–1860*, 190–217.
Edited by Waldo W. Braden with the assistance of J. Jeffrey Auer
and Bert E. Bradley. Baton Rouge: Louisiana State University
Press, 1970.

Petrie, George. "William F. Samford, Statesman and Man of Letters."
In *Transactions of the Alabama Historical Society, 1899–1903*,
IV: 465–86. Edited by Thomas McAdory Owen. Montgomery:
Alabama Historical Society, 1904.

Phillips, Ulrich B. *Georgia and State Rights*. Yellow Springs, Ohio:
Antioch Press, 1968.

————. *The Course of the South to Secession*. Edited by E. Merton
Coulter. New York: D. Appleton-Century Company, 1939.

————. *The Life of Robert Toombs*. New York: Macmillan Company, 1913.

Potter, David M., and Don E. Fehrenbacher. *The Impending Crisis,
1848–1861*. New York: Harper & Row, 1976.

Pressly, Thomas J. *Americans Interpret Their Civil War*. New York: The
Free Press, 1962.

Ranck, James Byrne. *Albert Gallatin Brown: Radical Southern Nationalist*. New York: D. Appleton-Century Company, Inc., 1937.

Rand, Clayton. *Men of Spine in Mississippi*. Gulfport, Miss.: The Dixie
Press, 1940.

Rawley, James A. *Race and Politics: "Bleeding Kansas" and the Coming of the Civil War*. Philadelphia: Lippincott, 1969.

Rayback, Joseph G. *Free Soil: The Election of 1848*. Lexington: University Press of Kentucky, 1971.

Rayback, Robert J. *Millard Fillmore: Biography of a President*. East
Aurora, N.Y.: Henry Stewart, Inc., 1972.

Roark, James L. *Masters Without Slaves: Southern Planters in the Civil
War and Reconstruction*. New York: W. W. Norton and Company,
1977.

Robert, Joseph Clarke. *The Road from Monticello: A Study of the Virginia Slavery Debate of 1832.* Historical Papers of the Trinity College Historical Society, Series 24. Durham, N.C.: Duke University Press, 1941.

Rothbard, Murray N. *The Panic of 1819: Reactions and Policies.* New York: Columbia University Press, 1962.

Schaper, William A. *Sectionalism and Representation in South Carolina.* American Historical Association *Annual Report,* 1900, vol. 1.

Schultz, Harold S. *Nationalism and Sectionalism in South Carolina, 1852–1860.* Durham, N.C.: Duke University Press, 1950.

Shanks, Henry T. *The Secession Movement in Virginia, 1847–1861.* Richmond: Garrett and Massie, 1934.

Sharp, James Roger. *The Jacksonians* versus *the Banks: Politics in the States after the Panic of 1837.* New York: Columbia University Press, 1970.

Shoemaker, Floyd Calvin. *Missouri's Struggle for Statehood, 1804–1821.* Reprint. New York: Russell & Russell, 1969.

Shryock, Richard H. *Georgia and the Union in 1850.* Durham, N.C.: Duke University Press, 1970.

Silbey, Joel. *The Partisan Imperative: The Dynamics of American Politics Before the Civil War.* New York: Oxford University Press, 1985.

Simpson, Craig M. *A Good Southerner: The Life of Henry A. Wise of Virginia.* Chapel Hill: University of North Carolina Press, 1985.

Sitterson, Joseph Carlyle. *The Secession Movement in North Carolina.* James Sprunt Studies in History and Political Science, vol. 23, no. 2. Chapel Hill: University of North Carolina Press, 1939.

Stampp, Kenneth M. *American in 1857: A Nation on the Brink.* New York and Oxford: Oxford University Press, 1990.

Stevens, William Oliver. *Charleston: Historic City of Gardens.* New York: Dodd, Mead & Company, 1939.

Taylor, William R. *Cavalier and Yankee: The Old South and American National Character.* Cambridge: Harvard University Press, 1979.

Thompson, William Y. *Robert Toombs of Georgia.* Baton Rouge: Louisiana State University Press, 1966.

Tise, Larry. Proslavery: *A History of the Defense of Slavery in America, 1701–1840.* Athens: University of Georgia Press, 1987.

Trent, William P. *William Gilmore Simms.* Boston: Houghton, Mifflin and Company, 1892.

Van Deusen, John G. *The Ante-Bellum Southern Commercial Conventions.* Historical Papers Published by the Trinity College Historical Society, Series 16. Durham, N.C.: Duke University Press, 1926.

Walther, Eric H. *The Fire-Eaters.* Baton Rouge and London: Louisiana State University Press, 1992.

Wellington, Raynor C. *The Tariff and Public Lands from 1828 to 1833.* American Historical Association *Annual Report,* 1911, vol. 1.

Wells, Damon. *Stephen Douglas: The Last Years, 1857–1861.* Austin: University of Texas Press, 1971.

White, Laura A. *Robert Barnwell Rhett: Father of Secession.* New York: The Century Company, 1931.

Wilson, Henry. *History of the Rise and Fall of the Slave Power in America.* 9th ed. 3 vols. Boston: Houghton, Mifflin and Company, 1872–77.

Wiltse, Charles W. *John C. Calhoun: Sectionalist, 1840–1850.* Indianapolis: Bobbs-Merrill Company, Inc., 1951.

Woods, James M. *Rebellion and Realignment: Arkansas' Road to Secession.* Fayetteville: University of Arkansas Press, 1987.

Wyatt-Brown, Bertram. *Yankee Saints and Southern Sinners.* Baton Rouge: Louisiana State University Press, 1985.

Yonge, J. E. D. "The Conservative Party in Alabama, 1848–1860." In *Transactions of the Alabama Historical Society, 1899–1903,* IV: 501–26. Edited by Thomas McAdory Owen. Montgomery: Alabama Historical Review, 1904.

Zacharias, Donald W. "The Know-Nothing Party and the Oratory of Nationalism." In *Oratory in the Old South, 1828–1860,* 218–33. Edited by Waldo W. Braden with the assistance of J. Jeffrey Auer and Bert E. Bradley. Baton Rouge: Louisiana State University Press, 1970.

Journal Articles

Allen, Jeffrey Brooke. "'All of Us Are Highly Pleased with this Country': Black and White Kentuckians in Liberian Colonization." *Phylon* 43 (Summer 1982): 97–109.

Barr, C. Alwyn. "The Making of a Secessionist: The Antebellum Career of Roger Q. Mills." *Southwestern Historical Quarterly* 79 (October 1975): 129–44.

Bates, William B. "The Last Stand for the Union in Georgia." *Georgia Review* 7 (Winter 1953): 455–66.

Bernstein, Barton J. "Southern Politics and Attempts to Reopen the African Slave Trade." *Journal of Negro History* 51 (January 1966): 16–35.

Binkley, William Campbell. "The Question of Texas Jurisdiction in New Mexico under the United States." *Southwestern Historical Quarterly* 24 (July 1920): 1–38.

Boucher, Chauncey S. *"In Re* That Aggressive Slavocracy." *Mississippi Valley Historical Review* 8 (June–September 1921): 13–79.

Broussard, Ray. "Governor John A. Quitman and the Lopez Expeditions of 1851–1852." *Journal of Mississippi History* 28 (May 1966): 103–20.

Brown, Walter L. "Rowing Against the Stream: The Course of Albert Pike from National Whig to Secessionist." *Arkansas Historical Quarterly* 39 (Autumn 1980): 230–46.

Brugger, Robert J. "The Mind of the Old South: New Views." *Virginia Quarterly Review* 56 (Spring 1980): 277–95.

Campbell, Randolph B. "Texas and the Nashville Convention." *Southwestern Historical Quarterly* 76 (July 1971): 1–14.

Carnathan, W. J. "The Proposal to Reopen the African Slave Trade in the South, 1854–1860." *South Atlantic Quarterly* 25 (October 1926): 410–29.

Cauthen, Charles Edward. "South Carolina's Decision to Lead the Secession Movement." *North Carolina Historical Review* 18 (October 1941): 360–72.

Cole, Arthur C. "The South and the Right to Secession in the Early Fifties." *Mississippi Valley Historical Review* 1 (December 1914): 376–99.

Crenshaw, Ollinger. "Christopher G. Memminger's Mission to Virginia, 1860." *Journal of Southern History* 8 (August 1942): 334–49.

_____. "The Knights of the Golden Circle: The Career of George Bickley." *American Historical Review* 47 (October 1941): 23–50.

_____. "The Speakership Contest of 1859–1860." *Mississippi Valley Historical Review* 29 (December 1942): 323–38.

"Documents Relating to Secession in Florida." *Florida Historical Quarterly* 4 (April 1926): 183–85.

Dodd, Dorothy. "The Secession Movement in Florida, 1850–1861." *Florida Historical Quarterly* 12 (July 1933): 3–24.

Donald, David. "The Proslavery Argument Reconsidered." *Journal of Southern History* 37 (February 1971): 3–18.

Durden, Robert F. "The American Revolution as Seen by Southerners in 1861." *Louisiana History* 19 (Winter 1978): 33–42.

Faust, Drew Gilpin. "The Rhetoric and Ritual of Agriculture in Antebellum South Carolina." *Journal of Southern History* 45 (November 1979): 541–68.

Fleming, Walter Lynwood. "The Buford Expedition to Kansas." *American Historical Review* 6 (October 1900): 38–48.

Fornell, Earl W. "Agitation in Texas for Reopening the Slave Trade." *Southwestern Historical Quarterly* 60 (October 1956): 245–59.

Foster, Herbert D. "Webster's Seventh of March Speech and the Secession Movement of 1850." *American Historical Review* 27 (1921–22): 245–70.

Gage, Larry Jay. "The Texas Road to Secession and War: John Marshall and the *Texas State Gazette*." *Southwestern Historical Quarterly* 62 (October 1958): 191–226.

Garner, Alto L., and Nathan Scott. "William Lowndes Yancey: Statesman of Secession." *Alabama Review* 15 (July 1962): 190–202.

Garner, James W. "The First Struggle Over Secession in Mississippi." *Publications of the Mississippi Historical Society* 4 (1901): 89–104.

Gonzalez, John E. "Henry Stuart Foote: A Forgotten Unionist of the Fifties." *Southern Quarterly* 1 (October 1963): 129–39.

Greer, James K. "Louisiana Politics, 1845–61." *Louisiana Historical Quarterly* 12 (October 1929): 570–610.

Harmon, George D. "Douglas and the Compromise of 1850." *Journal of Illinois State Historical Society* 21 (1929): 453–99.

Hodder, Frank H. "The Authorship of the Compromise of 1850." *Mississippi Valley Historical Review* 22 (March 1936): 525–36.

Holder, Ray. "The Brown-Winans Canvass for Congress, 1849." *Journal of Mississippi History* 40 (November 1978): 353–73.

Howard, Victor B. "John Brown's Raid at Harper's Ferry and the Sectional Crisis in North Carolina." *North Carolina Historical Review* 19 (Autumn 1978): 396–420.

Huff, A. V., Jr. "The Eagle and the Vulture: Changing Attitudes Toward Nationalism in Fourth of July Orations Delivered in Charleston, 1778–1860." *South Atlantic Quarterly* 73 (winter 1974): 10–22.

Keller, Mark, and Thomas A. Belser, Jr., eds. "Albert Pike's Contributions to the *Spirit of the Times,* Including his 'Letter from the Far, Far West.'" *Arkansas Historical Quarterly* 37 (Winter 1978): 318–53.

Kibler, Lillian Adele. "Unionist Sentiment in South Carolina in 1860." *Journal of Southern History* 4 (August 1938): 346–66.

Ledbetter, Billy D. "The Election of Louis T. Wigfall to the United States Senate, 1859: A Reevaluation." *Southwestern Historical Quarterly* 77 (October 1973): 241–54.

Mathis, Robert Neil. "Preston Smith Brooks: The Man and His Image." *South Carolina Historical Magazine* (October 1978): 296–310.

McCrary, Peyton, Clark Miller, and Dale Baum. "Class and Party in the Secession Crisis: Voting Behavior in the Deep South, 1856–1861." *Journal of Interdisciplinary History* 8 (Winter 1978): 429–57.

McCrary, Royce, ed. "The Authorship of the Georgia Platform of 1850: A Letter by Charles J. Jenkins." *Georgia Historical Quarterly* 54 (Winter 1970): 585–89.

Meador, John. "Florida and the Compromise of 1850." *Florida Historical Quarterly* 29 (1960–61): 16–33.

Mellen, G. F. "Henry W. Hilliard and William L. Yancey." *Sewanee Review* 17 (January 1909): 32–50.

Miller, William T. "Nullification in Georgia and in South Carolina as Viewed by the West." *Georgia Historical Quarterly* 14 (December 1930): 286–302.

Neighbors, Kenneth F. "The Taylor-Neighbors Struggle over the Upper Rio Grande Region of Texas in 1850." *Southwestern Historical Quarterly* 61 (April 1958): 431–63.

Parks, Joseph H. "John Bell and the Compromise of 1850." *Journal of Southern History* 9 (August 1943): 328–56.

Perkins, Howard C. "A Neglected Phase of the Movement for Southern Unity, 1847–1852." *Journal of Southern History* 24 (Fall 1958): 38–55.

Perritt, Henry Hardy. "Robert Barnwell Rhett: Disunionist Heir of Calhoun, 1850–1862." *Southern Speech Journal* 24 (Fall 1958): 38–55.

Phillips, Ulrich Bonnell. "The Course of the South to Secession: VI. The Fire Eaters." *Georgia Historical Quarterly* 22 (March 1938): 41–71.

Rezneck, Samuel. "The Depression of 1819–1922: A Social History." *American Historical Review* 39 (October 1933): 28–47.

Riggs, David F. "Robert Young Conrad and the Ordeal of Secession." *Virginia Magazine of History and Biography* 86 (July 1978): 259–74.

Roed, William. "Secessionist Strength in Missouri." *Missouri Historical Review* 72 (July 1978): 412–23.

Roland, Charles P. "Louisiana and Secession." *Louisiana History* 19 (Fall 1978): 389–99.

Sandbo, Anna Irene. "Beginning of the Secession Movement in Texas." *Southwestern Historical Quarterly* 18 (July 1914): 41–73.

_____. "First Session of the Secession Convention in Texas." *Southwestern Historical Quarterly* 18 (October 1914): 162–94.

Sellers, Charles Grier, Jr. "Who Were the Southern Whigs?" *American Historical Review* 59 (1954): 335–46.

Sioussat, St. George L. "Tennessee, the Compromise of 1850, and the Nashville Convention." *Mississippi Valley Historical Review* 2 (December 1915): 313–47.

Somers, Dale A. "James P. Newcomb: The Making of a Radical." *Southwestern Historical Quarterly* 72 (April 1969): 449–69.

Stephenson, Nathaniel W. "Southern Nationalism in South Carolina in 1851." *American Historical Review* 36 (1931): 314–55.

Stuckey, Sterling. "Remembering Denmark Vesey." *Negro Digest* 15 (February 1966): 28–41.

Takaki, Ronald. "The Movement to Reopen the African Slave Trade in South Carolina." *South Carolina Historical Magazine* 66 (January 1965): 38–54.

Terrel, A. W. "Recollections of General Sam Houston." *Southwestern Historical Quarterly* 16 (October 1912): 113–36.

Venable, Austin L. "The Conflict Between the Douglas and Yancey Forces in the Charleston Convention." *Journal of Southern History* 8 (May 1942): 226–41.

Wade, Richard. "The Vesey Plot: A Reconsideration." *Journal of Southern History* 30 (May 1964): 148–61.

White, Laura A. "The Fate of Calhoun's Sovereign Convention in

South Carolina." *American Historical Review* 34 (July 1929): 757–71.

_____. "The National Democrats in South Carolina, 1852–1860." *South Atlantic Quarterly* 28 (October 1929): 370–89.

White, M. J. "Louisiana and the Secession Movement of the Early Fifties." *Proceedings of the Mississippi Valley Historical Association* 8 (1916): 277–88.

White, William W. "The Texas Slave Insurrection in 1860." *Southwestern Historical Quarterly* 52 (January 1949): 259–86.

Wilson, Major L. "'Liberty and Union': An Analysis of Three Concepts Involved in the Nullification Controversy." *Journal of Southern History* 33 (1967): 331–55.

Wish, Harvey. "The Revival of the African Slave Trade in the United States in 1855–1860." *Mississippi Valley Historical Quarterly* 27 (March 1941): 569–88.

Wooster, Ralph A. "The Florida Secession Convention." *Florida Historical Quarterly* 36 (April 1958): 373–85.

Unpublished Sources

Barnwell, John G., Jr. "'Love of Order': The Origins and Resolution of South Carolina's First Secession Crisis." Ph.D. diss., University of North Carolina, 1979.

Coussons, John Stanford. "Thirty Years with Calhoun, Rhett, and the *Charleston Mercury:* A Chapter in South Carolina Politics." Ph.D. diss., Louisiana State University, 1971.

Draughon, Ralph Brown, Jr. "William Lowndes Yancey: From Unionist to Secessionist, 1814–1852." Ph.D. diss., University of North Carolina, 1968.

Gardner, John Cooper. "Winning the Lower South to the Compromise of 1850." Ph.D. diss., Louisiana State University, 1974.

Greenberg, Kenneth S. "The Second American Revolution: South Carolina Politics, Society, and Secession, 1776–1860." Ph.D. diss., University of Wisconsin, 1976.

Hunt, Alfred Nathaniel. "The Influence of Haiti on the Antebellum South, 1791–1865." Ph.D. diss., University of Texas at Austin, 1975.

Huston, James Lynn. "The Panic of 1857 and the Coming of the Civil

War." Ph.D. diss., University of Illinois at Urbana-Champaign, 1980.

Kell, Charles Lewis. "A Rhetorical Study of James Hamilton, Jr.: The Nullification Era in South Carolina, 1816–1834." Ph.D. diss., University of Kansas, 1971.

Mallonee, Frank Buckner, Jr. "The Political Thought of Jefferson Davis." Ph.D. diss., Emory University, 1966.

Rachleff, Marshal J. "Racial Fear and Political Factionalism: A Study of the Secession Movement in Alabama, 1819–1861." Ph.D. diss., University of Massachusetts, 1974.

Index

Adams, John H., 122, 170
Adams, John Quincy, 11
Aiken, William, 133
Alabama, 4, 13–17, 40, 49–52, 58, 62–64, 66, 67, 69, 71, 72, 75, 88–90, 93, 94, 104, 105, 109, 111, 122, 123–25, 129, 134, 139, 144–46, 148, 149, 151, 152, 153, 155, 157, 159, 163–65, 171, 173, 177, 178, 183, 185, 186; delegates to Nashville, 49; and Nashville Convention, 33–34; secession of, 174; Whig party in, 25
Alabama Platform, 15–16, 33, 89, 93, 122, 125, 139, 145–46, 151, 153
Aldrich, A. P., 166
Alston, J. Motte, 105
Anderson, Robert, 167, 171
Arkansas, 30, 67, 111, 126, 149, 151, 153; secession of, 184; Whig Party in, 25
Association of 1860, 163, 170
Atchison, David Rice, 63, 82, 126–27
Avery, Waightstill, 148

Bachman, John, 156, 169
Banks, Nathaniel, 141
Barksdale, Ethelbert, 115, 137, 148

Barksdale, William, 172
Barnwell, Robert W., 26, 51, 63, 64; as emissary to Washington, 170; on extremism, 92; and Hammond's "Plan for State Action," 98; and Orr's movement, 107; replaces Calhoun in Senate, 79; in South Carolina legislature, 87
Barry, William S., 173
Bayard, James A., 152
Bell, John, 32, 162
Bell, Peter H., 30, 60, 62, 113
Bellinger, Edward, 94
Benjamin, Judah P., 177
Benning, Henry L., 40; on Calhoun, 38; and Confederate cabinet, 186; on consolidated republic, 73; ineffective in 1860, 148; lack of influence of, 183; at Nashville, 50, 51; and Pierce, 104; on Whig disintegration, 121
Benton, Thomas Hart, 31, 39, 40, 115
Berrien, John M., 22, 82, 101
Bethune, James N., 67
Bickley, George, 163
Bigler, William, 149
Bird, Thomas, 112
Bluffton Movement, 24, 106

Bonham, Milledge L., 104
Botts, John Minor, 111, 162, 180
Boyce, William, 111
Bragg, Thomas, 165
Branch, Lawrence O'Bryan, 162
Breckinridge, John, 157, 162
Bright, Jesse D., 149, 152
Brooks, Preston, 107, 111, 112, 127–28
Brooks, Whitelaw, 112
Brown, Aaron V., 58, 67, 68
Brown, Albert Gallatin, 54; and
  Compromise of 1850, 63; on congres-
  sional slave code, 137, 147; description
  of, 27; and Douglas, 136; 1849 cam-
  paign of, 27; and 1850 secession move-
  ment, 65; and 1860 campaign, 162; and
  Freeport Doctrine, 135; lack of influ-
  ence of, 183; and Pierce, 104; on
  President Davis, 121, 187; and radical-
  ism, 103, 107; as reformer, 109; on
  secession, 172–73
Brown, Bedford, 37, 162
Brown, John, 140, 163. *See also* Harpers
  Ferry
Brown, Joseph E., 129–30, 165, 168, 175,
  185
Brown, Thomas, 32
Brownlow, W. G., 164
Buchanan, James, 55; against Douglas in
  1860, 149; and Lecompton Constitution,
  129–30; and Missouri Compromise line,
  52; and secession crisis, 169; and
  Robert Walker, 128; warned against
  coercion, 171; and Yancey, 125
Buford, Jefferson, 49, 103, 126
Burt, Armistead, 13, 172
Butler, Andrew Pickens, 26, 63, 90, 92,
  98, 127, 128
Butler, Benjamin F., 151

Cabell, Edward C., 32
Calhoun, John C., 31, 65; and Cuba, 84;
  death of, 36; and 1848 election, 18; 4
  March 1850 speech, 35; Hammond

aspires to place of, 95–96; Houston's
  opposition to, 29; against indifference,
  66; influence of, 7, 36–38; memory of,
  39; on Mississippi action, 28; and
  Northern attitudes, 18–19; and
  Nullification, 8–9; and Oregon contro-
  versy, 13; and Rhett, 24–25, 109;
  Simms's opinion of, 96; and South
  Carolina, 26, 105–6; and Southern
  unity, 21, 22; successors to, 53, 76, 79;
  and Texas annexation, 12; and Wilmot
  Proviso, 13
California, 26, 29, 34, 53, 56, 63
Call, Richard K., 111
Campbell, John A., 15, 49, 51, 58, 89, 93,
  103, 125, 144
Carroll, J. P., 112
Cass, Lewis, 14–15, 17–18, 52, 93
Chalmers, David, 181
Chapman, Reuben, L., 52, 110
Charleston, 24, 149–50, 168, 170
Chase, Salmon P., 6, 82
Chatham Platform, 75
Chesnut, James, Jr., 133, 161, 166, 168
Cheves, Langdon, 10, 50–51, 68, 87, 98
Claiborne, John Herbert, 41
Clay, Clement C., 148, 177
Clay, Henry, 31, 34, 41, 44, 57, 61, 80–81,
  83, 106
Clemens, Jeremiah, 63, 110, 104
Clingman, Thomas L., 31
Cloud, Noah B., 134
Cobb, Howell, 72, 93, 121; and Buchanan,
  129, 176; and Constitutional Union
  party, 93; defeat of McDonald in 1851,
  93; effectiveness of, 183; and Hunter in
  1860, 147; on Rhett, 58; and Southern
  Democratic bolt, 154; and Stephens,
  175
Cobb, Thomas R. R., 161, 175
Cobb, W. R. W., 104
Colcock, William F., 166
Collier, Henry W., 34, 66, 68, 69, 93
Colquitt, Walter T., 40, 50, 54, 67, 71, 175

Compromise of 1850, 34, 63, 101, 103, 106
Connor, James, 166
Cooper, Thomas J., 10
Cooper, William J., 82, 83
Cooper Institute (New York City), 164
Crittenden, John J., 111, 177
Cross, Charlotte (Mrs. Louis Wigfall), 112
Cunningham, John, 111
Cushing, Caleb, 150, 169

Davis, Jefferson, 27, 52; on Brown, 107, 121, 136, 137; on California's admission, 63; and Cuba, 84; and 1848 election, 17; and 1850 secession movement, 65; and 1851 governor's race, 93; and 1860 convention, 149; Foote's dislike of, 39; and Fugitive Slave Law, 83; and Mississippi Democrats, 148; and Mississippi's secession, 183; at Pierce's War Deptartment, 102; as president of the Confederacy, 186; on Quitman's vice-presidential bid, 84; on secession, 172–73; and Senate, 136, 177; on South Carolina's secession, 169
Davis, Reuben, 172
Dawson, A. B., 103
DeBow, J. D. B., 116–17, 122, 129
Democratic Party: in Alabama, 58, 88–89, 104, 124; and Alabama Platform, 15, 33, 138; Charleston as 1860 convention site, 140; demise of predicted, 121; Douglas and Southerners in, 135; 1848 convention of, 14, 16, 84; 1852 campaign heals wounds of, 104; 1852 convention of, 103, 104, 107; 1856 convention of, 111, 114; 1860 convention of, 119, 138, 171; factionalization of, 130; fire-eaters, attitude about, 3; in Georgia, 33, 40, 93, 104, 121, 129; and Harpers Ferry Raid, 140; and Hunter, 146; influence of, 17; and Kansas-Nebraska Act, 110; and Know-Nothings, 112; and Lincoln's election,

162; misjudgment about disruption, 149; in Mississippi, 107, 136, 137; and Nashville Convention, 48, 56; and radicals, 3, 122, 136; Rhett's criticism of, 140; secession a doctrine of Southern wing of, 69; and South Carolina, 26, 106, 111, 148, 155; Southern withdrawal in Baltimore from, 157; Southerners in, 35, 36; and Southern Rights party, 75; and Texas controversy, 12; in Texas, 29; Unionists in, 68, 88, 93, 137, 155; in Virginia, 26; and Wilmot Proviso, 14; and Yancy, 18, 125
Dew, Thomas R., 43
Dickinson, Platt, 170
Dillard, Anthony W., 153
Donelson, Andrew Jackson, 32, 68
Douglas, Stephen A.: and Compromise of 1850, 61, 62; and 1848 election, 17; and 1860 Democratic convention, 145–47, 149, 152, 153, 186; and Freeport Doctrine, 135, 136; and Kansas-Nebraska Act, 125, 126; and Lecompton Constitution, 130; in Montgomery, 163; and Northern Democrats, 110; Southern opinion of, 23; Sumner's castigation of, 127; and Yancey, 145, 164
Drayton, William, 10
Duvall, William P., 60

Ellis, John W., 165, 172, 184, 187
Elmore, Franklin, 79
Elmore, John A., 58, 103
English, William H., 130
Eufaula Regency, 66, 134
Eustis, George, 111

Faneuil Hall, 164
Fillmore, Millard, 39, 61, 62, 70, 85
Fisher, George, 147
Fitzhugh, George, 118–19
Fitzpatrick, Benjamin, 17, 34, 88, 124, 134–35, 177

Florida, 7, 15–17, 25, 51, 63, 67, 70, 111, 149, 153, 157, 165, 183; character of Nashville delegates, 49; and Alabama Platform, 33; and Nashville Convention, 32–33; secession of, 173–74
Flournoy, George M., 178
Flournoy, W. C., 116
Floyd, John B., 41
Foote, Henry S., 28, 50, 137; and Benton, 39, 40; California, departure for, 102, 103; and the Compromise, 80; on Mississippi, 84; in Mississippi governor's race, 92; after Nashville, 65; Rhett's castigation of, 81; on secessionist conspiracy, 94; on Tucker, 43
Fort Sumter, 171–72, 181
Freeport Doctrine, 135–36
Frémont, John C., 136, 161
Fugitive Slave Law (also Act), 63, 81–83, 90, 122

Garnett, James M., 4
Garnett, M. R. H., 41, 90, 179
Garrison, William Lloyd, 11
Gavin, David, 111, 165–67
Gayle, G. W., 109
Geary, John W., 128
Georgia, 11, 22, 25, 38, 51, 54, 57, 58, 60, 64, 66, 67, 68, 71–77, 82, 86, 89, 93, 101–4, 110, 111, 115, 117, 121, 122, 129, 130, 134, 147–49, 153, 154, 157, 161–65, 168, 173–76, 183, 185; delegates to Nashville, 50; elections in 1850, 40; and Nashville Convention, 33
Georgia Convention, 66, 71, 74–76, 86
Georgia Platform, 75–76, 103, 122, 130
Giddings, Joshua, 13, 63
Gilchrist, J. G., 103
Gilmer, John, 180
Gist, William Henry, 140, 142, 144, 165–66
Goldwaithe, George, 49, 58, 59
Gordon, William F., 49, 67
Gott, Daniel, 21
Gourdin, Henry, 167

Green, Duff, 43
Green, Thomas Jefferson, 128, 148, 171
Gregg, Maxcy, 91–92, 98, 122, 134
Gregg, William, 117
Grinnan, Robert, 180

Hale, John P., 82, 83
Hamilton, James, 9, 10, 71
Hamlin, Hannibal, 82
Hammond, James Henry, 66; and "A Plan for State Action," 95, 97, 98; on Calhoun's ideas, 37; on California, 26; on Douglas's enemies, 149; and 1840 governor's race, 112; and family scandal, 46, 47; on League of United Southerners, 132; at Nashville, 51; on Nashville Convention, 47; on Nashville Address, 53; parochialism of, 105; political aspirations of, 109; in retirement, 96, 97; on Rhett, 63, 156–58; and Senate, 133, 166; on secessionists, 170; and South Carolina, 102; and South Carolina convention, nomination to, 87; on Southern agrarianism, 120; and Tucker, 43, 45, 69; on Tucker's Nashville speech, 55; on Washington, D.C., 21
Hampton, Wade, 133
Hampton, Wade, II, 46
Harper, William, 43
Harpers Ferry, 140–44, 185
Harris, Wiley P., 155
Hartford Convention, 4
Hartridge, Julian, 175
Harvie, Lewis E., 111, 115, 142, 180
Hayne, Isaac W., 86, 87, 156
Hayne, Robert Y., 8–9
Helper, Hinton, 41, 120, 141
Hemphill, John, 178
Henderson, James P., 49
Henderson, John P., 57, 85–86
Henry, Patrick, 165
Hibernian Hall, 57
Hill, Benjamin H., 111, 176
Hilliard, Henry W., 34, 93, 110, 163

Holmes, John, 4
Holt, Edwin, 117
Hooper, Johnson J., 163
Houston, Sam, 49; on disunion, 29; 1859 victory for governor, 148; and Know-Nothing party, 111; and Texas's secession, 178; Wigfall's opposition to, 113, 121, 124
Hunter, R. M. T., 63, 90, 142, 152; presidential aspirations of, 108, 132, 146; on South Carolina's secession, 169; and Virginia's secession, 180; warns of future disruptions, 165; Wise, rivalry with, 121

Institute Hall (Charleston, S.C.), 150
Iverson, Alfred, 141, 148

Jackson, Andrew, 9, 11, 21, 25, 37, 70
Jamison, David F., 169
Jefferson, Thomas, 4
Jenkins, Charles J., 74
Johns, Clement R., 178
Johnson, Cave, 55
Johnson, Herschel V., 76, 155, 176
Johnson, Isaac, 30
Johnson, Robert W., 30, 115
Judge, Thomas, 54

Kansas, 49
Kansas-Nebraska Act, 110, 113, 125–26, 186
Keitt, Lawrence M., 107, 111, 128–29, 141–42, 157, 170
Kentucky and Virginia Resolutions, 8, 36
King, Preston, 13, 16, 63
King, Rufus, 3, 11, 82
King, Thomas Butler, 154
King, William R., 17, 88
Knights of the Golden Circle, 163, 185
Know-Nothing party, 110–14, 124

Lamar, L. Q. C., 172
Lane, Joseph, 157

League of United Southerners, 130–32, 134
Lecompton Constitution, 129–30
Lee, Robert E., 84
Letcher, John, 132, 142, 144, 156, 181
Lewis, Dixon Hall, 15, 17
Lincoln, Abraham, 1, 156, 161, 162, 164
Logan, John A., 147
Lopez, Narciso, 84
Loughery, Robert W., 29
Louisiana, 4, 25, 30, 40, 49, 63, 75, 92, 111, 122, 125, 149, 151, 153, 165, 170, 171, 173, 177, 178, 187
Lyon, Francis S., 144

McClernand, John A., 147
McCrea, John H., 51, 54, 103
McCune, R. W., 74
McDonald, Charles J., 50, 57, 68, 71, 93–94, 99
McGehee, John C., 67, 173, 183
McGrath, Andrew Gordon, 133, 166, 168
McGrath, Edward, 133
McQueen, John, 111
Macon, Nathaniel, 5
Madison, James, 5
Mallory, Stephen, 173–74, 177, 183
Manning, John, 107
Mason, George, 82
Mason, James M., 35, 40, 63; on Brown's resolutions, 148; and grandfather's anti-slavery remarks, 82; and Harpers Ferry Raid, 143; on secession, 157; Union, swears devotion to, 90; and Virginia's secession, 180
Means, G. H., 92, 95, 98
Memminger, Christopher G., 107, 141–42, 144, 167, 187
Miles, William Porcher, 129, 141–43, 152, 167–68, 171
Mississippi, 33, 39, 51, 57, 58, 62–65, 67, 68, 72, 75, 81, 83–86, 88, 91, 92, 102, 103, 107, 117, 121, 128, 136, 137, 144, 148, 149, 151, 153, 155, 162, 165, 172–174, 180, 183, 187; calls for

Mississippi *(continued)*
  Southern convention, 28; delegates to
    Nashville, 50; in Southern movement,
    27; secession of, 173; Whig party in, 25
Missouri, 3–4, 6, 11, 25, 31, 32, 42,
    52–54, 63, 67, 71, 82, 125–26, 135, 184
Missouri Compromise, 4–6
Missouri Compromise line, 4, 67; and
    Dred Scott decision, 135; extension of,
    29, 52–54, 63, 71; removed by Kansas-
    Nebraska Act, 125
Monroe, John, 60
Montgomery, James, 184
Montgomery Regency, 124, 135, 144, 155
Moore, Andrew B., 165, 174
Moore, Thomas E., 165
Morton, Jackson, 32, 63

Nashville, 47–48, 66–67
Nashville Convention, 29, 89; activities
    after, 57; Address of, 53, 54, 56, 59;
    appeal of, 28; and Compromise of 1850,
    35; resolutions of, 53–54; second ses-
    sion of, 66–68; and Southern states,
    30–34
Native American party. *See* Know-
    Nothing party
New England Emigrant Aid Society, 126
New Mexico, 27
Newton, Willoughby, 117–19, 131–32,
    180–81
Nicholson, A. O. P., 67–68
North Carolina, 25, 40, 61, 67, 68, 117,
    142, 148, 162, 165, 170, 172, 184; and
    Nashville Convention, 31; secession of,
    185
Nullification, 8, 36, 105

Olmstead, Frederick Law, 77
Omnibus Bill, 61
Oregon controversy, 12, 13
Orr, James L., 138; and Brooks's death,
    128; and 1860 convention, 148; as emis-
    sary to Washington, 170; on extremism,
    92; on Know-Nothings, 111; and nation-
    alism, 121; popularity of, 109; Rhett,
    comparison to, 168; South Carolina pol-
    itics, leading of, 105–6

Palmer, Benjamin Morgan, 177
Panic of 1819, 8
Payne, Henry B., 146
Pennington, William, 142
Perry, Benjamin F., 10–11, 70, 105, 111,
    106, 130
Petit, John, 14
Pettus, John J.: and Davis, 148; on
    Lincoln's victory, 162; and Mississippi
    congressional delegation, 172–73; and
    Mississippi military, preparation of,
    155; and Nashville Convention, refusal
    to attend, 50; runs for governor, 137;
    and secessionists, 165
Pickens, Francis W.: and Buchanan, 169;
    as candidate for Senate, 133; on
    Confederate government, 172; elected
    governor, 168; offered 1860 vice-presi-
    dential nomination, 152; opposes
    Know-Nothings, 111; as U.S. minister
    to Russia, 114
Pierce, Franklin, 126, 128
Pike, Albert J., 111, 115–16, 184
Pillow, Gideon, 50, 54, 58, 67
Polk, James K., 12, 22
Polk, William H., 49
Preston, John S., 86, 133
Prioleau, John C., 82
Pryor, Mrs. Roger, 80
Pryor, Roger A., 115, 123, 131–32,
    179–80
Pugh, George E., 147, 151
Pugh, James L., 172, 178
Purcell, Jack, 82

Quitman, Eliza, 84
Quitman, John A., 99; accused of conspir-
    ing with Rhett, 94; on Buchanan, 129;
    career of, 84; and Cuban filibustering,
    83–86; on Davis, 102; death of, 136;
    and 1850 secession movement, 64–65;

on Foote for governor, 92–93; after
Nashville, 57; presidential nomination
of, 103; in the Senate, 136; South
Carolina secession promised to, 92; and
Texas–New Mexico border dispute, 62
Quitman, Rosalie, 76

Randolph, John, 5–7, 10, 43, 82
Randolph, Robert, 179
Reagan, John H., 124, 183, 185
Republican party, 5, 110, 112, 115, 161
Rhett, Edmund, 133, 140, 156
Rhett, Robert Barnwell, 89; advocates sep-
arate state action, 63, 91, 186; on
aggression against federal installations,
95; barred from power, 187; bewildered
by events, 122; career of, 23–24;
Cheves and Barnwell, suspicions of, 87;
and compromise, refusal to accept, 77;
Confederate administration, denied
place in, 186; and 1848 election, 17; and
1860 campaign, 164; after 1860
Democratic disruption, 155–56;
Democratic conventions, objects to participation in, 140; influence of, 94, 109,
157, 158, 166–168, 170, 183; on Know-
Nothings, 111; on Lecompton
Constitution, 130; in legislature, 70; at
Macon meeting, 71; at Nashville
Convention, 50–51, 53, 57–58; and
Nullification, 9–10; and Oregon controversy, 13; parochialism of, 105; on reconciliation, 171; on reform, 110; in
retirement, 101–2, 132–33, 137–38; and
Ruffin, meeting with, 175; in the Senate,
79–81, 83, 90; Senate resignation, 98;
and slave trade, 123; on South Carolina,
26, 114, 169; and Southern Commercial
Conventions, 115; Southern decisive-
ness, hope for, 24–25; on Upper South,
166; and Virginia's secession, 179; at
Walterboro, 72; and Yancey, comparison
with, 139
Rhett, Robert Barnwell, Jr., 142, 153, 154,
156

Richardson, John P., 112
Richardson, William A., 147
Richmond Junto, 108
Ritchie, Thomas, 41, 90, 93, 108
Rives, Timothy, 180
Rives, William Cabell, 180
Ruffin, Edmund, 47, 98; agricultural activ-
ities of, 102; and Association of 1860,
163; bewildered by events, 122; Border
States, hears opinion of, 184; on
Charleston fortifications, 171; on
DeBow, 117; and Florida's secession,
173; and Fort Sumter, 181; and
Georgia's secession, 174–75; and
Hammond, 96; and Harpers Ferry Raid,
143; and Kansas-Nebraska Act, 125;
and League of United Southerners,
131–32; on Northern corruption, 118;
on Pickens, 168; political aspirations of,
109; on reform, 110; and Rhett, 69, 114;
and slave trade, 122; and South
Carolina, 155; and Southern
Commercial Conventions, 114–15; and
Southern cooperation, hopes for, 167;
and Texas's secession, 178; and
Tidewater influence, 119; and Tucker,
43; and Virginia, 41, 108, 142, 156, 179,
180; on Wigfall, 113; and Yancy, 123,
157, 165
Ruffin, Edmund, Jr., 18, 38, 42, 69, 90,
172, 180
Ruffin, Julian, 42
Runnels, H. R., 114, 124
Rusk, Thomas J., 29, 62
Rutherford, William, Jr., 68

Samford, William F., 134
Sanders, George, 147, 152
Schenck, David, 185
Scott, Dred, decision, 114, 135, 139, 186
Seabrook, Whitemarsh B., 63–64, 66, 70,
73, 79, 97, 165
Seddon, James A., 17, 108, 146, 156, 179
Seibels, J. J., 66, 93, 124, 134–35, 144–45
Seward, William, 28, 50–51, 63, 136–37

Sherman, John, 141, 152

Shorter, John Gill, 134

Simms, William Gilmore, 41; on Democratic disintegration, 121; and Georgia moderation, complaints about, 73; as Hammond's advisor, 66, 96–97; as Jamison's friend, 169; and Rhett, 91; and South Carolina convention, 87; and Texas border dispute, 59; and Tucker, 43–44, 69–70; and Virginia, 90

Singleton, Ortho R., 172

Slaughter, James, 130

Slave trade, 122–24

Slidell, John, 16, 149, 152, 162, 177

Smith, Cotesworth Pinckney, 85

Soulé, Pierre, 63

South Carolina, 7–10, 14, 17, 21, 23–28, 30, 33, 36, 37, 40, 41, 46–51, 53, 62–64, 66, 67, 69–72, 75–77, 79, 80, 82, 86–88, 90–98, 102, 104–9, 111, 112, 114, 117, 122, 127, 128, 132, 133, 138, 140–44, 148, 151, 153, 155, 157, 163, 165, 166, 169–72, 177, 184, 185; delegates to Nashville Convention, 49–51; rivalry with Georgia, 72; Whig party in, 25–26

Southern Address, 22, 25, 29, 34–35, 53

Southern Commercial Conventions, 114–16, 122–24

Southern Rights Associations, 57, 69, 88, 91, 93–94, 115

Spalding, Thomas, 74

Spratt, Leonidas W., 122, 124

Stallworth, James A., 111

Stephens, Alexander H., 66; and Constitutional Union party, 93; and Democratic reconciliation, 104; and English bill, 130; at Georgia legislature, 175–76; Georgia Platform, claims authorship of, 74; and Kansas-Nebraska Act, 125; on McDonald, 94; on public indifference, 119; on secession, consequences of, 184; on Southern Democratic bolt, 154; on Texas–New Mexico border dispute, 60; as vice-president

of the Confederacy, 186; and Whig party, 110

Stuart, Charles E., 147, 152–53

Stuart, Hamilton, 124

Sumner, Charles, 127

Taber, William R., 133

Tait, Charles, 4, 5

Tallmadge, James 3

Taylor, John, of Caroline, 5

Taylor, Zachary: and Compromise of 1850, 34; compromise, refusal to endorse, 56; death of, 61; election of, 17; and Mexican War, 12; as presidential candidate, 14; and Texas–New Mexico border dispute, 59; and Tucker, 44, 69

Tazewell, Littleton W., 11, 17

Tennessee, 31–33, 42, 48, 49, 51, 55, 58, 61, 63, 67, 68, 74, 75, 96, 102, 164; delegates to Nashville, 49–50; and Nashville Convention, 31–32

Tertium Quids, 5

Texas, 13, 27–30, 34, 52, 56–64, 70, 105, 111, 112, 113, 114, 118, 121, 122, 124, 126, 143, 148, 149, 151, 153, 163, 179, 185; annexation of, 12; and border dispute with New Mexico, 27, 53, 56, 59, 60, 62; delegates to Nashville, 49; secession of, 178; in Southern movement, 28–29

Thomas, Jesse B., 4

Thomas, William H., 142

Thompson, Meriwether Jefferson, 184

Toombs, Robert, 33, 66; in Confederate cabinet, 186; and Constitutional Union party, 93; effectiveness of, 183; and 1860 convention, 148; and Hunter in 1860, 147; and Know-Nothings, 110; Senate resignation, 166, 168; on Southern Democratic bolt, 154; on Southern protective tariff, 117; and Stephens, 175–76; on Walker, 128–29; and Whig party, 110

Towns, George W., 33, 64, 73–75, 77, 129
Townsend, John, 163
Trescott, William Henry, 90, 114
Troup, George M., 103
Tucker, Beverley, 65, 90; on Calhoun, 38;
  career of, 42–43; on egalitarianism, 108;
  and Hammond, 96; irrationality of, 44;
  and Nashville Convention, 41, 44–45,
  52, 54–55; in South Carolina, 69–70; on
  Virginia moderation, 42
Tucker, John Randolph, 179
Tucker, St. George, 5, 43
Tunnard, William H., 170–71
Turnbull, Robert J., 8, 11
Turner, Nat, 82
Turney, Hopkins L., 32, 63, 102

Utah Territory, 27

Van Buren, Martin, 12, 17
Venable, Abraham W., 31
Vesey, Denmark, 11, 82
Virginia, 5, 8, 11, 16–18, 25, 26, 30,
  35–36, 38, 43, 45, 47, 51, 60, 61, 67, 69,
  70, 82, 90–91, 98, 102, 111, 116–18,
  121–24, 131–32, 135, 140–44, 146–48,
  156, 157, 162, 166, 187; and Alabama
  Platform, 33; delegates to Nashville, 49;
  Democratic party in, 108; divisions
  within, 40–41; political complexion of,
  26; secession of, 179–81; Whig party in,
  25–26
Virginia Resolutions, 30

Wadley, Sarah Lois, 187–88
Walker, Leroy P., 15, 49, 153, 186
Walker, Percy, 15, 103, 110
Walker, Robert J., 128–30
Walker, William, 135
Watts, Thomas H., 174
Webster, Daniel, 9, 11, 35, 37, 39, 61, 80
Webster-Hayne Debates, 8
Whig party, 24, 25, 88, 110, 121; criticized
  by Rhett, 24; disintegration predicted,

121; drifts away from Southern movement, 23; in Mississippi, 28; nature
  of, 25; and Northern schools, 23; Southerners in, 21; and Taylor administration, 22
Wigfall, Louis T., 49; Brooks, duel with,
  127; and Brown, 148, 172; career of,
  112–114; and 1860 campaign, 164; on
  compromise efforts, 177; and Houston,
  121; lack of influence of, 183; as mem-
  ber of Galveston committee, 29; on
  President Davis, 186–87; after seces-
  sion, 178–79; and slave trade, 122–24;
  and South Carolina, 105
Wilcox, John A., 107
Wilkinson, J. W., 87
Williams, David R., 170
Williams, George W., 67
Williams, John Nicholas, 170
Williams, Shadrach, 81
Williams, Thomas, Jr., 58
Wilmot, David, 12–13
Wilmot Proviso, 13–15, 17–18, 26, 43, 53,
  81, 91, 185
Wiltse, Charles, 37
Winans, William, 27
Winston, John A., 49, 153
Winthrop, Robert, 36
Wise, Henry A.: declares for Douglas,
  147; and Harpers Ferry Raid, 143;
  Hunter, rivalry with, 108, 121; on
  Nashville nomination, 42; as reformer,
  109; and Virginia's secession, 180–81
Wood, George T., 30, 113
Woodbury, Levi, 15, 147

Yancey, William Lowndes, 99; and
  Alabama 15, 88, 138, 145, 174; barred
  from power, 187; and Border States,
  184; and Buchanan, 129; after
  Compromise of 1850, 66; Democratic
  disruption, blame for, 154; and Douglas,
  opposition to, 148–49; and 1848 election, 17–18; and 1851 secession move-

Yancey, William Lowndes *(continued)*
    ment, 89–90, 93–94; after 1851, 102;
    and 1860 Democratic convention, 151,
    186; 1860 tour of, 164–65; and Harpers
    Ferry Raid, 144; influence of, 33, 183;
    and Know-Nothing party, 111; and
    League of United Southerners, 130–31;
    at Macon meeting, 71; and Nashville,
    49, 57, 59; oratorical style of, 34, 59;
    and Oregon controversy, 13; and radi-
    calism, 103; reemergence of, 124, 125;
    as reformer, 109; Rhett, compared to,
    139; Senate try, 134–35; and slave
    trade, 122–23; and South Carolina, 105;
    and Southern Commercial Conventions,
    115; and vice-presidential nomination in
    1860, 152; and Wilmot Proviso, 14
Yulee, David L.: and California, admission
    of, 63; career of, 32; and 1848 conven-
    tion, 15; and Florida's secession,
    173–74; lack of influence of, 183; and
    Northern hypocrisy, 23; Senate resigna-
    tion, 177; and South Carolina's seces-
    sion, 169